THE MYTH OF INDEPENDENCE

The Myth of Independence

How Congress Governs the Federal Reserve

Sarah Binder

Mark Spindel

PRINCETON UNIVERSITY PRESS

PRINCETON AND OXFORD

Copyright © 2017 by Princeton University Press

Published by Princeton University Press,
41 William Street, Princeton, New Jersey 08540

In the United Kingdom: Princeton University Press,
6 Oxford Street, Woodstock, Oxfordshire OX20 1TR

press.princeton.edu

Jacket photograph: Federal Reserve Chairman Ben Bernanke testifies before the
Senate Banking, Housing and Urban Affairs Committee Hearing on the "Semiannual
Monetary Policy Report to the Congress," 2011 © James Berglie / Zuma Press

ISBN 978-0-691-16319-2
The myth of independence
Library of Congress Cataloging in Publication Control Number: 2017014304

British Library Cataloging-in-Publication Data is available

This book has been composed in Adobe Text Pro and Gotham

Printed on acid-free paper. ∞

Printed in the United States of America

10 9 8 7 6 5 4 3 2 1

For our daughters

CONTENTS

ILLUSTRATIONS

TABLES

ACKNOWLEDGMENTS

This project took root in 2008 when we discovered our mutual interest—professor and practitioner—in the political, economic, and policy implications of the global financial crisis. The Federal Reserve's dominant role in rescuing the economy posed a puzzle: If lawmakers blame the Fed when the economy tanks, why does Congress typically react by giving central bankers more power? Remarkably, Congress's complicated relationship with the Federal Reserve had largely escaped scholarly attention. And yet understanding the interaction of the two institutions was critical for academics probing the allocation and accountability of economic power as well as market participants grappling with the effects of the Fed's and legislature's existential roles in the wake of the crisis. This book represents the fruits of our collaboration.

Like the federal government, we accumulated many debts in writing this book. We appreciate the willingness of former and current central bankers—Ben Bernanke, Narayana Kocherlakota, Don Kohn, Jeffrey Lacker, Larry Meyer, Paul Tucker and Kazuo Ueda —to engage our questions and offer us invaluable perspective on the Fed's relations with Congress during and after the crisis. We are grateful as well for insightful discussions, advice, and support from many colleagues in Washington, DC, and beyond: Liaquat Ahamed, James Aitken, Joe Beaulieu, Seth Carpenter, Peter Conti-Brown, Jason Cummins, Mike Feroli, Stephen Kaplan, Eric Lawrence, Alan Levenson, Forrest Maltzman, Nolan McCarty, Bill Nelson, Nobuya Nemoto, Eric Patashnik, Brian Sack, Wendy Schiller, Nathan Sheets, Rick Valelly, Chris Varvares, Phil Wallach, David Wessel, Darrell West and the Brookings Governance Studies program, Russell Wheeler, and David Zervos. The book also benefited from conversations with many journalists covering the Federal Reserve in the wake of the crisis, including Binyamin Appelbaum, Katy Burne, Kate Davidson, Sam Fleming, Robin Harding, Jon Hilsenrath, Jeff Kearns, Ylan Mui, Robert Samuelson, Craig Torres, and Josh Zumbrum.

We appreciate too the helpful feedback we received at presentations at the Brookings Institution, Columbia University, the Government Accountability Office, Ohio State University, Texas A&M, the University of California at Berkeley, the University of Georgia, William and Mary, and Yale University as well as the annual meeting of the American Political Science Association in Washington, DC (2010), the Congress and History Conference held at Brown University (2011), the DC Area American Politics Workshop (2012), and the Congress and Policy Making in the 21st Century conference held at the University of Virginia (2013). We also benefited greatly from research assistance from colleagues at the Brookings Institution, the Federal Reserve Board, George Washington University, and Potomac River Capital, including Peter Andersen, Josh Bleiberg, Katie Bowen, Doug Cohen, Curtlyn Kramer, Tara Kutzbach, Alyx Mark, Mark Miller, Benny Miller-Gootnicht, Molly Reynolds, Jonathan Robinson, Kris Vajs, and Raffaela Wakeman. At Princeton University Press, we appreciate the many contributions of Eric Crahan, who carefully shepherded this project from manuscript to publication, the editorial and production assistance of Karen Carter, Cindy Milstein, and Hannah Zuckerman, and the invaluable feedback from two anonymous reviewers. We believe their collective insights helped improve the book immeasurably.

Portions of the book appeared previously in print. An earlier version of chapter 3 appeared as "Monetary Politics: Origins of the Federal Reserve," *Studies in American Political Development* 27, no. 1 (2013): 1–13. Parts of chapter 2 appeared in "Congress and the Federal Reserve: Independence and Accountability," in *Congress and Policy Making in the 21st Century*, ed. Jeffrey A. Jenkins and Eric M. Patashnik (New York: Cambridge University Press, 2016), 187–209. Both are reprinted with the permission of Cambridge University Press. Figure 3.3 is adopted from Richard Franklin Bensel, *Sectionalism and American Political Development, 1880–1980* (Madison:

University of Wisconsin Press, 1984), and is reprinted with the permission of the University of Wisconsin Press. The epigraph for chapter 8 is from Ben S. Bernanke, *The Courage to Act: A Memoir of a Crisis and Its Aftermath* (New York: W. W. Norton and Company, 2015), and is used with the permission of W. W. Norton and Company, Inc.

Finally, we are ever thankful for our Wissioming families and Washington friends who never stopped asking, "When are you going to finish that book?!" Years later, we remain grateful for their love and support, and our own collaboration and friendship.

THE MYTH OF INDEPENDENCE

1

Monetary Politics

When the Federal Reserve celebrated its centennial in December 2013, it bore only passing resemblance to the institution created by Democrats, Progressives, and Populists a century before. In the wake of the devastating banking Panic of 1907, a Democratic Congress and President Woodrow Wilson enacted the Federal Reserve Act of 1913, creating a decentralized system of currency and credit, and sidestepping Americans' long-standing distrust of a central bank. After the Fed failed to prevent and arguably caused the Great Depression of the 1930s, lawmakers rewrote the act, taking steps to centralize control of monetary policy in Washington, DC, while granting the Fed some independence within the government. Decades later in 2007, another global financial crisis retested the Fed's capacity to overcome policy mistakes and prevent financial collapse. Congress again responded by significantly revamping the Fed's authority, bolstering the Fed's financial regulatory responsibilities while requiring more transparency and limiting the Fed's exigent role as the lender of last resort. By the end of its first century, the Federal Reserve had become the crucial player sustaining and steering the nation's and, to a large extent, the world's economic and financial well-being—a remarkable progression given the Fed's limited institutional beginnings.

What explains the Federal Reserve's existential transformation? In this book, we explore the political and economic catalysts that fueled the development of the Fed over its first century. Economic historians have provided excellent accounts of the Fed's evolution, focusing on the successes and failures of monetary policy. Still, little has been written about why or when politicians wrestle with the Fed, each other, and the president over monetary policy, and who wins these political contests over the powers, autonomy, and governance of the Fed, or why. Moreover, in the wake of economic and financial debacles for which Congress and the public often blame the Fed, lawmakers respond paradoxically, amending the act to expand the Fed's powers and further concentrate control in Washington. Why do Congress and the president reward the Fed with new powers and punish it for poor performance? In this book, we contextualize Congress's existential role in driving the evolution of the Fed—uncovering the complex and sometimes-hidden role of Congress in historical efforts to construct, sustain, and reform the Federal Reserve.[1]

By concentrating on Congress's relationship with the Fed, we challenge the most widely held tenet about the modern Fed: central bankers independently craft monetary policy, free from short-term political interference. Instead, we suggest that Congress and the Fed are *interdependent*. From atop Capitol Hill, Congress depends on the Fed to both steer the economy and absorb public blame when the economy falters. Indeed, over the Fed's first century, Congress has delegated increasing degrees of responsibility to the Fed for managing the nation's economy. But by centralizing power in the hands of the Fed, lawmakers can more credibly blame the Fed for poor economic outcomes, insulating themselves electorally and potentially diluting public anger at Congress.

In turn, the Fed remains dependent on legislative support. Because lawmakers frequently have revised the Federal Reserve Act over its first century, central bankers (despite claims of independence) recognize that Congress circumscribes the Fed's alleged policy autonomy. Fed power—and its capacity and credibility to take unpopular but necessary policy steps—is contingent on securing as well as maintaining broad political and public support. Throughout the book, we highlight the interdependence of these two institutions, exploring the political-economic logic that shapes lawmakers' periodic efforts to revamp the Fed's governing law.

The concentration of monetary control in Washington has been politically costly for the Federal Reserve, particularly in the wake of the Great Recession and continuing into the 2016 presidential campaign. Beginning in 2008, the Fed's DC-based Board of Governors vastly expanded the breadth of monetary policy. The Fed extended and stretched its emergency lending powers, purchased unprecedented levels of government, mortgage, and other debt, and more generally, played a critical role in the selective extension of credit to US industry and finance—often working closely with the US Treasury and Federal Reserve Bank of New York (one of the Fed's twelve regional reserve banks that share power with the Board to make monetary policy).[2] Those choices, which at one point more than quadrupled the size of the Fed's balance sheet, reinserted the Fed into the midst of political discussions about fiscal policy, and more existentially, how far and in what ways the central bank should intervene to prevent and contain financial crises as well as bolster economic growth.

By extending credit to specific institutions and demographic cohorts, the Fed's actions during and after the 2007 crisis blurred the line between monetary and fiscal policy, making the central bank a target of critics across the ideological spectrum, tarnishing its reputation. Over 90 percent of respondents in public opinion polls in the late 1990s during the "Great Moderation" (a nearly quarter-century period of low and stable inflation) applauded the performance of the Federal Reserve as either excellent or good. As shown in figure 1.1, less than a third of the public approved of the Fed at the height of the Great Recession a decade later in 2009.[3] Even the perennially hated Internal Revenue Service polled higher. Liberals and conservatives criticized the lack of transparency surrounding the Fed's emergency lending programs. Conservatives objected to the Fed's large-scale asset purchases (LSAPs), on the unproven grounds that the Fed was foolishly stoking inflation. And while many Democrats welcomed the Fed's focus on reducing unemployment, Republicans pushed for eliminating the employment component of the Fed's dual

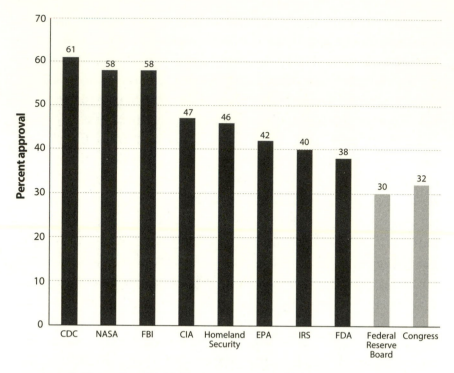

FIGURE 1.1. Public standing of Federal Reserve, Congress, and federal agencies, 2009. Question wording for agency, department, and Federal Reserve Board evaluations: How would you rate the job being done by [agency]? Would you say it is doing an excellent, good, only fair, or poor job? Approval calculated as percent responding excellent/good. Question wording for Congress evaluations: Do you approve or disapprove of the way Congress is handling its job? Gallup Organization, Gallup News Service Poll: July Wave 1, July 2009 (dataset). USAIPOGNS2009-12, Version 2, Gallup Organization (producer). Storrs, CT: Roper Center for Public Opinion Research, Roper*Express* (distributor), accessed November 30, 2015, https://ropercenter.cornell.edu/CFIDE/cf/action/home/index.cfm.

mandate—a bank-friendly move that would force the Fed to concentrate exclusively on price stability.

Intense partisan and ideological criticism of the Fed made it harder for President Barack Obama to secure Senate confirmation of his appointments to the Fed, even after Democrats in November 2013 revamped Senate procedures to allow simple majorities to block filibusters of Obama's nominees. Nor did the judiciary defer to the Federal Reserve: the Supreme Court in 2010 refused to come to the defense of the central bank when Bloomberg News sued to force disclosure of the identities of borrowers from the Fed's discount window. And in the 2016 presidential campaign, Republican nominee Donald J. Trump accused chair Janet Yellen and the Federal Reserve of playing politics with interest rates—claiming that she was doing the bidding of the White House to help elect Trump's opponent (Davidson 2016). In short, the Fed's autonomy was put at risk in the wake of the global financial crisis and afterward as the Fed faced tough choices about how to respond to the crisis and roll back its unconventional efforts as the economy improved. Even years after the crisis, lawmakers and market participants continue to scrutinize the Fed as it decides how to tighten monetary policy. How the Fed balances conflicting demands from politicians and industry against both its own preferences and a unique, dual mandate from Congress to maximize employment and keep inflation at bay will shape the reputation, power, and effectiveness of the Fed in its second century.

The Political Transformation of the Fed

The image of the Federal Reserve as a body of technocratic experts belies the political nature of the institution. By defining the Fed as political, we do not mean that the Fed's policy choices are politicized. To be sure, policy making within the Federal Open Market Committee (FOMC) is rarely a matter of applying partisan prescriptions to generate appropriate monetary policy, although accusations as such are common. Given internal frictions, especially during times of economic stress, the Fed chair faces the challenge of building a coalition within (and beyond) the FOMC to support a preferred policy outcome, akin to committee or party leaders in Congress, or Supreme Court justices working to secure majorities for proposals or opinions. Former Fed chair Ben S. Bernanke once described a central challenge of leading the Fed in precisely this way: "In Washington or any other political context you have to think about: how can you sell what you want to do to others who are involved in the process" (Dubner 2015). That said, the Fed is not just another partisan body reflecting the views of the presidents who appoint the Board of Governors in Washington or boards of directors who select the Fed's reserve bank presidents who then vote on monetary policy. Decision making inside the Fed surely involves technocratic, macroeconomic policy expertise, even within a political institution.

We deem the Fed "political" because successive generations of legislators have made and later remade the Federal Reserve System to reflect temporal, political, and economic priorities. Most important, because the Fed is a product of and operates within the political system, its power derives from and depends on the support of elected officials. Institutions are political not because they are permeated by partisan decision making but rather because political forces endow them with the power to exercise public authority on behalf of a diverse and at times polarized nation.

The Fed is an enduring political institution—its powers, organization, and governance evolving markedly over its first century. As such, the Fed is similar to many institutions that "have been around long enough to have outlived, not just their designers and the social coalitions on which they were founded, but also the external conditions of the time of their foundation" (Streek and Thelen 2005, 28). Given the difficulty of eliminating organizations once they are embedded in statute, political actors often try to adapt old rules and authorities to new purposes or to meet new demands (Pierson 2004). Indeed, reformers frequently target old organizations mismatched to new environments by seeking to remold them for new times. In other words, bureaucracies originally created to address past sets of interests can be transformed to serve the purposes of newly empowered coalitions. Old institutions become proving grounds for politicians eager to secure their policy goals without having to invest time and resources creating new organizations from scratch.

The Federal Reserve offers a prime example of historical "conversion" (Streek and Thelen 2005, 26), or more colloquially, "mission creep." Democrats and Populists in 1913 placed high priority on devising a reserve system that would address the needs of the credit-starved, agrarian South. Creating regional reserve banks, empowering Democrats to determine where to locate the reserve banks, and providing for an "elastic currency" that would expand the money supply to meet regional as well as national credit needs served lawmakers' goals well. Importantly, Wall Street bankers no longer controlled agrarian Democrats' access to credit. The new decentralized reserve system, however, made it difficult to devise national monetary policy when banks began to fail again in the late 1920s. Innovation by the twelve district reserve banks (for example, creating an informal monetary policy committee to coordinate government debt purchases) proved insufficient during the Great Depression, leading Congress and the president to enact new banking acts in 1933 and 1935, thereby creating a more formal, system-wide monetary policy committee. The evolution of the economy, monetary theory, and the financial system—and crucially, the electoral map—all but guaranteed that future political coalitions would periodically revisit the handiwork of their predecessors. As a result, the Fed has been transformed over its long history: successive generations of politicians respond to economic downturns by battling over the appropriate authority, governance, and mission of the Fed.

In this book, we explore the Fed's political transformation. The growth of the US economy and concomitant transformation in the size, scope, and complexity of the financial system has naturally helped to expand the Fed's global economic influence. But congressional action has also made a difference. First, Congress has increasingly centralized monetary authority and power within the Federal Reserve System. Second, Congress has made the Fed more transparent and accountable to its legislative overseer. To be sure, Congress periodically clips the Fed's power and rejects centralizing reforms. But lawmakers' efforts to revamp the Fed have on balance made the Fed more powerful and more transparent. With more power, of course, comes more responsibility—allowing Congress to routinely blame the Fed for its policy failures. Below, we preview these twin transformations of the Fed and propose a political-economic theory to explain the dynamics of congressional reform of the Fed.

A MORE CENTRALIZED AND POWERFUL FED

The 1913 Federal Reserve System was highly decentralized: twelve privately owned reserve banks operated regional "discount windows" and set their own interest rates—thereby controlling lending to member banks in their districts. The Federal Reserve Act empowered a president-appointed, Senate-confirmed Federal Reserve Board in Washington to approve the regional banks' discount rates. But as Milton Friedman and Anna Schwartz (1963) documented in their history of monetary policy in the United States, the Board typically took a back seat to more assertive reserve banks, including the Federal Reserve Bank of New York. Because the DC-based board did not have its own lending facility, the power to devise and implement monetary policy rested largely in the hands of the regional, district banks. We show in chapter 3 that this hybrid, public-private agreement was the price of enactment for agrarian Democrats who otherwise would have rejected a more centralized, Wall Street–dominated, national bank.

The modern Fed bears little in common with the 1913 original. The institution is significantly more centralized, and has far greater powers and responsibility than it did a century ago. At its inception, the Fed's monetary policy extended only to member banks of the Federal Reserve System. Today, the Fed's authority reaches far beyond institutions that belong to the reserve system. The twelve reserve banks retain supervisory power over member banks in their districts, but the reserve banks have lost their autonomy over regional lending decisions. Moreover, centralized open market operations long ago replaced discount window lending as the key tool for affecting national interest rates and the allocation of credit more generally.[4] Today, the twelve reserve banks are largely local research arms that ensure the consideration of regional economic and macroprudential factors within the Federal Reserve System.[5]

Instead, the president-appointed, Senate-confirmed, Washington-based Board of Governors dominates monetary policy making through its voting cohesion on the FOMC. Moreover, the Board exploits its so-called 13(3) emergency lender-of-last-resort powers to direct credit without the input of reserve bank presidents.[6] The reserve bank presidents retain voting rights on the FOMC, but their representation is partial and rotating. Since 1935, only five of the FOMC's twelve voting seats are reserved for the regional reserve presidents, and since 1942, one has always been saved for the New

York Fed. In other words, a cohesive and fully staffed Board of Governors can always outvote the reserve bank presidents.

Why did Congress gradually concentrate power over money and credit in Washington? When lawmakers originally drafted the Federal Reserve Act in 1913, the nation's historical aversion to a strong central bank discouraged lawmakers from centering control of monetary policy in Washington or New York City.[7] At the time, policy makers foresaw a relatively limited role for the Fed: the new central bank's discretion would be curtailed by adherence to the gold standard—an arrangement that restricted the money supply to the nation's gold stock. As we explore in chapter 3, a decentralized reserve system was the opponents' price for creating a central bank. Lawmakers thus gave the Fed only limited lending powers, placing control of credit into the hands of regional financial agents, thereby institutionalizing access to credit beyond the nation's power centers. To centralize and empower the Fed, lawmakers ultimately would have to unravel the compromise that lay at the heart of the original Federal Reserve Act.

Our theory suggests that recurring economic crises, electoral change that often follows a crisis, and institutional competition encouraged lawmakers to concentrate greater authority in the Fed in Washington—unwinding the original deal. Monetary centralization affords Congress an easy target to blame when the economy sours, and facilitates easier oversight by Congress—useful when lawmakers are eager to escape blame for economic malaise. As we look at in chapter 4, for example, centralization of power within the Fed in 1935 was part and parcel of President Franklin Roosevelt's New Deal, the Democrats' policy program that aimed to fix the economy in the wake of the Great Depression. Indeed, FDR's pick to head the Fed in 1935, Marriner Eccles, agreed to accept the position only if Congress could be convinced to give the Board in Washington greater control over the conduct of monetary policy.

Given Congress's success in centralizing Fed authority in Washington, the resilience of the regional reserve system is curious. Why has Congress failed to fully centralize the Fed? Even after a century of technological, demographic, and economic change, each of the reserve banks remains in its original location. As we examine throughout the book, lawmakers could not completely uproot the Fed at every turn: past institutional choices about the organization of the Fed generated coalitions that benefited from maintaining the status quo—constraining future efforts to fully centralize the Fed. Today, the central bank remains a *federal* reserve system, with some modicum of power over monetary policy still lodged in regional reserve banks around the country.

A MORE ACCOUNTABLE, TRANSPARENT FED

Monetary policy poses a dilemma for politicians. Electoral incentives encourage short-term economic stimulants, but come with long-term costs: increased chances of inflation and higher odds of a recessionary payback. The solution worldwide has been to try to insulate central bankers from political interference (particularly in the run-up to an election) that might otherwise induce monetary policy makers to keep interest rates too loose for too long.[8] That is the root of politicians' dilemma: fully autonomous central banks would preclude lawmakers from micromanaging macroeconomic policy and holding central bankers accountable for their policy mistakes. In short, lawmakers face the challenge of empowering and controlling central bank decisions.

In return for giving the Fed more power, Congress periodically demands greater accountability. Critics charge today that the Fed's monetary policy decisions remain too insulated from public view. But the trajectory of the Fed over its first century has been toward greater accountability to its congressional overseers. As we explore in detail in later chapters, accountability requirements take different forms. Creating or revising the Fed's statutory mandates, imposing new reporting requirements, subjecting the Fed to audits—these and other reforms create potential avenues for greater congressional oversight of the Fed. And over the Fed's history, both parties have demanded greater transparency. For example, in the wake of the 2007 financial crisis, Republicans continue to champion "audit the Fed" legislation. But populist Democrats first proposed auditing the Fed more than a half century ago in an effort to force the Fed to be more accountable to the views of the congressional Democratic majority.

With rare exception, the Fed routinely fights congressional efforts to increase scrutiny of monetary policy choices. Central bank resistance to greater congressional oversight is not surprising: when Congress puts in place new mechanisms for overseeing the central bank, the Fed's autonomy weakens. Mandating new goals for the Fed to guide its conduct of monetary policy, for instance, necessarily constrains and could even tilt the Fed's discretion in setting interest rates. Similarly, requiring regular reporting to Congress of the Fed's monetary policy targets creates additional economic performance benchmarks against which lawmakers can ostensibly hold the Fed accountable for its performance. By forcing the Fed to justify its policy choices in real time, Congress makes it harder for the central bank to deploy unconventional tools at the height of a financial or economic crisis.

As we discuss in detail below, lawmakers asymmetrically demand more accountability from the Fed for its performance in managing the economy. When the economy is performing well, Congress pays relatively little attention to the Fed—allowing the central bank to seem independent from its political overseers. In contrast, public support for the Fed declines markedly when the economy suffers; lawmakers are more likely to criticize the Fed and propose new limits on the Fed's operational independence. Whether congressional criticism fuels public distrust or vice versa, the result is the same: lawmakers demand more accountability from the Federal Reserve—over time transforming the Fed into a far more transparent institution.

A Political-Economic Theory of Reform

Our theory of monetary politics highlights why and when economics and politics interact to shape the nature as well as timing of Fed reform. Economic and financial crises typically encourage reelection-minded lawmakers to pay attention to the Fed.

Lawmakers' inherently reactive behavior means that congressional action is countercyclical. The Fed largely escapes scrutiny when the economy is sound. But a souring economy encourages Fed-blaming lawmakers to revisit the act, and reconsider the powers and governance of the Federal Reserve.

Simple changes in the economy are necessary but rarely sufficient to generate congressional action. Political and institutional forces on Capitol Hill and in the White House shape both the chances that Congress acts and the proposals it adopts. Given many legislative veto points and often competing partisan prescriptions, changes to the Federal Reserve Act are more likely when a single party controls both Congress and the White House. Still, majority parties rarely hold enough seats to act without some support from the opposition, so reform of the Fed inevitably requires the parties to compromise. Finally, conflict with the executive branch over how monetary policy should be made can shape lawmakers' preferred reforms. As we explain in chapter 5, the most dramatic such battle between the branches generated the Treasury-Fed Accord of 1951—a document that cemented the subordination of the Federal Reserve and monetary policy to Congress. In sum, economic, political, and institutional forces collectively generate a cycle of blame and reform, and mold the Fed's evolution as a political institution.

HOW CRISIS SHAPES REFORM OF THE FED

The Fed was born of crisis in the wake of the Panic of 1907. The existing privately controlled reserve system was incapable of stemming a full-blown banking crisis, and bank runs ended only when financier J. P. Morgan and a consortium of fellow bankers stepped in as "lenders of last resort" to provide banks needed liquidity. Despite the severity of the crisis, a Republican Congress reacted with baby steps: it passed the Aldrich-Vreeland Act of 1908 to authorize the Treasury to issue emergency currency during future panics and created the National Monetary Commission to study alternative reserve systems. In sync with financial conservatives who had for decades opposed government control of the reserve system (Ritter 1997), the 1910 Aldrich bill advocated a largely banker-controlled reserve system. Progressives and Democrats denounced the bill in their 1912 presidential party platforms, and deferred action on a new reserve system until after the election of 1912, in which the Democrats captured control of Congress and the White House for the first time in two decades. As we examine in chapter 3, newly elected Wilson made currency reform a high priority for the Democrats and signed the Federal Reserve Act into law just before Christmas in 1913.[9]

The creation of the Federal Reserve significantly dampened—but could not eliminate—banking crises or the deflation that had contributed to them. Indeed, deflation (falling prices) was pivotal to the onset of depression (falling output) in the late 1920s and early 1930s.[10] Congress responded to subsequent financial meltdowns and major economic crises by reopening the Federal Reserve Act to empower the Fed (and in the 1930s, the executive branch) to stem and reverse deflation. Lawmakers, for example, strengthened the Fed's lender of last resort powers in 1932, concentrated more power in political appointees heading a revamped Board of Governors in Washington in 1935, and imposed greater accountability in the wake of severe economic distress in both 1977 and 2010.

The Fed's financial crisis roots made subsequent reform even more likely. Legislative changes in the wake of a crisis typically fight the last fire, even though the next crisis frequently takes a different form and requires a new approach. If an institution cannot easily adapt, its policy failures often incite Congress to consider new reforms. Moreover, compromise demanded by the legislative process in creating or reforming an institution usually undermines the future effectiveness of the organization.[11] In the case of the Fed, the early compromises necessary for creating a decentralized institution in 1913 generated a structure that soon proved suboptimal for future crises. The original set of tools devised for the Fed in 1913 had become nearly obsolete when Congress revamped the Fed in the wake of the Great Depression. Financial crises   accompanied by an evolving understanding of monetary policy and macroeconomics—encouraged lawmakers to reshape the Fed even before its twentieth anniversary. The Fed's crisis-driven design, implemented in the early twentieth century amid world war and a historic depression, made subsequent changes to the Federal Reserve Act highly likely.

HOW CONGRESS'S REACTIVE BEHAVIOR GENERATES PRESSURE FOR REFORM

By affecting output, inflation, and employment, macroeconomic decisions by central banks are among the most important policy choices made in a democracy. Powerful fiscal and monetary policy trade-offs help to shape economic outcomes. And while the effects of fiscal policy decisions and institutions can outstrip the impact of central bank decision making, monetary policy affects interest rates immediately, which in turn shape the public's borrowing costs, the availability of credit, and ultimately economic growth and household wealth. As the public demand for goods and services grows, businesses and governments increase production and services as well as employ more workers. No other bureaucracy in the US political system has such a pervasive and enduring impact on the economic lives of citizens and businesses. This was especially so in the wake of the Great Recession when congressional stalemate over fiscal policy left the Fed, in the words of Senator Chuck Schumer (D-New York) in 2012, "the only game in town" (Menza 2012).

The distributional consequences of monetary policy play a central role in generating Congress's disproportionate attention to the Fed. As we show in chapter 2, legislators' focus on the Fed is typically reactive, rising and falling with the state of the economy. Congressional attention is thus countercyclical because the Fed is especially salient to "single-minded seekers of re-election" Mayhew (1974) when they seek to avoid blame for a bad economy. When monetary policy stokes inflation or contributes to job losses, lawmakers respond in two ways. First, they blame the Fed for the state of the economy and its impact on their constituents. Second, in particularly poor economic times, politicians are likely to prevent the Fed from making the same mistakes again, proposing and sometimes securing changes to the powers, mandate, or organization of the Fed.

Lawmakers' response to populist anger toward the Fed in the aftermath of the global financial crisis illustrates the dynamic starkly. The depth and breadth of public ire in hindsight are remarkable. Republicans warned that the Fed's unconventional cocktail of zero interest rates and unfettered purchases of government bonds would lead to imminent, uncontrollable inflation. Running for the GOP presidential nomination in 2008, Governor Rick Perry of Texas vowed that "if this guy prints more money between now and the election, I don't know what y'all would do to him in Iowa, but we— we would treat him pretty ugly down in Texas. Printing more money to play politics at this particular time in American history is almost treacherous—or treasonous in my opinion" (Keyes 2011). Perry's right-wing tirade echoed popular views across the ideological spectrum that the Fed's emergency actions during the crisis revealed a preference to rescue Wall Street before Main Street. On the Left, Occupy Wall Street rants in 2011 against rising levels of economic inequality spawned Occupy the Fed protests at barely known Federal Reserve regional banks. On the Right, public anger helped to propel Rep. Ron Paul's (R-Texas) "End the Fed" presidential campaign and his "Audit the Fed" legislative drive.

Fed officials at the time worried that populist criticism was taking a toll on the Fed's reputation and autonomy to conduct monetary policy.[12] Such concerns led a reportedly reluctant Fed chair Bernanke to appear twice on *60 Minutes*, conduct town hall meetings, teach a course about the Federal Reserve to college students at George Washington University, and appear at other unprecedented public and private engagements to explain the Fed's unconventional monetary policy in accessible terms. The *Washington Post* subsequently reported that "the goal was to convince the country—largely through the reassuring words of the soft-spoken Bernanke, a son of Dillon, S.C.—that the Fed was out to help the average American worker" (Goldfarb 2014). After leaving office, Bernanke summed up the challenge: "The natural reaction from the guy on Main Street is, well, how come you're bailing them out and not bailing me out? And the answer is complicated: by preventing the system from collapsing, we are protecting the economy and we are protecting you. It's a complicated argument to make" (Fitch 2014).

As we explore in chapter 7, such efforts failed to dissuade lawmakers from revamping the powers of the Fed in the wake of the global financial crisis. When Congress wrote the Dodd-Frank Wall Street Reform and Consumer Protection Act in 2010, lawmakers gave the Fed more supervisory powers over large financial institutions. But channeling public anger from the Left and Right about the Fed's unconventional policies during the crisis, Congress also imposed more transparency on the Fed and clipped its lender of last resort authority. Public anger compelled electorally motivated legislators to place reform of the Fed high on their postcrisis agendas and act to revamp the law.

WHY AND HOW PARTIES DIVIDE OVER MONETARY POLICY

The global financial crisis reminds us that in the wake of economic downturns, populist fringes of the two major parties are occasionally aligned in their criticism of the Fed and proposals to reform it. Over the broader arc of Fed history, however, the two parties typically hold markedly different views about the role of the government and central bank in managing the economy. Democrats and Republicans usually disagree about the appropriate trade-off between growth and inflation. More likely creditors than borrowers—today and in the past—Republicans have long been the party of financial conservatism. Even in the nineteenth century, Republicans opposed government management of the economy—instead favoring use of a gold standard along with Wall Street control of currency and credit.[13] In contrast, southern and western farmers were likely to have been Democrats, supporting more inflationary policies—including the adoption of a "bimetallic" standard of coining both gold and silver. Although the United States long ago abandoned the gold standard, differences between the constituency bases of the parties endure: contrasting attitudes about the appropriate trade-off between inflation and employment today still color Democratic and Republican views about how Fed power should be exercised.

That said, Congress does not give the Fed free rein to determine how to balance the goals of promoting jobs and limiting inflation. As we discuss later in the book, Democratic majorities at pivotal points in the Fed's history have dictated with increasing clarity the Fed's dual mandate: a statutory requirement that the central bank pursue both maximum employment and low, stable inflation. The parties, however, have fought over what the mandate should be and the tools that the Fed should have to pursue it. So long as the two parties represent divergent constituency interests, congressional parties will prescribe different fixes for the Fed. In short, contests over the powers and governance of the Fed reflect prevailing partisan or factional lines within the legislature. Still, neither party's majorities are typically large or cohesive enough to exclude the other party when considering reform of the Fed. In other words, majorities are often forced to compromise when they try to institutionalize their priorities into the Federal Reserve Act.

Internal party divisions also shape congressional moves to revamp the Fed. The most important such differences emerged within the Democratic Party with the rise of the Conservative Coalition in the late 1930s. For nearly a half century, Republican and southern Democratic conservatives joined forces to oppose key parts of the New Deal's economic (and later, racial) liberalism. Conservatives generally opposed the spread of federal economic power into the South, fearing that government intervention in the economy would threaten the South's racially segregated economy as well as social and political spheres. Throughout the book, we examine the impact of this ideological cleavage on reform of the Fed. We pay special attention to southern Democrats' fight to preserve the decentralized, federal character of the reserve system, even as their northern, more liberal colleagues pushed to centralize power in the Fed in Washington. Conservatives no longer rule the roost in the Democratic Party. But their imprint has been institutionalized in the governance and organization of the Fed.

INTERBRANCH CONTESTS TO CONTROL THE FED

Institutional fault lines—pitting legislators against the president—have also shaped contests over the powers and governance of the

Fed. Interbranch rifts are particularly likely when questions of Fed independence—from whom, to do what, and over what time horizon—arise. As we explore in chapter 5, such battles are not strictly partisan: the fight to secure the Fed's independence from the Treasury in the late 1940s and early 1950s, for example, occurred largely among Democrats. Indeed, the move in 1951 to free the Fed from monetizing Treasury debt was fought largely on institutional, not partisan, grounds. A small, bipartisan coalition of senators joined the Fed's struggle to free itself from executive branch control and Treasury Department subordination. Viewed more broadly, politicians' institutional positions can shape their views about the powers and accountability of the Fed. Lawmakers assert their constitutional power to manage the currency, while presidents exploit their executive power to push the Fed to support their administration's macroeconomic goals.

Still, Congress at times has pushed the executive to exert more control over monetary policy. As we investigate in chapter 4, Congress adopted several measures in the wake of the Great Depression that enhanced presidential influence over monetary policy. Empowering the president to take the country off the gold standard, creating a currency exchange fund within the Treasury—these and other legislative moves significantly enhanced the White House's potential influence over monetary policy and central bankers in the 1930s and 1940s. Recouping those powers became a key challenge for lawmakers seeking to cement the Fed's subordination to Congress and secure its support for Congress's postwar economic priorities. In sum, the interaction of economics, politics, and institutions indelibly shapes the evolution of the Fed.

Plan of the Book

Table 1.1 lists key legislation that transformed the Fed over its first century—from enactment of the Federal Reserve Act in 1913, adoption of the 1951 Treasury-Fed Accord, and reorganization of the financial regulatory system in the Dodd-Frank Act of 2010.[14] As we explore in detail throughout the book, political reforms can expand

TABLE 1.1. Key Episodes of Congressional Reform of the Fed, 1913–2015

Year	Reform
1913	Federal Reserve Act adopted
1917	First and Second Liberty Bond Acts
1922	Addition of agricultural seat to Federal Reserve Board
1923	Agricultural Credits Act of 1923
1927	McFadden Act
1932	Glass-Steagall Act (February) and Emergency Relief and Construction Act (July)
1933	Emergency Banking Act (March), Thomas Amendment (1933), and Banking Act (June)
1934	Gold Reserve Act of 1934
1935	Banking Act of 1935
1942	Second War Powers Act of 1942
1946	Employment Act of 1946
1951	Treasury-Fed Accord (nonlegislative)
1956	Bank Holding Company Act
1975	House Concurrent Resolution 133 (new reporting requirements)
1977	Federal Reserve Act Amendments
1978	Humphrey-Hawkins Full Employment Act
1980	Monetary Control Act
1991	Federal Deposit Insurance Corporation Improvement Act
2006	Financial Services Regulatory Relief Act
2010	Dodd-Frank Wall Street Reform and Consumer Protection Act

the power and mandates of the Fed, reorganize its governance and organizational structure, impose greater accountability, or strip the Fed of previously granted powers. Sometimes, Congress only empowers the Fed, and at other times it only clips its wings. Equally often, legislative packages become a common carrier for a broader range of changes to the Federal Reserve Act—coupling reforms that give the Fed more responsibility while imposing stronger oversight over the use of new or inherited powers.

Chapter 2 offers a broad view of patterns in the timing of proposals and successful congressional action to reform the Fed. Historical quantitative evidence allows us to apply our political-economic theory of reform to the history of the Fed, examining the conditions that encourage lawmakers to act. Chapters 3 through 7 dive chronologically into key episodes of reform, probing the particular political and economic circumstances that lead lawmakers to challenge the Fed as well as revamp the central bank's powers, organization, and governance. Chapter 8 takes broader stock of the Fed's transformation, and speculates about the political and economic challenges ahead for the Fed's second century.

We begin in chapter 2 by testing the fit of our theory to broader trends in the Congress-Fed relationship. How does the state of the economy shape both lawmakers' and the public's attention to the Fed? We marshal public opinion polls in recent decades to demonstrate that the public routinely blames the Fed when the economy falters, even as heightened partisanship among voters now colors citizen attitudes about the Fed. Using data on congressional bill sponsorship over a sixty-year period, we also establish lawmakers' reactive attention to monetary policy. Finally, we explore the conditions that foster major Fed reform, showing the impact of partisan alignments and economic distress on changes to the Federal Reserve Act. Overall, lawmakers' political efforts to avoid blame for major downtowns in the economy lead Congress to saddle the Fed with even more responsibility while often punishing it for poor performance.

We dive into the historical transformation of the Fed in chapter 3, looking at the dynamics that drove the adoption of the Federal Reserve Act in 1913. Acute financial crisis—coupled with electoral change in 1912—put creation of a central bank on Washington's agenda after nearly a century of US antipathy toward government control of currency and credit. The institution that emerged from congressional and presidential bargaining in 1913 was truly "federal": the Federal Reserve Act empowered quasi-private, regional district banks to conduct their own open market operations, even occasionally defying the Washington-based Board's efforts to set regional lending rates. Although the reserve system's framers sought to make the Fed independent of Wall Street financial interests, there was little enthusiasm for placing the new institution out of reach of political control. Placement of the comptroller of the currency and the Treasury secretary on the Federal Reserve Board in Washington cemented the Board as a public capstone on a broadly decentralized reserve system. In sum, although the original Fed did not rely on government funds to operate, the new institution was obviously decentralized and only marginally independent.

In chapter 3, we also examine how political and financial forces shaped the organization of the reserve system in 1914. Democrats choose a design that served their policy interests: Democrats broadened the regional footprint of the Fed to ensure greater access to credit for Populist and Democratic constituencies far from the Eastern Seaboard, and bolstered the economies of the underdeveloped South. Despite the assertion of the Reserve Bank Organization Committee (RBOC)—led by high-ranking Wilson political appointees—that only economic and financial criteria would guide its decisions about where to locate the new reserve banks, our analysis shows that Democrats' policy and political interests led them to spread access to credit beyond Wall Street and other turn-of-the-century financial hubs.

The regional design of the reserve system had political, institutional, and policy consequences. By placing reserve banks in communities across the country, Main Street political support for the new Federal Reserve was soon hardwired across the geographic array of districts and states that secured one of the twelve regional banks. Such geographically diverse support meant that "reserve bank" lawmakers would rally to the support of the Federal Reserve when future Congresses considered either cutting back the Fed's autonomy or granting it new powers. Ironically, it was the Fed's decentralized authority and structure that was partially to blame for the duration and severity of the Great Depression less than two decades later. Remarkably, the signature achievement of the RBOC lacked the monetary policy tools and structure to prevent another financial collapse in the run-up to the economic havoc of the 1930s.

In chapters 4 through 7, we explore the transformation of the Fed into a more powerful and accountable institution. Chapter 4 tackles congressional battles to reform the Fed amid financial and economic crises—first in the early 1920s, and later in the years following the stock market crash in 1929. The mid-1920s proved to be a period of experimentation within the Federal Reserve System as the regional reserve banks tried unsuccessfully to coordinate their "open market" buying and selling of government bonds to adjust the cost of borrowing and supply of credit. Coupled with the Board's limited power in

Washington, missteps by the Fed (including misreading the economy, raising interest rates, and letting banks fail) ultimately led to the 1929 collapse of the stock market and onset of the Great Depression. The electoral change that followed pushed politicians to bring control of monetary policy more tightly under the thumb of political appointees. Concentrating and coordinating open market operations in Washington and New York, creating new emergency lending authority for the Fed, and creating new monetary policy powers for the president and Treasury drove reform of the central bank after Roosevelt and large Democratic majorities took office in 1933.

We also show in chapter 4 the impact of a widening divide within the Democratic Party on reform of the Fed—examining political reactions when Roosevelt and Eccles pushed Congress to rewrite the Federal Reserve Act in 1935. One coalition, aligned with FDR and Eccles, sought to revamp the FOMC that had been created in 1933 and had only included heads of the reserve banks. The FDR-Eccles coalition pushed for greater centralization of monetary policy making, proposing to empower a newly created Board of Governors in Washington and strip reserve banks of their votes on the FOMC. A rival coalition—led by Senator Carter Glass (D-Virginia), the key architect of the 1913, decentralized system—sought to protect a role and voting rights for the regional reserve banks in the making of monetary policy. We explore Congress's institutional choices in revamping the Federal Reserve Act in 1933 and 1935, probing the partisan and electoral forces that gave rise to a split-the-difference compromise between the Eccles and Glass factions. The Fed emerged far more centralized than Glass's original design, albeit with vestiges of his federal system that guaranteed voting rights on monetary policy for leaders of the regional reserve banks. Moreover, Congress enhanced political control over monetary policy by granting the president tools that could be used to expand the money supply and take the country off the gold standard.

We turn in chapter 5 to the postwar period, including the adoption of the 1946 Employment Act and implementation of the 1951 Treasury-Fed Accord. Most accounts of the Accord depict it as the critical moment in the birth of the modern, independent Federal

Reserve. We recognize the importance of the Accord for the Fed's maturation as a central bank. We provide an alternative account of the dynamics that gave rise to the Accord. First, we emphasize that the Fed gained independence from the Treasury, but not from Congress. In fact, the Accord made the Fed more dependent on Congress. Second, we probe the conflict between Congress and the White House over the Fed's subordination to the Treasury—given pressures from Congress for the Fed to tackle inflation after the Korean War. We highlight the impact of lawmakers who encouraged the Fed to break its wartime pledge to keep interest rates pegged low to allow the Treasury to cheaply finance its war debts. Why did Congress get involved in this dispute between the president, Treasury, and the FOMC over the pegging of the Fed's interest rate on government debt? And why did congressional Democrats oppose their party's president, Harry S. Truman, by siding with the Fed over the Treasury? By highlighting lawmakers' role in the genesis of the Accord, we recast the implications of this existential transformation of the Fed.

In chapter 6, we turn our focus to Congress's rewriting of portions of the Federal Reserve Act in the 1970s given Democrats' frustration with the performance of the Fed. A severe economic downturn, the evolution of monetary theory, and partisan politics led to the establishment of the Fed's first explicit statutory mandate from Congress—one that required the Federal Reserve to secure price stability and maximize employment. We argue that stipulating a mandate and imposing new transparency requirements reduced the Fed's autonomy: the reforms made clear the policy grounds on which Congress would seek to hold the Fed accountable, and required the Fed to set and justify policy targets before Congress. We also compare the records of successive Fed chairs, Arthur F. Burns and Paul Volcker, in combating stagflation and restoring the economy, debunking conventional wisdom that Volcker's independent leadership sufficed to return the economy to health by the mid-1980s. We suggest instead that considerable support from the White House and key lawmakers contributed to Volcker's success. Far from a demonstration of Fed independence, the Fed's performance under

Volcker's leadership indicates that support from fiscal authorities is necessary for the Fed to sustain unpopular monetary policy.

In chapter 7, we examine congressional reaction to the Fed's performance in the run-up to and aftermath of the financial and economic crises that began in 2007. By exploiting its emergency lending power, and extending billions of dollars of credit to a broad range of businesses, investment firms, banks, and nondepository institutions, the Fed stirred debate over the appropriate role of central banks in stemming crisis along with restoring the financial system and economy. The choices of the Fed in 2008—especially decisions to facilitate the acquisition of Bear Stearns by J. P. Morgan, rescue AIG and make its counterparties whole at par, and stand by while the Lehman Brothers went bankrupt—and secrecy with which the Fed acted fueled significant criticism of the Fed as well as efforts to reform it when Congress and the president turned to rewiring the financial regulatory system in 2009.

Disagreements over the appropriate powers and organization of the Fed surfaced in the drafting of the Dodd-Frank Act in the wake of the crisis. The administration and Democratic leaders contended with three competing coalitions. One group fought for new macroprudential supervisory and regulatory powers for the Federal Reserve as the regulator of systemically important institutions. Another coalition—led by two senators representing states that housed Federal Reserve district banks—sought to protect the power of the regional banks in the face of pressure to strip them of their supervisory roles and revise the process for selecting their leaders. Yet another coalition emerged to push for greater transparency in the Fed's use of its emergency lending powers. Ultimately, legislators approved new audits of the Federal Reserve, defeated efforts to strip the regional banks of their supervisory role, pared back the Fed's lending powers, and gave the Fed new supervisory and regulatory powers. In chapter 7, we demonstrate that financial crisis and partisan politics interacted to drive a Democratic Congress to reward the Fed with additional authority and expand its mission, all the while sustaining its regional structure and requiring greater transparency for its lending decisions.

Chapter 8 concludes, placing the transformation of the Federal Reserve into a broader, democratic context. Driven by the interaction of politics and economics, the Fed's evolution into the world's dominant central bank illustrates the double-edged sword of congressional empowerment. One side of the sword gives lawmakers expressly what they wish for: a central bank with a reputation for independence and sufficiently centralized authority to act as the uber regulator of the financial system, a global lender of last resort during severe economic downturns, and a receptor of more blame and power when the nation steps back from the economic abyss. In the current, polarized era in which politicians routinely stalemate over more aggressive fiscal stimulus, the burden of generating economic growth in the wake of the crisis and recession rests even more firmly on the Fed's shoulders.

The other side of the sword is problematic. The Fed's dominant macroeconomic role exposes it to severe criticism, especially in the wake of crises when the Fed attracts considerable political oversight and criticism of its policy choices. Such criticism compromises the Fed's reputation for independence. As political scientist Daniel Carpenter (2010) argues, institutional reputations are "organizational assets"; they are critical to sustaining and expanding an institution's power and autonomy over time. Has the Fed's reputation and credibility been irreparably harmed by its actions during and after the recent crisis? How will the Fed withstand its critics on the Left and Right as it continues to unwind its massive balance sheet? Will unified Republican control of government in 2017 and the elevated threat of reform alter the Fed's approach to monetary policy? We conclude our study by speculating about the likely institutional future of the Federal Reserve, given its historical path and the magnitude of the policy-making challenges it will continue to face in the years ahead.

2

The Blame Game

> As an institution, the Federal Reserve must continue to be willing to make tough decisions, based on objective, empirical analysis and without regard to political pressure. But . . . we must also recognize that the Fed's ability to make and implement such decisions ultimately depends on the public's understanding and acceptance of our actions. . . . Ultimately, the legitimacy of our policies rests on the understanding and support of the broader American public, whose interests we are working to serve.
>
> —BEN S. BERNANKE, "CONCLUDING REMARKS"

The Federal Reserve's evolution into a powerful, more macroeconomic focused policy maker and financial regulator capable of making tough decisions belies its persistent dependence on political support. By highlighting the importance of public acceptance for the Fed's monetary decisions, Bernanke reveals that Congress—the national institution that channels public discontent and holds exclusive authority to rewrite the Federal Reserve Act—is the proximate audience for Fed policy makers. "Congress is our boss," he told his successor, Yellen (Federal Reserve 2013).

In chapter 1, we proposed that the transformation of the Federal Reserve into a more powerful and transparent institution stems from a century of political interactions between Congress and the Fed. Contrary to notions of an independent central bank, Congress and the Fed are interdependent institutions. We argued that recurring cycles of crisis, blame, and reform drove the Fed's creation, and continue to shape its evolution today. Crisis spurs lawmakers to pay heed to the Fed's and Congress's own failures in managing the economy. Avoiding blame for a poor economy compels Congress to revise the Federal Reserve Act—often empowering the Fed or paring back its powers, and usually demanding greater transparency from the central bank.

In this chapter, we offer initial tests of our theory by modeling the cycles of blame and reform that drive the evolution of the Fed. First, we use public opinion surveys to track changes in the Fed's public standing and determine the forces that shape approval of the Fed. In particular, we look for evidence that the public blames the Fed for economic downturns. If the Fed's reputation is associated with economic health, one should expect blame-avoiding, election-seeking lawmakers to hold the Fed accountable when the economy falters. Second, we investigate the conditions that encourage lawmakers to propose changes to the Fed's powers, governance, and organization. These efforts typically fold before Congress rewrites the Federal Reserve Act. But mapping the political economy of legislative threats is important: lawmakers send key signals to the Fed about the nature and intensity of their concerns about the Fed's performance, and lay the groundwork for future reform. Analyzing legislators' bill portfolios allows us to pinpoint the forces that drive the timing and shape of reform.

Third, we test empirically the main claims of the book: that crisis begets blame and blame begets reform. Using the historical set of major of changes to the Federal Reserve Act outlined in chapter 1, we examine the economic and political forces associated with amendments to the law. As we show in subsequent chapters and as contemporary critics continue to call for additional reform, the cumulative impact of legislative changes is a more powerful, more transparent, and ultimately more congressionally accountable central bank. In sum, the powers and transparency of the modern Fed emerge from a century of economic crises and political interactions between these two interdependent institutions.

Public Perceptions of the Economy and the Federal Reserve

When Alan Greenspan stepped down as chair of the Fed in 2006 (after almost nineteen years at the helm), he enjoyed a 65 percent approval rating—befitting a central banker commonly referred to as "the maestro." In contrast, when Bernanke completed his second term as chair in January 2014, 40 percent of the public reflected favorably on his performance (Dugan 2014). Of course, snapshots of public approval can mislead and fail to reveal the full set of forces shaping confidence in the Fed. In particular, such glimpses of the Fed's approval do not tell us whether or how closely the public holds the Fed accountable for the state of the economy. If the public fails to recognize the centrality of the Fed to the nation's economy, it would be unusual for Congress to scapegoat the Fed when the economy sours.

To investigate the forces that shape the Fed's public standing, we examine two sets of opinion data: a time series of public attitudes over the past forty years, and a 2014 poll that delves into views about Yellen's stewardship of the Fed. Figure 2.1 reports every poll available in the Roper Center's Public Opinion Archives between 1975 and spring 2015 that addresses public approval of, confidence in, or support for the Federal Reserve, its chair, or its monetary policy choices. Granted, pollsters do not consistently ask the same question about the public's views of the Fed, suggesting that the survey results might tap different but related dimensions of public approval. But given the relatively few number of survey questions asked over the period, we combine the responses into a single measure of public support for the Fed.

Two trends stand out. First, pollsters periodically ignore the Fed. After a burst of attention during Volcker's controversial inflation-squelching rate increases in the late 1970s and early 1980s, pollsters

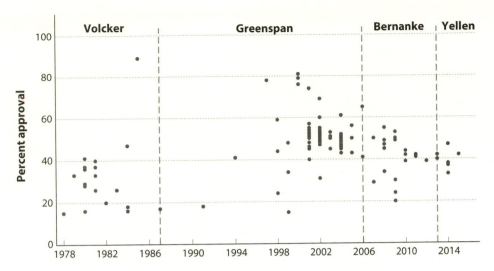

FIGURE 2.1. Public approval of the Federal Reserve, 1979–2015. The figure includes every poll available in the Roper Center's Public Opinion Archives between 1975 and spring 2015 that addresses public approval of, confidence in, or support for the Federal Reserve, its chair, or its monetary policy choices. The polls are located via a "Federal Reserve" search. Note that Bernanke's last poll was taken in January 2014, but is coded for presentation purposes as taken in 2013. All other 2014 polls were conducted during Yellen's tenure as chair of the Federal Reserve Board of Governors. Storrs, CT: Roper Center for Public Opinion Research, Roper*Express* (distributor), accessed November 30, 2015, https://ropercenter.cornell.edu/CFIDE/cf/action/home/index.cfm. Citations for individual polls available from authors on request.

focused elsewhere until the middle of the Greenspan era. The sparse data midstream limits our generalizations about the forces shaping opinion over the longer term. Second, as shown in figure 2.2, tougher economic times dampen confidence in the Fed. Regressing approval ratings for the Volcker, Greenspan, Bernanke, and Yellen Feds against annual unemployment and inflation rates, we find that an improving economy (with less inflation and fewer unemployed) is associated with slightly higher approval ratings for the Fed and its leaders.[1]

We can use the model's predicted levels of approval to assess whether particular Fed chairs are especially prone to gain or lose the public's confidence. Controlling for the state of the economy, Bernanke, for example, faced far tougher sledding than expected during 2010 and 2011, after securing confirmation in the wake of the

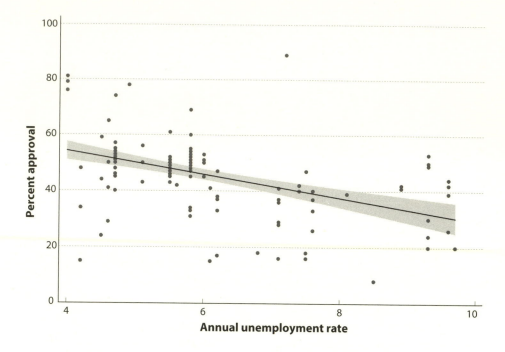

FIGURE 2.2. The economy and public approval of the Fed, 1979–2015. Using data from figure 2.1, we plot percent approval as a function of the annual unemployment rate. We calculate predicted approval as a function of unemployment and plot the resulting line with a 95 percent confidence interval. We use the nonseasonally adjusted, annual unemployment rate reported in Bureau of Labor Statistics, "Labor Force Statistics from the Current Population Survey," 2015. Accessed January 1, 2017, http://data.bls.gov/timeseries/LNU04000000?years_option=all _years&periods_option=specific_periods&periods=Annual+Data.

Great Recession for a second term.[2] We suspect that conservatives' steady and harsh criticism of the Bernanke Fed's unconventional monetary policies (as we explore in chapter 7) tarnished Bernanke's public reputation. Bernanke fared better than predicted, however, in 2012 and 2013, during the last two years of his second term. Perhaps the "all-out campaign" by the Fed to win back public support had begun to pay dividends (Goldfarb 2014).

Digging deeper into a national opinion poll affords us a better understanding of the sources of public sentiment toward the Fed.[3] Ten months into Yellen's term as chair, the Gallup Organization in November 2014 asked a national sample of adults, "How would you rate the job being done by . . . the Federal Reserve Board? Would you

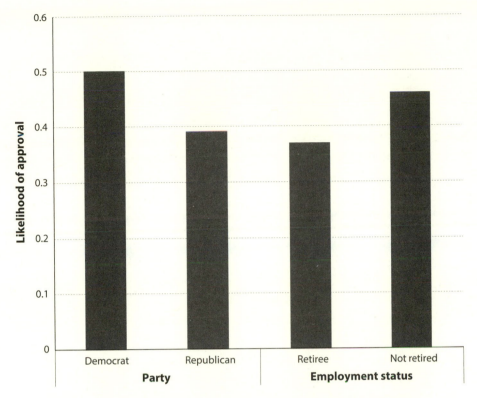

FIGURE 2.3. Likelihood of approving Fed's performance, 2014. The approval is simulated as a function of respondent income and education level. Gallup Organization, Gallup Poll, November 2014 (survey question). USGALLUP.112014A.R01C, Gallup Organization (producer). Ithaca, NY: Cornell University, Roper Center for Public Opinion Research, iPOLL (distributor), accessed July 10, 2016, https://ropercenter.cornell.edu/CFIDE/cf/action/home/index.cfm.

say it is doing an excellent, good, only fair, or poor job?" Even with the average unemployment rate in the United States at 5.8 percent that month and inflation barely over 1 percent, half of the respondents gave the Fed a fair or poor rating; 38 percent judged the Fed's performance good or excellent.

Looking more closely, partisan and financial factors shaped the respondents' views. As shown in figure 2.3, controlling for education and household income, Republicans and retirees disproportionately disapproved of the Fed's economic stewardship.[1] When we simulate support for the Fed, controlling for education, income, and work status, roughly half of Democrats approve of the central bank's performance, compared to just 37 percent of Republicans. In our simulations, a similar gap divides attitudes of retirees from those still working: nearly half of those in the workforce approve of the Fed, compared to just a third of retirees.

With the 2014 White House in Democratic hands—and Yellen appointed by President Obama—the results confirm that partisanship colors the public's economic evaluations. Similarly, retirees' negative views of the Fed are not unreasonable given the common criticism that the Fed's low interest rates disproportionately harm income-dependent older Americans. Still, these patterns are important: they reinforce the conditionality of public attitudes about the Fed. Americans do not perceive the Fed as a technocratic body of experts. In fact, they see the central bank as they might perceive any other political institution: partisan and economic heuristics mold evaluations of the Fed's performance.

Few Americans follow the details of monetary policy closely. Most everyone, though, understands their own economic situation. Such evaluations—whether aggregated over several decades or taken as a snapshot of recent opinion—reveal the strength of the Fed's public credibility as an economic policy maker and the efficacy of monetary policy itself. Lawmakers, of course, are electorally attuned to heed such shifts in public sentiment. As we show below, such economic alarms motivate legislators to criticize the Fed and threaten to revisit its governing law. As Bernanke observed, central bankers take these threats seriously. They wish to safeguard the Fed's powers and autonomy, and understand and rely on strong political support to succeed.

Legislative Signals to the Fed, 1947–2014

Our theory suggests that cycles of crisis, blame, and reform drive the institutional and statutory evolution of the Fed. In this section, we closely examine the first part of the cycle: How, if at all, do changes in the nation's economic health influence lawmakers' attention to and proposals for reforming the Fed? As evidence for the theory, we anticipate three trends in the nature and timing of lawmakers' legislative proposals that would affect the powers or governance of the Fed.

First, we expect reelection-oriented lawmakers to react to economic downturns by shifting blame to the Fed, and proposing changes to its governance and powers. As we explore in detail below, this dynamic should be visible in the timing of legislative proposals to amend the Federal Reserve Act, nature of those proposals, and identity of the lawmakers who champion such proposals.

Second, because the state of the economy shapes party fortunes at the ballot box, we expect a partisan cast to legislative proposals that target the Fed. Lower-income, Democratic voters are more likely to be impacted by economic downturns, so Democratic lawmakers might be more prone to attack the Fed when unemployment is high. Conversely, representatives of typically higher-income Republican creditors might be more likely to focus on the Fed when inflation rises. Still, the Fed's dual mandate from Congress directs the Fed to both maximize employment and stabilize prices. It is thus possible that Democrats' attention to the Fed waned after the dual mandate was clarified in the 1977 amendments to the Federal Reserve Act. Once Congress legally cemented the Fed's dual mandate for boosting jobs and fighting inflation, the pressure on Democrats to threaten changes to the Fed's toolbox might have slipped. In contrast, GOP attention to the Fed might have increased after the 1977 amendments, as Republicans reacted to the dual mandate by advocating that the Fed prioritize fighting inflation under a single mandate.

Third, like most national institutions, the Federal Reserve has been caught in the cross hairs of contemporary partisan polarization. Congressional disagreements with the performance of the Fed in recent years lead us to expect that recent congressional and executive attacks on the Fed might emerge from the more ideologically intense fringes of both parties.

In short, during severe economic times, we should expect both parties to revisit the Federal Reserve Act. Because lawmakers are prone to fighting the last war (a sign of their reactive, election-motivated policy making), legislators could easily justify limiting Fed powers or, counterintuitively, expanding them. Sometimes lawmakers view restrictions on the Fed's authority or more oversight as sufficient. Alternatively, by granting the Fed *more* power after economic crises, blame-averse lawmakers establish additional reasons to attack the Fed during the next, inevitable economic downturn.

LEGISLATIVE AGENDAS DATA

We measure lawmakers' attention to monetary policy by tracking the introduction of bills between 1947 and 2014 that address the power, structure, and governance of the Federal Reserve. We treat lawmakers' bill portfolios as statements of their issue agendas: regardless of whether legislators' efforts become law, sponsoring a bill signals a lawmaker's policy and political priorities.[5] We code the content of each bill along several dimensions, including whether the bill seeks to constrain or empower the Federal Reserve, increase or decrease its independence, centralize or decentralize power within the Federal Reserve System, or alter the makeup of the Federal Reserve's Board of Governors.[6] Overall, 879 bills were introduced in the House and Senate over these 6.5 decades, representing the legislative efforts of 333 House and Senate lawmakers.

Bill Sponsorship

We start by examining trends in bill sponsorship. Figure 2.4 shows the number of bills introduced each year.[7] We overlay a smoothed "misery index" on the data to demonstrate the relationship between congressional attention to the Fed and the state of the economy.[8] The data suggest that legislative interest rises with economic downturns, recurring in the late 1950s and early 1960s, the mid-1970s and early 1980s, and today. Similar to the rarity of polls focused on the Greenspan Fed, congressional attention drops precipitously during the Greenspan-led, mid-1980s' Great Moderation.

Bill sponsorships also provide a window into the two parties' relative interest in the Fed, as shown in figure 2.5's display of the annual proportion of Federal Reserve bills introduced by Democrats and Republicans. Between the end of World War II and the stagflationary 1970s, Republicans seemed disinterested in the Fed and

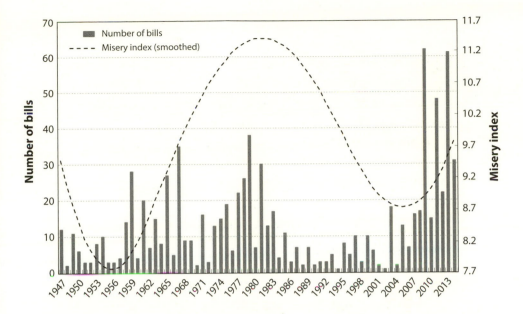

FIGURE 2.4. Number of bills introduced addressing the Fed, 1947–2014. For bill introduction data, see Adler and Wilkerson n.d.; Proquest n.d.; http://thomas.loc.gov. For economic data, see https://research.stlouisfed.org/fred2/.

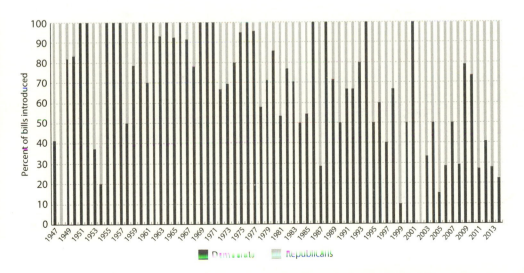

FIGURE 2.5. Congressional attention to the Fed, by party, 1947–2014. For bill introduction data, see Adler and Wilkerson n.d.; Proquest n.d.; http://thomas.loc.gov.

its powers. Granted, Democrats typically outnumbered Republicans in the House and Senate over this long period of Democratic control of Congress. Republican interest in the Fed nonetheless begins to grow (as Democratic interest wanes) after formal adoption of the dual mandate in 1977, long before the onset of GOP majorities in the 1994 elections. Once Democrats successfully added employment maximization to the Fed's mandate, their incentives to seek further changes in the powers of the Fed diminished.

With the onset of the Great Recession and implementation of unconventional monetary policy tools (after the Fed had lowered interest rates to effectively zero), the parties appeared to care equally about the central bank and its policies. Between 2007 and 2012, Democrats and Republicans introduced roughly the same number of bills, although Republicans' legislative activity climbed markedly in 2013 and 2014.[9] Partisans often differed in their prescriptions for the Fed. Representative Barney Frank of Massachusetts, the ranking Democrat on the House Financial Services Committee in 2011, proposed stripping reserve bank presidents of their votes on the FOMC—a move that would empower presidential appointees and centralize power considerably within the DC-based Board of Governors; in 2012, Republican Kevin Brady of Texas wanted all twelve reserve bank presidents to vote at each FOMC meeting (versus the current rotating scheme that limits reserve bank presidents to five votes each meeting). As a group, district bank presidents tend to be more hawkish than the Board members, making it tougher for the Board to monopolize monetary policy. Still, on some issues— especially related to transparency—coalitions sported odd bedfellows: liberal Bernie Sanders (I-Vermont) and conservative David Vitter (R-Louisiana) advocated audits of the FOMC in 2010.

Substantive Focus

A clear pattern also emerges when we examine the content of the bills. First, we assess bills that would directly empower or constrain the Fed. Empowering bills provide the Federal Reserve System with new authority, such as extending the Fed's authority to purchase obligations directly from Treasury. Constraining bills limit the Fed's

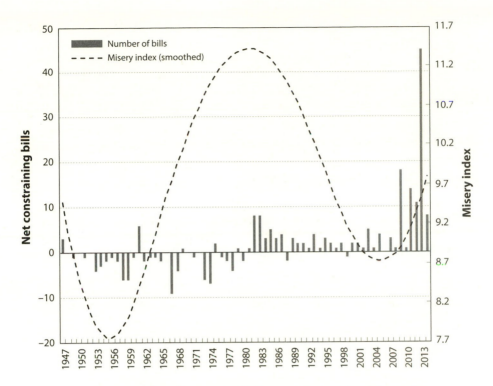

FIGURE 2.6. Constraining bias of congressional bills, 1947–2014. For bill introduction data, see Adler and Wilkerson n.d.; Proquest n.d.; http://thomas.loc.gov. For economic data, see https://research.stlouisfed.org/fred2/.

authority by, for example, preventing the Fed from purchasing certain obligations from foreign governments or mandating new action by the Fed (such as requiring the Board of Governors to establish monthly targets for interest rates).[10] To determine the net sentiment across lawmakers sponsoring bills each year, we subtract the total number of empowering bills from the total number of constraining bills each year.

Figure 2.6 captures lawmakers' collective views about reining in the powers of the Fed over the postwar period (again with the smoothed misery series overlaid).[11] Congressional attitudes about the powers of the Fed vary with the state of the economy. When the economy slips, lawmakers advocate clipping the powers of the Fed and limiting its policy-making discretion. Granted, these are proposals, not new laws. Regardless of how lawmakers legislate in

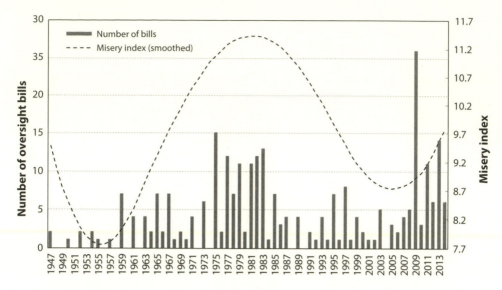

FIGURE 2.7. Number of bills introduced increasing congressional oversight of the Fed, 1947–2014. For bill introduction data, see Adler and Wilkerson N.d.; Proquest n.d.; http://thomas.loc.gov. For economic data, see https://research.stlouisfed.org/fred2/.

times of crisis, congressional sentiment leans toward new limits on Fed autonomy during economic downturns.

Second, we chart variation in the number of bills that would increase oversight of the Fed, such as bills to shorten the term of governors on the Board or expand government audits of the FOMC. We see a now-familiar countercyclical pattern in figure 2.7. Lawmakers more frequently propose greater oversight when the economy falters. The trend is most noticeable in the early 1980s, as we explore in chapter 6. Lawmakers from both parties reacted to Fed chair Volcker's push to hike interest rates when the Fed moved to tame inflation by inducing a deep recession. Democrats advocated changes to the Fed's organization and powers, including the expansion of the Fed's Board of Governors. By "packing the court" with additional president-appointed, Senate-confirmed governors to the Board, Congress would weaken the influence of reserve bank presidents and potentially dilute the chair's influence over monetary policy. Republicans pushed for more audits as well as synchronizing the terms of presidents and Fed chairs.

LEGISLATIVE REACTIONS AND
COUNTERCYCLICAL ATTENTION

For a more precise understanding of the dynamics of legislative attention to the Fed, we model the total number of sponsored bills each year as a function of the inflation and unemployment rates.[12] When each party's legislative measures are combined, we find initial evidence that lawmakers' interest in the Fed follows economic downturns. We find no effect for the inflation rate on the number of bills introduced, but legislators sponsor more bills targeting the Fed as unemployment rises. Modeling the parties separately, we see that economic conditions help shape Democratic lawmakers' priorities: Democrats pay more attention to the Fed when the unemployment rate is high (even after controlling for the rate in the previous year). This suggests that blame avoidance for a poor economy might shape Democrats' focus since they turn their attention elsewhere as the economy improves. That said, after a Democratic Congress gave the Fed its dual mandate in 1977, Democrats' overall interest in the Fed waned. Legally mandating that the Fed maximize employment while maintaining stable prices might have lessened Democrats' perceived need to empower or constrain the Fed through micromanaged legislative threats. In short, both electoral and policy goals drive Democrats' attention to the Fed.

In contrast, the state of the economy seems to matter less in generating Republican proposals (see table 2.1, column 3). We find that GOP activism rose markedly after the dual mandate was created in the 1970s, and see spikes in GOP bills in the late 1970s (following runaway inflation during the Carter administration), and again just before and after the Great Recession. Perhaps GOP misperceptions—for example, worrying recently about inflation in the absence of evidence—weaken any relationship between economic conditions and its party's activism more broadly. Low levels of GOP attention to the Fed before the late 1970s might also explain the broken link, shortening the period over which we can detect the impact of economic misery. Finally, we observe that the recent rise in GOP attention to the Fed largely reflects the party's effort to

TABLE 2.1. Variation in Congressional Attention to the Fed, 1947–2014

Independent variables	(1) Total number of bills	(2) Democratic bills	(3) Republican bills
Inflation rate	0.032 (0.051)	0.059 (0.052)	−0.018 (0.078)
Inflation rate (lagged)	−0.041 (0.055)	−0.026 (0.059)	−0.043 (0.073)
Unemployment rate	0.257 (0.107)*	0.332 (0.109)**	0.235 (0.162)
Unemployment rate (lagged)	0.008 (0.105)	−0.035 (0.108)	−0.034 (0.153)
Dual mandate	−0.137 (0.248)	−0.764 (0.260)**	1.091 (0.384)**
Constant	1.056 (0.426)*	0.574 (0.449)	−0.234 (0.632)
Observations	67	67	67

Notes: The dependent variable is the number of bills introduced in the House and Senate each year. Negative binomial regression estimates are calculated in Stata 14.2's *nbreg* command. Standard errors in parentheses. * significant at $p < 0.05$; ** $p < 0.01$ (two-tailed tests). Data include bills addressing monetary or regulatory policy.

repeal Dodd-Frank. Republicans' recent legislative activism might, per Occam's razor, simply be political—driven more by GOP desire to reverse Democrats' regulatory gains than by concern about the state of the economy.

Quarterly patterns in bill introduction (1973 through 2008) afford a closer view of lawmakers' reactive behavior. As we show in table 2.2, lawmakers tend to ramp up legislative efforts after quarters in which the Fed raises rates—even after controlling for changes in unemployment.[13] The relationship is stronger before the Great Moderation, when lawmakers turn their attention elsewhere. Importantly, prior to the Great Recession, lawmakers treated the Fed equally regardless of which party had appointed the Board chair. Attention to the Fed varies, but we do not see any coordinated, consistent out-party attacks over the longer period studied here.

Variation in who targets the Fed reveals additional dynamics that drive lawmakers' monetary focus. The 112th Congress features a Democratic White House along with split party control of the House and Senate. In that Congress, Democratic House incumbents with narrow electoral margins were more likely to sponsor bills to reform the Fed. One might expect the opposition party to launch

TABLE 2.2. Interest Rate Hikes and Legislative Attention, 1973–2008

Independent variables	Coefficient (standard errors)
Quarterly change in unemployment rate	0.362 (0.218)*
FOMC rate increase	−0.207 (0.165)
FOMC rate increase (lagged one quarter)	0.444 (0.160)**
Dual mandate	−0.440 (0.194)*
President–Fed chair party match	−0.092 (0.152)
Number of bills (lagged one quarter)	0.180 (0.028)**
Constant	2.013 (0.260)**
Observations	143
Log likelihood	−258.382
LR chi2	93.64**

Notes: The dependent variable is the number of bills targeting the Fed introduced in the House and Senate each quarter. Negative binomial regression estimates are calculated in Stata 14.2 *nbreg* command. Standard errors in parentheses. * significant at $p < 0.05$; ** $p < 0.01$ (one-tailed tests). Data include bills addressing monetary or regulatory policy. Model includes quarterly dummy variables for each two-year Congress (using first quarter as excluded category). Coefficients for quarterly dummies significant at $p < 0.01$.

more attacks on the Fed given that its members lack the power to nominate Fed leaders. Counterintuitively, the Fed is an attractive target for vulnerable members of the president's party who seek to deflect blame for a struggling economy, potentially distancing themselves from an unpopular president (table 2.3).[14] Members of the House financial services panel are also more likely to address the Federal Reserve, as are more liberal Democrats.

In contrast, Republican attention to the Fed seems divorced from electoral circumstance: only GOP members of the House financial services panel are disproportionately more likely to call out the Fed for reform in their legislative agendas. Such attention could reflect panel members' stronger interests in monetary policy. Alternatively, many members of the Financial Services Committee hail from districts whose economies rely heavily on the financial industry. Sponsoring measures addressing the Fed might still be constituent driven, as attention to their district's economic interests would be electorally valuable for committee members.

In the Senate, electoral considerations matter (table 2.3, column 3). Senators up for reelection in 2012 were slightly more likely to introduce bills affecting the Fed compared to their colleagues

TABLE 2.3. Who Pays Attention to the Fed? (112th Congress, 2011–12)

Independent variables	(1) House Democrats	(2) House Republicans	(3) All senators
First-term lawmaker	0.735 (1.278)	0.012 (0.586)	1.339 (0.913)
Ideology	−5.999 (1.621)***	1.922 (1.374)	0.805 (0.758)
Electoral vulnerability	1.441 (0.547)**	0.028 (0.671)	—
Running in 2012	—	—	1.508 (0.773)*
District bank in state	0.450 (0.497)	0.177 (0.613)	−0.074 (0.918)
Financial/banking panel	1.039 (0.417)**	2.367 (0.455)***	1.60 (0.580)**
State unemployment rate	—	—	−0.234 (0.149)
Constant	−6.381 (1.105)***	−3.813 (0.677)***	−1.172 (1.296)
N	191	238	100
Wald chi2	19.29**	41.91***	12.81*

Notes: The dependent variable is whether or not a lawmaker introduced a bill targeting the Fed during the 112th Congress. Estimates calculated in Stata 14.2's *logit* command. Robust standard errors in parentheses. * p < 0.05; ** p < 0.01; *** p < 0.001 (one-tailed tests, except for two-tailed Wald chi2 test).

who were earlier in their electoral cycles. Institutional position also plays a role: senators serving on the chamber's banking panel were disproportionately more likely to sponsor bills targeting the Fed. Nevertheless, state-specific economic conditions do not appear to directly motivate senators when they craft legislative agendas addressing the Fed. Nor are rookie senators or those from reserve bank states more likely to target the Fed in their bill portfolios.

Overall, political and economic considerations drive legislators' attention to the Fed in distinct ways. First, the timing and competitiveness of elections—as well as legislators' policy interests—mold individual lawmakers' activism toward the Fed. Those more at risk of losing their seats or immersed in financial issues in Congress disproportionately propose changes to the Federal Reserve Act. Second, a clear partisan pattern emerges from congressional proposals targeting the Fed. The parties vary in their attention to the Fed over the postwar period: Democrats' interest initially waned after creation of the Fed's dual mandate in 1977, while Republican interest rose with the Fed-induced recession in the early 1980s.[15] Third and most important, economic conditions drive lawmakers' prescriptions for the Fed. When the economy is sound, lawmakers propose fewer changes to the Federal Reserve Act; when the economy falters, or more alarmingly, when high inflation and high unemployment indicate the Fed is failing on its mandates, lawmakers renew calls for reform. Politicians' reactive legislative attention to the Fed— especially when elections approach—highlights lawmakers' instinct for avoiding blame.

Audit Politics on Capitol Hill

The twenty-first century, Republican-led Audit the Fed campaign closely illustrates how partisan and electoral forces shape legislators' interventions in monetary policy over the postwar period. At issue is the authority of the Government Accountability Office (GAO) to annually review FOMC deliberations, decisions, or actions on monetary policy. By law, Congress empowers the GAO to audit the Fed, but since 1978 has exempted monetary policy from its purview.[16] Fed officials and their defenders oppose new audits; they argue that GAO scrutiny of monetary policy would facilitate congressional meddling in monetary policy with adverse economic effects—undermining the key justification for delegating monetary policy to the central bank. Supporters of expanded audits suggest that GAO review of monetary policy would enhance congressional oversight of an insufficiently transparent Fed.

Audit the Fed is recently associated with Senator Rand Paul (R-Kentucky) and his father, former House member Ron Paul (R-Texas), as noted above. But the Pauls are newcomers to the campaign. In figure 2.8, we compile all legislative proposals introduced in the House or Senate between 1947 and 2014 that authorized audits of the Federal Reserve. We plot the year of each bill's introduction against its sponsor's ideology.[17] Three patterns stand out.

First, Representative Wright Patman (D-Texas) introduced the original postwar audit measure more than sixty years ago. Patman was a longtime populist critic of the Fed who wanted to end the Fed's budgetary independence, placing it back under the thumb of the Treasury Department and White House, and subjecting it to annual appropriations like every other government agency. He eventually

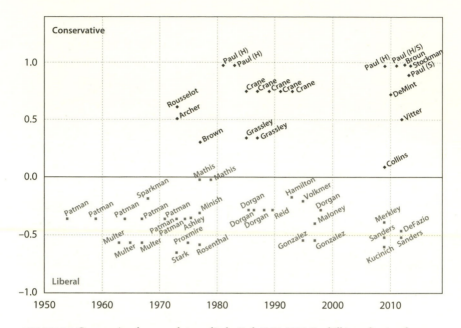

FIGURE 2.8. Congressional proposals to audit the Fed, 1947–2014. For bill introduction data, see Adler and Wilkerson n.d.; Proquest n.d.; http://thomas.loc.gov. For economic data, see https://research.stlouisfed.org/fred2/.

bowed to the political reality that the Fed's budgetary autonomy was untouchable. Instead, Patman pushed to restore the power of the GAO to audit the Fed's operations—a power the GAO had held from 1921 until 1933 (Kettl 1986, 154). Over the years, he offered sixteen audit proposals—eight of them in 1975 alone. Congress finally empowered the GAO to audit the Fed after lawmakers reached a compromise in 1978 to carve out a monetary policy exemption.

More generally, Democrats, not Republicans, have been the biggest boosters of Fed audits—sponsoring twice as many measures to audit the Fed as the Republicans over the broader postwar period. Still, although we see a clear partisan cast to the proposals, members of the president's and opposition's parties drop audit bills into the legislative hopper with roughly equal frequency over this period. At least based on the audit proposals, legislators appear equally likely to threaten tougher oversight of the Fed, regardless of whether they hail from the president's party or the party that appointed the Fed chair.

Similar to our earlier polling analysis, no one wants to audit the Fed in good economic times. The economy's Great Moderation—in place from the mid-1980s through 2006—dampened congressional distrust of the Fed. Congress's reactive, countercyclical attention—heeding the Fed's performance only when the economy sours—gave the Fed a respite from most audit proposals starting in the economically robust 1990s and lasting until the onset of the most recent financial crisis.

Third, with the exception of a measure by moderate Senator Susan Collins (R-Maine) to audit the Fed's emergency lending programs in 2009, recent audit proposals come exclusively from party fringes. Senator Paul—one of the most conservative members of the Senate GOP conference—has been the most recent standard-bearer for the Fed's Far Right critics. Granted, the political center has all but disappeared in Congress, yet the absence of centrist critics of the Fed today is still striking given that prominent moderates of the past—for example, Lee Hamilton (D-Indiana)—offered versions of audit proposals decades ago.

These trends illustrate how politics and economics interact to drive lawmakers' prescriptions for the Fed. From today's vantage point, Republicans seem to "own" the audit issue. Attacking the Fed's unconventional monetary policy in the wake of the financial crisis and recession, Republicans doggedly pursue new audits with little Democratic support. Viewed more broadly over the postwar period, no party monopolizes the campaign for new oversight authority. Patman, after all, was the audit's populist standard-bearer in an earlier era. Indeed, Democrats could co-opt Republican proposals should Democrats find a need to blame the Fed for economic failings or policy incoherence.

The Political Economy of Legislative Reform of the Fed

Lawmakers—particularly those up for reelection—signal their dissatisfaction with the Fed when the economy worsens, championing legislative proposals to reshape Fed power and governance. Do similar political and economic dynamics drive the timing of actual

changes to the Federal Reserve Act? Unlike sponsoring bills, amending law requires action, not merely talk: lawmakers must build majorities for measures that would change the way the Fed manages
the economy or alter the contours of congressional accountability.
As such, we would only expect lawmakers to seriously advance
reforms when the stakes are highest and the electoral rewards are
greatest—as they are in the wake of a severe financial or economic
crisis. That is when the public would be most likely to support congressional efforts to prevent a future crisis. In contrast, when the
economy is performing well, politicians are unlikely to rock the boat.
As Joseph Stiglitz (1998, 224) argued during the Great Moderation
that stretched from roughly the mid-1980s until the onset of the
global financial crisis in 2007:

> There is an old saying that "if it's not broken, don't fix it." Many
> people believe that our monetary institutions, if not perfect, have
> been doing a remarkably good job. There is a collective amnesia
> at work. We forget the criticism our monetary institutions are
> repeatedly subjected to when the economy goes into a down-
> turn, or when it does not live up to its potential over protracted
> periods of time.

Acute crisis trumps chronic problems. Given this dynamic, amendments of the Federal Reserve Act will likely be conditional on the
severity of economic decline.

Partisan alignments in Washington also likely shape the timing
of reform. Legislative changes should be more likely when a single
party controls the White House and both chambers of Congress
(Binder 2003). During unified party government, we typically see
stronger policy agreement across the branches about legislative priorities since partisans tend to hold similar policy views and share a
common electoral interest in burnishing their party's reputation at
election time. Unified party control also clarifies for voters which
party to reward for its efforts in the wake of a crisis. In contrast, when
parties divide power between the branches, collective action on behalf of a legislative agenda is harder to secure. Moreover, divided
party control diffuses responsibility for acting when the economy

fails: voters have a harder time knowing which party to blame for inaction when the parties divide power between the branches.

To test our expectations, we model the incidence of consequential changes to the Federal Reserve Act over the Fed's first century. We build a list of important changes to the Federal Reserve Act from several sources (see table 1.1), including major reforms noted in histories of the Fed (such as Allan Meltzer's multivolume Fed chronicle) as well as lists of legislative changes recorded in annual reports of the Federal Reserve Board (1913–34) and the Board of Governors (1935–2014). We compile these reforms into a single, dichotomous dependent variable that indicates whether or not major reforms were enacted in each year between 1913 and 2015.[18] Major legislative reforms occurred in 18 of the 103 years in this time period.[19] Some reforms clip the autonomy of the Fed, such as the 1970s' reforms discussed in chapter 6 that required greater transparency from the Fed to make it more accountable to Congress for its policy choices. Other amendments empower the Fed, such as the Depression era creation of the Fed's emergency lending authority. And in several instances, legislative reforms marry new limits on the Fed's authority with new grants of power.[20] Overall, the list of 18 major reform episodes is nearly evenly balanced between empowering and constraining packages.

To estimate the impact of political and economic forces on the incidence of reform, we begin with several annual measures of the state of the economy: inflation and unemployment rates as well as the number of months (if any) that the US economy was in recession in any given year, according to the National Bureau of Economic Research's (2010) "peak to trough" measure for each recession in the period studied.[21] To determine the extent to which partisan alignments are associated with congressional action, we control for the presence or absence of unified party control of Congress and the White House. We also control for the party alignment between the White House and Fed chair to determine whether Congress is more likely to target the Fed when an incumbent president inherits a Fed chair from the opposite party.[22] For example, Bernanke—originally appointed by George W. Bush—served under both Republican and Democrat presidents.[23]

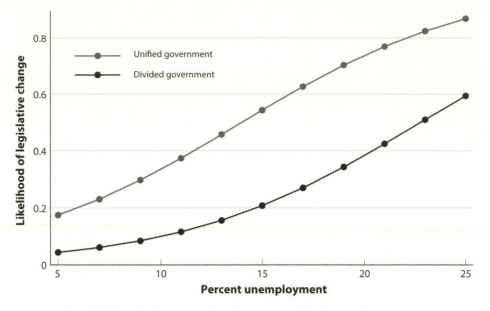

FIGURE 2.9. Likelihood of changes to Federal Reserve Act, 1913–2014. The figure shows the simulated likelihood of legislative action, conditional on economic and political forces (as described in the text). The model controls for unemployment and inflation rates, the number of months the economy was in recession in any given year, and whether the president's party appointed the sitting Fed chair. The results for the underlying model are available from the authors.

As expected, electoral alignments and a faltering economy correlate with Fed reform. Controlling for the duration of any recession, legislative changes are more likely when the nation experiences higher rates of inflation or unemployment. We also find a strong effect of party control, with legislative action more likely when a single party holds both ends of Pennsylvania Avenue. In contrast, partisan alignment of White House and Fed leadership makes little difference to the timing of successful reform.

Figure 2.9 illustrates how economic and partisan forces drive major changes to the Fed's powers and governance. The figure plots the likelihood that Congress and the president will amend the act, conditional on the severity of the recession and party alignments. First, our simulated likelihood of reform rises with a weakening economy. When unemployment is low, chances for reform are slight—regardless of whether a single party controls the levers of government. As a higher proportion of Americans find themselves out of work, amendments to the act become more likely—especially so if a single party controls Congress and the White House. At Depression era levels of unemployment, action is all but guaranteed—especially in periods of unified party control. Our simulation suggests that even divided governments marshal majorities for change when the economy slips into a deep depression, although we lack actual cases after the creation of the Fed during which divided governments presided over an economic crisis of such magnitude.

Overall, lawmakers are more prone to act after a crisis than before one. Such "fire alarm" behavior is endemic to Congress; it follows from legislators' electoral incentives (McCubbins and Schwartz 1984). In an environment that rewards legislators for the positions they take (rather than for the policies that ensue), politically efficient lawmakers often wait until someone else rings an alarm instead of prowling for problems as if they were cops on the beat. Such a strategy is no doubt economically suboptimal, though: it leads lawmakers to ignore chronic problems within the Fed's mandate—such as the Fed's lax regulation of subprime lending in the years running up to the global financial crisis. Moreover, voters frequently throw out governing majorities in times of severe economic crisis—as was the fate of Republican majorities with the onset of the Great Depression and, decades later, global financial crisis—suggesting that lawmakers can pay a steep electoral price for lax oversight of the Fed. Those who withstand the electoral backlash soon thereafter reopen the Federal Reserve Act, clipping the Feds wings, giving it more power, or imposing greater transparency. Such reforms deflect blame from Congress to the Fed and set up the Fed to take the fall during the next, inevitable recession.

Conclusions

> The fact that monetary policy involves trade-offs . . . has one clear implication in a democratic society. The way those decisions are made should be representative of the values of those that comprise society. At the very least, they should see as their objective the application of their expertise to reflect broader societal values.
> —JOSEPH STIGLITZ, "CENTRAL BANKING IN A DEMOCRATIC SOCIETY"

As economist Stiglitz warns, insulating central banks from democratic politics raises the risk that central bankers will fail to deliver macroeconomic outcomes consistent with societal preferences. Importantly, the economic and political priorities of lawmakers and their parties evolve over time, often generating conflicting views within and between congressional parties as well as between the branches about whether or how to reform the Fed. Economic shortfalls and financial crises focus lawmakers' attention on the Fed's performance, and frequently spark congressional contests and action to renegotiate the central bank's mandate, organization, and accountability.

Reflecting on legislative challenges to the Fed in the wake of the financial crisis of 2008–9, Bernanke noted to us, as he did to his successor, that Fed officials must take their Hill bosses seriously. He explained that "the last three presidents—Clinton, Bush, and Obama—have all been proponents of Fed independence. Absent the support of some future White House, although it might be difficult to get passed and signed legislation that poses a serious challenge to the basic powers of the Fed, it unfortunately would not be impossible."[24] The election of Trump and a Republican Congress in November 2016 places Bernanke's warning in stark relief. As we explore in chapter 7, Republican lawmakers in the wake of the global financial crisis targeted the Fed for reform—including proposing a monetary rule to limit the Fed's decision-making discretion, returning the Fed to a single mandate of price stability, and empowering the GAO to audit FOMC deliberations. Trump's campaign pronouncements on the Fed were erratic, ranging from endorsing monetary accommodation to excoriating chair Yellen for keeping rates too low. Coupled with a Republican Congress, prospects for major reform after years of a sluggish, postcrisis recovery suddenly seem much higher at the start of the Trump presidency.

As we discuss in the coming chapters, most Fed leaders seem to understand the need to secure public and congressional support for their policies—lest economic shortfalls catalyze congressional action to revisit and revise the Federal Reserve Act. To be sure, after controlling for economic trends, we found little evidence of a tidy correlation between the timing of bill introductions and FOMC rate choices. Moreover, it is challenging to demonstrate the counter-factual: How would the Fed have acted in the absence of legislative threats? In the chapters that follow, we turn to qualitative evidence of Congress-Fed interdependence, examining key episodes in which short-term political pressures weigh on Fed officials as they aim to craft policy for the longer term.

Ultimately, even if Congress fails to act, its attacks reflect and amplify public anger toward the central bank, contributing to the decline in the Fed's standing. Criticism complicates the Fed's ability to convince the markets, businesses, and the public that its often-complex, sometimes-temporizing policy decisions are consistent with Congress's directive. Years after the global financial crisis, a robust recovery remains elusive, public trust of the Fed is fragile, and critics continue to call for new limits on and interfere with the Fed's goals and discretion.

3

Creating the Federal Reserve

No ordinary central bank, the Federal Reserve weighs a powerful, president-appointed, Senate-confirmed, Washington-based board against twelve quasi-private regional reserve banks located in cities across the country. In this chapter, we apply the political-economic logic sketched and tested in the opening chapters to explain the enactment and implementation of the Federal Reserve Act after the election of 1912. Blame avoidance and partisan politics in the wake of the devastating 1907 financial panic generated sufficient momentum to create a politically viable, if organizationally awkward, institution.

Today, despite a century of ever-increasing centralization and empowerment of the Fed, the United States' central bank retains its federal roots: the original twelve district banks have survived, albeit with less authority to set monetary policy. Paying special attention to the politics that gave rise to the Fed's hybrid structure, we argue that a decentralized reserve system that diluted public control was the high price of enactment. As we show in the following chapters, the Fed's structure would prove economically cumbersome but politically invaluable. Specifically, the initial dispersal of power complicated monetary policy making, but hardwired support for the Fed far from the corridors of power and credit in Washington and New

York—insulating the Fed from future coalitions eager to dilute or even dispatch the Fed's monopoly on monetary control.

Why 1913?

When President Andrew Jackson vetoed renewal of the Second Bank of the United States in 1832, his nascent Democratic Party killed the United States' experiment with central banking. His veto came two decades after James Madison's Democratic-Republican Party had retired the charter for Alexander Hamilton's Federalist Party brainchild, the First Bank of the United States. As Jackson (1832) argued in his veto message,

> If we can not at once, in justice to interests vested under improvi-
> dent legislation, make our Government what it ought to be, we
> can at least take a stand against all new grants of monopolies and
> exclusive privileges, against any prostitution of our Government
> to the advancement of the few at the expense of the many, and
> in favor of compromise and gradual reform in our code of laws
> and system of political economy.

Reflecting Jeffersonian distrust of the banking industry and concentrated national power more generally, the impact of Jackson's veto was remarkably enduring. Decades later, even depression-inducing financial panics in 1873 and 1893 could not compel lawmakers to overcome public opposition to a central bank. Our political-economic perspective helps to explain how, in the wake of the 1907 Panic and nearly a century of animus toward a Hamiltonian central bank, the perfect storm of financial crisis, electoral change, and partisan opportunism generated sufficient political momentum and majorities for comprehensive monetary reform.

Anti–central bank ideology flourished in both political parties over the course of the nineteenth century. Within the Democratic Party, opposition was strongest within the party's southern and western agrarian wings (Sanders 1999), whereas conservative northeastern Democrats more often aligned with bank-friendly Republicans. Well into the early years of the twentieth century, agrarian

Democrats—who would have benefited most from currency reform—remained implacably opposed to a central bank (Lowenstein 2015, 19). Instead, most Democrats preferred inflationary policies, especially the outright printing of money. Their monetary commitments fused ideological, partisan, and economic values, contributing to the late nineteenth-century partisan divide between gold standard adherents and supporters of bimetallism (who supported the more inflationary, free exchange of gold and silver). Democratic members of Congress, whose constituents included indebted farmers, would have been hard-pressed to pursue hard-money, low inflationary policy solutions. In short, inflation reduced the value of their constituents' mortgages and raised the value of their crops.

Northeastern establishment Republicans, with supporters in portions of the Midwest and West, also opposed reintroducing a central bank. The party of financial conservatism (Ritter 1997) resisted government management of the currency or credit as well as any measures that would dilute Wall Street's ultimate control over the nation's banking reserves. As the financiers of industrialization, Republican creditors supported hard-money inflation control, preferring that the United States abandon the inflationary coinage of silver and commit to a gold standard.

With Republicans abhorring the idea that the government should ever intervene in the financial sector and Democrats opposed to allowing bankers to control the money supply, ideology and economics generated bipartisan antipathy to reinstating a central bank. Moreover, a highly competitive party system of the mid- to late nineteenth century that frequently produced divided party control of Congress and the White House ensured that government control for any one party was often brief. Combined with Democratic divisions over monetary affairs, the electoral landscape sharply limited prospects for reform.

The United States paid a steep economic price for the parties' resistance to creating a central bank. Coupled with national law that prohibited "branch banking" (a system of banking that might have diffused rather than concentrated risk within local banks), the lack of any form of central bank subjected the economy to periodic disasters

(Calomiris and Hadley 2014). Bank runs occurred frequently when economic shocks led holders of illiquid bank notes to demand conversion of their claims into cash (Calomiris and Gorton 1991). Without access to emergency funding to meet customer withdrawals, banks would close their doors, leading to financial panic as word spread locally, regionally, or nationally. Charles W. Calomiris and Gary Gorton (1991, 114) count ten full-fledged panics between 1789 and the creation of the Fed in 1913 when banks suspended note-to-cash conversion.

Consistent with the analysis in chapter 2 that pegged legislative action on monetary control to the electoral fallout from financial crises, the Panic of 1907 arrested decades of muddling through in response to banking panics and the economic collapse that often ensued. After nearly a century of US resistance to central banking, the Democratic, Republican, and Progressive Parties scrambled to put currency reform high on their respective agendas; in 1912, each party's national platform included planks on monetary policy. Why did the 1907 panic galvanize the parties to act when the 1873 and 1893 crises did not? In 1907, the limits of previous, jerry-built solutions to financial distress—coupled with electoral currents in both parties at the turn of the century—produced sufficient force to overwhelm deep-rooted opposition to a government role in managing the currency. We consider each of these forces in turn.

First, the limitations of the federal government's crisis-fighting tools were evident by the turn of the century. Government interventions were precarious, primitive, partial, and probably illegal. Without a lender of last resort, the federal government had limited tools and authority to aid ailing sectors in the wake of financial or economic crisis, let alone prevent them in the first place. On one such occasion recounted by Roger Lowenstein (2015, 20), a gold shortage led President Grover Cleveland in 1895 to privately engineer a bonds-for-gold swap with financier Morgan. The government gave Morgan thirty-year bonds (which he then sold to investors), and in exchange Morgan bailed out the government with an infusion of gold. More generally throughout the late nineteenth-century banking panics, Treasury secretaries used tariff-driven government surpluses (when they existed) to buy up investors' holdings of government debt, in what today would amount to open market operations by a central bank (Wicker 2000).

Improvised solutions in the 1890s foreshadowed Morgan's role in 1907 when the nation's private reserve system again proved incapable of stopping a banking panic and the ensuing financial crisis. This time, the Treasury exhausted its own surplus after making deposits to failing New York City banks. Once again, Morgan intervened as an informal and extralegal lender of last resort (Lowenstein 2015, 66). Morgan and an assembled group of financial colleagues evaluated bailout-seeking trust banks, and determined which the group would lend to and against what collateral. At one point during the three-week crisis, Morgan even engineered an emergency loan to keep New York City afloat (ibid., 65). That the seventy-year-old Morgan was indispensable to stopping the panic likely drove home to Republicans the precariousness of private arrangements in the absence of a formalized reserve system and lender of last resort for the banking system.

Second, turn-of-the-century partisan dynamics helped to break the logjam blocking currency reform. Democrats—who controlled both chambers of Congress and the White House during the banking panic of 1893—had shouldered blame for the panic turned depression, enabling Republicans to sweep national elections in 1894 and 1896, and usher in two decades of unified GOP control of government. The emergence of large Republican majorities outside the South made possible the 1900 Gold Standard Act—ending the coinage of silver as an alternative monetary standard. The split of the GOP into progressive and conservative wings soon thereafter, however, fractured the GOP's stranglehold on currency reform. The coincidence of another devastating financial crisis in 1907 and divided Republican Party created an opening for Democrats to simultaneously blame Republicans for the economic morass and gain control of the government in the panic's aftermath.

Remarkably, despite the severity of the crisis, Republicans reacted with modest innovations and delays. A Republican Congress and GOP president William Howard Taft first enacted the Aldrich-Vreeland Act of 1908, authorizing the Treasury to issue emergency currency during future panics. The act also authorized the creation of the National Monetary Commission, a sixteen-member panel (eleven Republicans and five Democrats) to study alternative reserve systems abroad. Senator Nelson Aldrich (R–Rhode Island) in 1910 then journeyed with several colleagues in disguise to Jekyll Island, Georgia, to write up what became known as the "Aldrich bill." In sync with financial conservatives who had for decades opposed government control of the reserve system (Ritter 1997), the Aldrich bill advocated a largely banker-controlled reserve system.

The bill became a focal point for debating currency reform during the 1912 presidential election. The party platforms of both Teddy Roosevelt's Bull Moose Progressives and the Democrats denounced the Aldrich bill.[1] Democrats argued that "banks exist for the accommodation of the public, and not for the control of business," while Progressives opposed the Aldrich bill because it "would place our currency and credit system in private hands, not subject to effective public control." In contrast, the Republican platform reaffirmed the party's support for the gold standard, and warned that the banking and currency system should be protected from "domination by sectional, financial, or political interests."

In the three-way race for the presidency that year, the splintering of the Republican Party into rival conservative and progressive wings allowed Democrats to capture the White House and Senate as well as hold onto the House—producing the first unified Democratic government in two decades. Exploiting the electoral fallout of the financial crisis, Democrats took control in 1913 by successfully pinning blame on Republicans for the economic morass. Whereas Republican factionalism had kept monetary reform in limbo, newly elected Wilson turned quickly to currency reform as a central plank of his first term agenda.

The Price of Enactment

We center our analysis of the creation of the Federal Reserve on the politics that gave rise to the regional reserve system in the Sixty-Third Congress (1913–15). As we showed in the last chapter, legislative attention to monetary policy increases in the wake of crisis, and law-makers are more likely to act when electoral change brings unified party control to Washington. Still, as we argued in chapter 1, partisan and institutional fault lines over how monetary policy should be con-ducted typically force majority parties to compromise in devising new monetary institutions. In the case of the creation of the Fed in 1913, disagreements within and across the two parties and branches about the organization as well as control of a new central bank complicated reform. As we explore in more detail below, southern Democrats and midwestern Populists rejected any private, Wall Street–controlled central bank. Republicans preferred a centralized reserve system, but opposed affording Washington any public control. And Progres-sives favored an independent bank out of reach of banker control. The compromise that emerged—a decentralized reserve system limiting Washington power at the top—was the price of enactment.

Importantly, despite divisions about how a new reserve system should be organized and who should control it, lawmakers gener-ally agreed on the underlying goal of currency reform. Most legisla-tors shared the aim of creating an elastic currency (one that would expand and contract with business and agricultural demand), so as to limit recurring banking panics and economic crises. To be sure, Republicans prioritized making the financial system more stable, while Democrats' wanted fairer and easier access to credit. Nota-bly absent from these debates, however, was the more idealized goal of an independent monetary authority to prevent opportunis-tic politicians from inflating their way to reelection. As Gyung-Ho Jeong, Gary J. Miller, and Andrew C. Sobel (2009) demonstrate, independence was the by-product—not the intent—of coalitions competing over how the new reserve system would be organized and governed. In fact, the final version of the Federal Reserve Act placed the secretary of the Treasury and comptroller of the currency on the Washington-based Reserve Board, conceptually affording the administration influence within the Board. Still, the original Federal Reserve Act gave relatively little power to the new Board, limiting the capacity of the president's lieutenants to shape monetary policy within the reserve system.[2]

Two key disputes emerged when the Democratic Congress began work on currency bills in 1913.[3] First, how should Democrats balance demands by eastern, primarily Republican bankers to centralize authority in a new reserve system, and those by agrarian Populists and Democrats in the South and West to devolve control of the flow of credit? Second, how should Democrats treat GOP demands for private control of a central bank against Democratic, Populist, and Progressive expectations for greater public control? Ultimately, by all accounts, President Wilson played a critical role by devising a compromise on which a winning coalition would eventually agree (Jeong, Miller, and Sobel 2009; Lowenstein 2015).

Disagreements over centralization and the degree of public control were resolved in contests over the size, governance, and construction of a federal-style reserve system. Rural Populists, farmers, and small-city bankers (largely Democrats) lobbied for a system of forty-eight regional banks—one per state (Timberlake 1993). A reserve bank "at every major crossroad," William Jennings Bryan supposedly urged (Nelson 1973). Such a system would maximize local control over the seasonal flow of credit, and coupled with a president-appointed board in Washington, make financial panics less likely and limit Wall Street influence in resolving crises when they inevitably occurred. The bill originally proposed by the chair of the House Banking and Currency Committee, Glass, came closest to advancing Populist interests by mandating twenty regional reserve banks. Under pressure from Wilson, however, the House-passed version of the bill reduced the number of reserve banks to a minimum of twelve and maximum of twenty (Jeong, Miller, and Sobel 2009). Out of concern that a Federal Reserve Board in Washington could be dominated by banking interests, the House bill delegated the choice of reserve cities to an outside organizing committee (rather than a newly appointed Federal Reserve Board) that would be composed of Wilson's top Democratic appointees.

Bankers made greater headway toward a more centralized reserve system in the Senate, where Democrats were divided over how to resolve factional and partisan conflict over the size and control of the reserve system. Large-city bankers—typically Republicans from the

Northeast—preferred a single, central bank dominated by bankers. With Democrats in control of both the White House and Congress, and Progressives favoring public control, prominent New York bankers acquiesced to three or four regional reserve banks. Senate Banking Committee Democrats, though, were unable to resolve the conflict over the size and control of the reserve system. Instead, under lobbying from the banking community, the Senate Banking Committee approved two different versions of the currency bill.[4]

Senator Gilbert Hitchcock (D-Nebraska)—attracting the support of Republicans on the Senate Banking Committee—proposed four regional banks, directing the Federal Reserve Board to appoint a majority of each reserve bank's directors. Robert Owen (D-Oklahoma), chair of the Senate Banking Committee, advocated a solution that came closer to the House-passed bill. Owen's proposal mandated a minimum of eight and maximum of twelve regional banks, each of which would be owned by its subscribing member banks. Both versions dropped the House proposal for an executive branch–dominated committee to organize the reserve system. Instead, the Senate bills empowered the Federal Reserve Board (which bankers expected to dominate) to determine the cities in which the regional reserve banks would be located. Bank-friendly Democrats who preferred the Hitchcock bill were outnumbered within their party caucus. The Senate Democratic Conference—newly energized in 1913 to bind its members to party positions on key priorities—bound its members to support the Owen proposal, leading to its adoption on the Senate floor.[5]

We offer two observations about the final compromise that emerged from conference negotiations over the weekend before Christmas in 1913. First, final decisions largely amounted to horse trading. That was perhaps inevitable given the approaching holiday. In fact, Democrats had already formally bound themselves in their party caucus to either finish the bill before Christmas or come back on December 26 to complete it (Ritchie 1999, 147). In short, negotiators split the difference. They adopted the Senate provision on the number of banks, requiring at least eight but no more than twelve district banks. And they authorized the RBOC to design the districts rather than entrusting the job to the soon-to-be-established Federal Reserve Board.

Second, chamber votes on the conference report had a partisan cast. Nearly every House and all Senate Democrats voted in favor; a majority of House Republicans and 90 percent of Senate Republicans were opposed.[6] This is not surprising given Republican senators' objections after Democrats moved to bind its members on the currency bill. "A tightening of party lines," one reporter observed, "would drive them [the Republicans] into concerted opposition to the bill."[7] Still, House Republicans did not uniformly reject the compromise; their more moderate members voted in favor. Just over half the GOP who hailed from states won in the 1912 presidential election by Progressive Roosevelt voted in favor of the House compromise, joined by thirteen out of fifteen House Progressives.[8] But even with Progressive support, a majority of Democrats favored the bill and a majority of the GOP was opposed. The partisan edge belies the received wisdom that the Federal Reserve System was a legislative deal acceptable to all parties.

Compromises embedded in the new federal system of regional reserve banks cemented legislative majorities for currency reform after decades of stalemate over how or even whether to create a central bank. As our theory expects, no single party faction got precisely what it sought when lawmakers inked the final version of the Federal Reserve Act, fostering the Fed's awkward, hybrid organizational structure. Importantly, the law's dispersal of power prevented any single coalition from monopolizing control of the reserve system. As Jeong, Miller, and Sobel (2009) remind us, the system owed its independence to that diffusion of power, rather than explicit steps that lawmakers might have taken to insulate the reserve system from political and banker influence. Nearly a century after Jackson's veto, devolving the flow of credit from Washington and Wall Street into the coffers of regional reserve banks anchored a uniquely US "central" bank. The federal system of reserve banks was the linchpin of Democrats' success in enacting the law.

Organizing the Reserve System

Studies of the creation of the Fed typically conclude at the law's enactment—leaving an impression of the original Fed as a broadly accepted, bipartisan compromise. The post-passage politics of the Federal Reserve Act cast a different light on the political origins of the institution. In crafting the final agreement, Democrats granted their party complete discretion over the organization of the regional reserve system.[9] Past studies diminish the importance of partisan politics in the location of the reserve banks, arguing that the RBOC sought an economically optimal system. In contrast, we show below that Democrats exploited their delegated power to mold a politically optimal system—one that would simultaneously attract the support of the system's member banks and benefit the credit-poor, Democratic South.[10] Drawing from archival materials from the RBOC's operations, we analyze the activities of the committee and its efforts to entrench Democrats' political priorities into the organization of the system.

The task of organizing the reserve system loomed after Wilson signed the Federal Reserve Act into law. Directed by the new law, Wilson appointed the comptroller of the currency along with the secretaries of Treasury and Agriculture to serve on the RBOC, charging the panel with selecting the number of reserve districts, choosing the cities in which the reserve banks would be located, and drawing the geographic boundaries of the districts. Funded by a $100,000 congressional appropriation, the RBOC (comprised of Treasury secretary William McAdoo, Agriculture secretary David Houston, and the yet-to-be-confirmed comptroller of the currency, John Williams) took preparatory steps in winter 1914. First, the committee conducted a survey of bankers in the more than seven thousand national banks that were required by the new law to join the new reserve system. The poll sought to determine where bankers most preferred the reserve banks be located (see fragment of polling results in figure 3.1). Second, McAdoo and Houston embarked on a ten-thousand-mile "listening tour" of eighteen cities to allow local officials to press their case to house a reserve bank in their hometown. Houston (1926, 108) claimed in his memoirs that the poll

FIRST-CHOICE VOTE FOR RESERVE-BANK CITIES.

RESERVE BANK ORGANIZATION COMMITTEE,
Washington, D. C., June 24, 1914.

SIR: The reserve bank organization committee has the honor to acknowledge the receipt of a copy of the resolution of the House of Representatives, dated April 15, 1914, which reads as follows:

Resolved, That the organization committee of the Federal Reserve Board be, and it is hereby, directed to send to the House of Representatives the ballots, or a tabulated statement thereof, cast by the various national banks of the United States to determine their choice for reserve cities according to a request made to said banks by the organization committee of the Federal Reserve Board.

In compliance therewith there is herewith transmitted the information called for.

Respectfully,

W. G. McADOO,
D. F. HOUSTON,
JNO. SKELTON WILLIAMS,
Reserve Bank Organization Committee.

THE SPEAKER OF THE HOUSE OF REPRESENTATIVES.

First-choice vote for reserve-bank cities, by States.

	First.	Second.	Third.		First.	Second.	Third.
ALABAMA.				**ARKANSAS.**			
Atlanta	8	35	14	Chicago		14	8
Birmingham	53	9	1	Dallas	1	2	
Chattanooga		2	3	Fort Smith			1
Cincinnati	1	2	4	Kansas City	2	16	5
Louisville		2	3	Little Rock		1	2
Memphis		1	1	Memphis		6	2
Mobile		1		New Orleans		4	12
Montgomery	4	1	2	New York			3
Nashville		3		St. Louis	51	3	
New Orleans	3	9	27				
St. Louis	1		3	Total	54	46	33
Savannah	3	2	6				
				CALIFORNIA.			
Total	73	67	64	Chicago		3	4
ARIZONA.				Denver			2
				Fresno	1	1	2
Chicago			1	Kansas City		3	2
Denver		1	2	Los Angeles	24	81	9
El Paso	1		1	New York	2	4	
Kansas City	1	1		Oakland		4	1
Los Angeles	2	5		Portland		9	15
Phoenix			1	Reno			1
St. Louis			1	Sacramento		2	5
San Francisco	8	3	1	Salt Lake			2
				San Francisco	208	25	2
Total	12	10	7	San Diego			5
				St. Louis			2

1923

3

FIGURE 3.1. Excerpt from poll of national banks on location of Reserve Banks, 1914. RBOC 1914a.

results "aided us immensely, helping to confirm opinions which we had developed during our trip."

The committee cataloged a diverse set of documents, ranging from letters by Chicago bankers to a statement on the mail facilities of El Paso, Texas (RBOC 1914b). Most cities highlighted their centrality to commerce in the region, such as maps showing railroad lines and travel times between their city and surrounding locales. Cities also explicitly compared themselves to their competitors. Summing up his city's claim, for example, one banker argued that "Kansas City, ranking sixth in bank clearings, seventh in postal receipts, second as a live stock market and tenth in manufacturing, proves her supremacy in this great Southwestern territory (RBOC 1914c, 1908–9). Chatta-nooga, Tennessee, with just three national banks compared to Kansas City's twelve (or New York's thirty-five), promoted its

> 40 miles of paved streets, 80 miles of sewers, a most efficient and well-equipped police and fire department, a low rate of in-surance, 64 miles of street railway, an excellent school system, a very complete public library, and a very fine system of public parks and recreation center . . . all the safeguards, comforts, and conveniences which would have to be considered in locating a reserve bank. (RBOC 1914b, 35)

Thirty-seven cities submitted formal applications for a reserve bank: each provided data on national banking activity in their city, including the volume of capital, loans, discounts, deposits, bonds, and bank reserves.[11] The RBOC's statutory assignment was to ap-portion the country into eight to twelve reserve districts and then choose the cities that would host the new reserve banks. Below, we offer alternative explanations to account for the RBOC's selections and then use archival records to show how the RBOC settled on a final map for the system.

Financial versus Political Strategies

Among the few scholars who have examined the RBOC's choices, the consensus view holds that the committee looked to place the reserve banks in the most active financial and commercial communities among the thirty-seven applicant cities (Bensel 1984; McAvoy 2006). That was McAdoo's rationale at the time, opening up each meeting on the RBOC's (1914c, 1809) cross-country tour with an apolitical statement of the panel's mission: "This is an economic and not a political problem, and what the committee is after is facts. . . . Those facts that will enable us to determine as intelligently as possible the customary courses of business and what will best conserve the convenience of business throughout the country in the organization of this system."

Still, some doubted at the time that economic considerations mattered most to the RBOC. When Wilson signed the Federal Reserve Act into law, one Republican senator observed about the RBOC that "these men would have the right to designate regional districts to suit themselves and to leave on the new system a deep partisan mark."[12] Even the RBOC's staff director hinted a decade later that the committee viewed its task as both a political and economic problem. As Henry Parker Willis (1923, 586–87) noted in his retrospective account of the RBOC's work, the reader was left to "draw his own conclusions concerning the degree to which the principles . . . had been put into application in any given place." Willis's implication is clear: financial capacity and commercial activity alone cannot explain the location choices made by the RBOC.

Conflicting historical signals suggest two strategies—one financial, and the other political—that the RBOC might have followed in locating the reserve banks. The accounts are not mutually exclusive: the RBOC might have sought a system that both protected Democrats' interests and was financially optimal. We articulate the logic that underpins each strategy and then use archival evidence to establish the fit of the accounts to the RBOC's final map.

FINANCIAL MODEL

The RBOC claimed to follow an apolitical strategy of placing the banks in the most financially important cities. Such a strategy would have been consistent with the limited statutory guidance written into the Federal Reserve Act, which specified that the "districts shall be apportioned with due regard to the convenience and customary course of business."[13] Given the concentration of capital in a small number of cities and the law's requirement that each regional reserve bank have subscribed capital from its member banks of more than $4 million to open its doors, the RBOC could hardly avoid placing banks in preexisting financial capitals. In particular, New York, Chicago, and St. Louis had long been designated as "central reserve cities" under nineteenth-century banking acts.[14] As staff for the RBOC (1914d) noted early in the process, placing federal district banks in those cities "must be regarded as practically predetermined."

The RBOC maintained that it considered a number of factors in mapping districts to best serve the "convenience and customary course of business." Financial activity and strength of the national banks in each city were paramount. The RBOC took into account each area's transportation networks and general business activity. Indeed, the applicant cities went to great lengths to demonstrate the centrality of their cities to regional commerce. Chattanooga, for example, reproduced regional train schedules in its application to the RBOC to demonstrate its accessibility to banking centers in the region (RBOC 1914b, 31). The RBOC's decision to survey bankers about the location of reserve banks also suggests that the RBOC cared about the preferences of the banking industry. Thus, if the RBOC located the reserve banks in the most financially active of the applicant cities, the financial model likely guided the RBOC's decisions.

POLITICAL MODEL

In contrast, Democrats might have exploited their control of the RBOC to pursue partisan priorities in drawing the map. Creating a regionally diversified reserve system, regardless of the financial activity of the selected cities, would have advantaged Democratic constituencies. In particular, given the historic concentration of financial capital in the Northeast, locating some of the reserve banks beyond the Eastern Seaboard would have helped to address credit deficits in the Democratic, agrarian South and West. That, after all, was one of the Democrats' top goals in creating the Federal Reserve:

developing an elastic currency and devolving authority over monetary policy to spread access to credit beyond the Republican-dominated Northeast, lowering interest rates and limiting the recurrence of financial panics.[15]

According to documents provided to the RBOC during its cross-country tour, civic leaders across the South made precisely that argument in lobbying for a reserve bank in their relatively undeveloped region. As Dallas business leaders noted, "The unassailable fact is—St. Louis and Kansas City will not dispute it—that when Texas needs money to move its crops its banks can not borrow money in any considerable quantities in either St. Louis or Kansas City, and must go to Chicago or the Atlantic seaboard (RBOC 1914b, 118). Moreover, Dallas leaders tied southern support for Wilson's Federal Reserve directly to the assumption that the administration would place reserve banks in their region: "The currency bill when under consideration attracted to its support those who believed that the present administration would locate the banks regionally . . . [and] those who thought that the old order was passing (ibid., 120).

Because the South was solidly Democratic at the time, placing reserve banks in southern cities would have provided an economic shot in the arm expressly for Democratic constituencies. So if the RBOC wanted to exploit its authority to protect Democrats' interests, we might see them disproportionately place banks in credit-starved areas in the South—rather than in the similarly credit-poor Republican West. To be sure, regional diversification of the reserve system would have served both the Democrats' political interest in broadening the footprint of the reserve system and their partisan interest in bolstering the economies of the underdeveloped Democratic South. It is impossible to distinguish between Democrats' potential motives since the two accounts are confounded: party and region are coterminous in this period. There were no Republican cities in the South and few Democratic cities in the West for the RBOC to consider. In short, the regional division of the parties complicates analysis of the allocation of the reserve banks. Yet evidence that the RBOC looked beyond cities' financial activity would suggest that the conventional wisdom overestimates the exclusive importance of local commerce and finance in shaping the location of the reserve banks.

Alternatively, the president's electoral needs for 1916 might have shaped the location decisions of the RBOC. As Scott James (2000) argues, Wilson's policy agenda in his first term was partially aimed at attracting Progressive Republicans into the Democratic fold for the 1916 elections. Wilson understood that he was unlikely to have the good fortune of running in a three-way race in 1916, with two Republicans splintering the opposition vote. Thus, Wilson needed to secure support of Progressive Republican voters in the West and Midwest. If so, it is possible that applicant cities from Progressive-leaning states (particularly those whose Republican legislators voted in favor of the bill) would be especially likely to secure a bank. That said, Progressives' antipathy toward the Federal Reserve Act was well known, shaped in part by their preference for greater public control over the system. That might have diminished the RBOC's interest in locating a reserve bank in Progressive strongholds.[16]

Testing Competing Accounts

We take two approaches to decipher the RBOC's decision making. First, we use Richard Bensel's (1984) research on turn-of-the-century trading patterns to construct a counterfactual financial map. If the RBOC had selected the reserve bank locations exclusively with "due regard to the convenience and customary course of business," the selected cities should closely fit a mapping of the nation's financial hubs at the turn of the century. Second, we use RBOC archival records to model the political and financial forces that might have shaped the committee's location choices.

CONSTRUCTING THE FINANCIAL MAP

Building on "central place theory," Bensel identifies two component parts of trade areas: an urban center, and the surrounding hinterlands (rural areas and lesser cities). An urban center provides for the financial needs of the region, making it the dominant transportation, banking, and insurance hub in the area. Bensel (1984, 422) uses two criteria to identify the trade areas and their urban centers at the turn of the century, and draw their territorial borders: a minimum of three railroad trunk lines connecting the city to other urban centers, and a population greater than fifty thousand. Cities within seventy-five miles of a larger urban center (say, New Haven, Connecticut, relative to New York City) were disqualified as urban centers. Ranking urban centers by population generates a list of the top fifty commercial hubs at the turn of the century. Given a strong correlation between each urban center's rank by population and its number of national banks, we can use the urban center ranking to determine the nation's top financial hubs. Thus, we use the ranked urban centers to create a counterfactual financial map and compare it to the RBOC's map: How closely did the RBOC follow the ranking of trade area urban centers in selecting reserve bank cities?

MODELING THE RBOC'S CHOICES

We use the RBOC archival materials to construct two models of the RBOC's decision making.

Model 1: Selecting the Cities

In the first model, we estimate the likelihood that the RBOC would have located a reserve bank in an applicant city.[17] The independent variables tap a range of financial and political factors, including:

> *Financial hub*: We use Bensel's trade center data to create a
> "trade center" dummy variable to denote whether or not
> each city was a designated trade area urban city. According
> to the financial model, trade centers should be more likely
> to secure a reserve bank than nontrade area centers.
> *Banker preferences*: We measure the intensity of banker
> preferences by recording (and logging) the aggregate
> number of bankers' first-choice votes for each applicant city
> (as shown in figure 3.1). If the RBOC placed the banks with

"due regard to the convenience and customary course of business," cities that are more popular with bankers should be more likely to secure a reserve bank.

South, Midwest, and West: We create three dummy variables to tap the regional location of each applicant city, treating northeastern cities as the "excluded" category. If the RBOC sought to break up the historic concentration of capital along the Eastern Seaboard, cities in one or more regions outside the East should be more likely to receive a reserve bank. A statistically significant estimate for the South would suggest that the RBOC sought regional diversity within the reserve system, disproportionately locating banks in the solid Democratic South (even after controlling for the applicant cities' financial and other characteristics).

Progressive strength: We tap each state's strength of the Progressive movement by measuring the percentage of Republican members from the state's congressional House delegation who voted for the conference report on the Federal Reserve Act in December 1913. If the RBOC sought to reward Wilson's Progressive supporters with a reserve bank to expand the Democratic coalition for 1916, Progressive areas should have a greater chance of securing a bank, even in light of their financial activity.

Model 2: Evaluating the Banker Survey

The second model explores how the RBOC responded to the views of the surveyed bankers. If the financial model provides the best fit for the RBOC map, and if the RBOC was responsive to the bankers, we would expect that bankers recommending prominent financial centers would be more likely to see their preferred cities selected to host a reserve bank. If the RBOC emphasized political factors in selecting the cities, we would expect nonfinancial features of the recommended cities to correlate with their likelihood of being selected for a reserve bank. The explanations of course are not mutually exclusive; the RBOC might have structured the map with an eye to financial network and partisan alignments.

VOTE FOR RESERVE-BANK CITIES.

FIRST-CHOICE VOTE FOR RESERVE-BANK CITIES, BY DISTRICTS.

DISTRICT NO. 5.

	Mary-land.	District of Co-lumbia.	West Virginia, southern district.	Virginia.	North Carolina.	South Carolina.	Total.
Richmond			16	96	44	11	167
Baltimore	95		21	11		1	128
Pittsburgh	1		34				35
Columbia						28	28
Cincinnati			26	1			27
Washington	1	12		9	2	1	25
Charlotte					18	1	19
New York	1			1			2
Total	98	12	97	118	64	42	431

FIGURE 3.2. Excerpt from poll of national banks, aggregated by Federal Reserve District, 1914. RBOC 1914b, 349.

To build the dependent variable, we exploit the RBOC's aggregation of the survey results by different groups of bankers—grouped either by state or subregion of a state. For example, as shown in figure 3.2, Maryland's bankers cast ninety-five first-choice votes for Baltimore, one for Pittsburgh, one for Washington, and one for New York. We treat each state banker–city choice dyad as a different observation, so that the Maryland bankers contribute four observations (Maryland-Baltimore, Maryland-Pittsburgh, Maryland-Washington, and Maryland–New York); the data include a total of 229 state-city dyad observations. We code the dependent variable "1" if the bankers' recommended city in the dyad secured a reserve bank, and "0" if otherwise.[18] The RBOC reported state banker preferences by the Federal Reserve district to which they were ultimately assigned. Hence, we use conditional logit to model the RBOC's choice of a reserve bank city from among the bankers' preferred cities within each reserve district, estimating the impact of state and city characteristics on the RBOC's calculus.[19] We include the following independent variables:

Financial strength: We include the number of national banks in each preferred city, as reported in the 1913 *Annual Report of the Comptroller of the Currency* as a measure of the financial strength of the city (Office of the Comptroller of the Currency 1914). The number of banks correlates highly with both city population and the volume of check clearings in each city.[20] Given the distribution of the data, we take the log of each city's number of banks.

South, Midwest, and West: We create three dummy variables to tap the regional location of the bankers' preferred city, with the Northeast region as the excluded category. If the RBOC sought to break up the historic concentration of capital along the Eastern Seaboard, and if the committee used the bankers' views to guide their decisions, cities preferred by bankers in one or more regions outside the Northeast should be more likely to receive a reserve bank.

Progressive strength: To test whether the RBOC was more responsive to bankers who hailed from Progressive states especially supportive of enacting the Federal Reserve Act, we include the Progressive strength measure described above.

Banker disagreement: As a control for the extent of banker consensus, we include a variable that captures divisions within each banking delegation over preferred cities. The measure divides the number of cities that received votes from each banker delegation by the proportion of delegation votes received by the most popular city. For example, Maryland's bankers split their votes across four cities, but gave 97 percent of their votes to Baltimore (scoring just over 4 on the metric of disagreement). In contrast, bankers from the southern portion of West Virginia also split their votes across four cities, but the most popular city garnered only 35 percent of the bankers' votes (scoring just over 11 on the metric). Across the twelve reserve districts, the measure of disagreement ranges from 1 (Washington, DC's bankers gave all their votes to DC) to over 32 (eastern Tennessee bankers split their votes over ten cities, and the most popular city garnered just over a third of the votes). The more fractured the state banking community, the less likely one of its preferred cities will be selected.

The Contours of a Politically Optimal Reserve System

The counterfactual financial map appears in figure 3.3. Given that the financial community typically preferred as few reserve banks as possible, we assume that the counterfactual system should include eight reserve banks in the country's most active financial hubs (marked in gray). The actual Federal Reserve System map and counterfactual map have six cities in common: New York (ranked first), Chicago (second), Philadelphia (third), St. Louis (fourth), Boston (fifth), and San Francisco (seventh). In placing the next five reserve banks in Cleveland (ninth), Minneapolis (fifteenth), Kansas City (eighteenth), Richmond (twenty-fourth), and Atlanta (twenty-seventh), the RBOC skipped over sixteen higher-ranked cities—including Baltimore (sixth) and Cincinnati (eighth). The twelfth and final reserve

Counterfactual Financial Map

1. Scranton
2. Baltimore
3. Pittsburgh
4. Cleveland   8. Louisville
5. Columbus   9. Evansville
6. Cincinnati   10. Nashville
7. Indianapolis   11. Grand Rapids

FIGURE 3.3. Counterfactual financial map: 1895 trade area boundaries, with top eight trade area urban centers. See Bensel 1984, 484.

TABLE 3.1. Cities' Likelihood of Securing a Reserve Bank

Independent variable	Coefficient (robust s. e.)
Financial hub	3.189 (1.209)***
Banker preferences (logged)	3.776 (1.452)***
Progressive strength	−1.817 (2.675)
South	4.825 (2.271)**
West	2.055 (1.778)
Midwest	1.547 (2.492)
Constant	−24.401 (9.092)***
N	36
Log pseudolikelihood	−8.274

Notes: The dependent variable measures whether or not the RBOC placed a reserve bank in an applicant city (1 = yes; 0 = otherwise). Estimates calculated in Stata 14.2 *logit* command. Robust standard errors in parentheses.
** $p < 0.05$ (one-tailed); *** $p < 0.01$; N = 36. Because Washington, DC, is unrepresented in Congress, we cannot calculate the level of Progressive support for the Federal Reserve Act in the relevant state's House delegation.

bank was given to Dallas, a city too sleepy to even qualify as one of the top fifty trade area urban centers in 1900.[21] Taken at face value, it seems that the RBOC placed the reserve banks in only some of the most active financial centers, exploiting its discretion to place reserve banks outside major commercial areas of the period.

Given thirty-seven applicant cities, what broader set of factors shaped the RBOC's map? Table 3.1 reports the results for our first model of the RBOC's decision making.[22] First, we confirm that trade area centers were more likely to receive reserve banks than non-center cities. Second, the greater the appeal of a city to the nation's bankers, the greater the chances that the RBOC would place a reserve bank in that city. Collectively, these two variables capture the overlap between the financial counterfactual map and final reserve system map. The RBOC approached its job by locating reserve banks in the most prominent financial hubs at the time.

Political factors also seem to weigh in the RBOC's decision making. After controlling for a city's popularity with bankers and its financial status, cities in the South had a greater chance of being selected to host a reserve bank than cities in the Northeast. Applicant cities in the Midwest and West, however, were no more likely to be selected than a northeastern city. Nor were cities in supportive Progressive states more likely to receive a reserve bank than other cities; if anything, they were especially unlikely to receive a bank. The findings suggest that the RBOC sought to make up for the deficit of credit in the South, and thus sought out southern locations when looking to extend the reserve system beyond the nation's financial centers in the East. In doing so, of course, the RBOC also placed a coveted financial resource in the heart of the Democratic South. Given the correlation between region and party, we cannot distinguish between these two potential RBOC motives. Yet the results indicate that the RBOC incorporated more than the interests of the financial sector in locating the reserve banks in the new federal system.

Archival evidence confirms the notion that the RBOC sought to dilute the importance of the New York district. For instance, Paul Warburg, the Republican banker behind Senator Aldrich's proposal for a centralized and privately controlled reserve system, certainly understood the RBOC's intentions. Writing in his memoirs in 1930, Warburg (1930, 427) recalled that "no plan should be considered which . . . might increase the power of New York." Or as the *New York Times* observed, the challenge facing the RBOC after its first day of hearings in New York City was that "it quickly developed that the committee had a difficult task on its hands and that it probably would be impossible to satisfy both New York and the rest of the country."[23] The creation of the Richmond district is also suggestive that the RBOC sought to extend the reserve system beyond the Northeast (New York) and mid-Atlantic (Washington). Addressing complaints about the Richmond reserve bank after the map was finalized, the RBOC noted that the Carolinas had objected to being assigned to either a southern or western reserve bank: "They said that their course of trade was northeast." But the RBOC (1914e, 24) reasoned that "it seemed undesirable to place a bank in the extreme northeastern corner or at Baltimore, not only because of its proximity to Philadelphia, but also because the industrial and banking relations of the greater part of the district were more intimate with Richmond than with either Washington or Baltimore." The RBOC clearly sought to locate reserve banks beyond the Eastern Seaboard.

We doubt our finding that southern cities had a leg up with the RBOC is an artifact of the types of cities that applied for a reserve bank. If it were true that southern cities perceived a bias against their region (unlikely, given the makeup of the RBOC), perhaps only marginal southern cities applied. If so, the southern effect we detect might simply reflect that only the strongest southern cities applied. We investigate this possibility by estimating the likelihood that a city from the hundred most populous cities (according to the 1910 census) applied to the RBOC. We find that central reserve or reserve cities under existing national banking laws (those with strong claims for a regional reserve bank) were more likely to apply, as were southern cities. Importantly, however, reserve cities in the South did not disproportionately apply (even after controlling for the level of bank clearings in 1913). The Democratic, southern cast of the RBOC and President Wilson, a Virginian, likely signaled to marginal southern cities that they faced a greater, not worse, chance of being awarded a prized reserve bank.

We build on these results in table 3.2, exploring how the RBOC responded to the reserve bank city choices revealed in the banker survey.[24] Financial considerations again appeared to matter. First, the greater the finances of a banking community's most favored city within a district, the higher the chances that city would be selected from among the locations mentioned in the banker survey. Consensus within each state also made a difference: the greater the disagreement among state bankers about where to place a reserve bank in their region, the less likely a preferred city received a reserve bank.

Still, politics also mattered. Even after controlling for the financial strength of the bankers' preferred cities, recommended cities in every region were not equally likely to secure a reserve bank. We find some limited evidence that the RBOC looked more favorably on bankers preferring midwestern cities to locations in the Northeast. Looking more closely, however, outside the three northeastern districts, only sizable numbers of bankers in the Cleveland district preferred East Coast locations for their reserve bank. When we drop the Cleveland district from the model, the result melts away. But if we look at the preferences of the Cleveland district bankers, the

TABLE 3.2. RBOC Response to the Banker Survey

Independent variable	Coefficient (robust s. e.)
Financial strength	3.150 (0.945)***
Progressive strength	−0.574 (0.216)
Banker disagreement	−0.056 (0.020)**
South	0.624 (1.272)
West	0.008 (1.230)
Midwest	2.719 (1.385)*
N	229
Log pseudolikelihood	−81.597
Pseudo R2	0.353

Notes: The dependent variable captures whether or not the RBOC placed a reserve bank in a city recommended by state-based groups of bankers. Coefficients are conditional logit estimates, grouped by federal reserve district and calculated in Stata 14.2 *clogit* command. Robust standard errors in parentheses. Details in the text.
* $p < 0.05$; ** $p < 0.01$; *** $p < 0.001$.

RBOC disproportionately heeded the views of those bankers who preferred a midwestern city for their reserve bank (thereby producing the midwestern effect noted above). Midwestern bankers desiring to venture east were more likely to be disappointed in securing a favored location.

The results in tables 3.1 and 3.2 are noteworthy. They suggest the RBOC looked beyond financial activity in locating the reserve banks. It did so in two ways. First, southern cities were disproportionately likely to secure a reserve bank compared to cities in the Northeast—even after controlling for economic activity in the cities (table 3.1). Second, we know the RBOC kept the regional shape of the reserve map in mind when considering the preferences of the bankers who lived on the eastern edge of the Cleveland district (table 3.2). The RBOC considered more than financial claims in organizing the regional reach of the reserve system.

The RBOC could have ignored the banker survey and located the reserve banks solely based on each city's financial merit. In fact, the panel chose locations with an eye toward where the bankers wanted the reserve banks. Just as the RBOC might have wanted to secure southern Democrats' support for the new reserve system, they might also have sought to build support for the newborn Fed among the nation's bankers far from Wall Street. Creating a reserve system that largely (although not entirely) followed the outlines recommended by banking communities allowed the RBOC to balance political and financial concerns in locating the banks.

The results also help us to explain the decision to place two reserve banks in Missouri. Willis (1923) argued that St. Louis was bound to receive a bank, given its longtime status as a central reserve city under nineteenth-century banking law. How to serve the region to the west of St. Louis was a thornier problem. Willis suggests that the choice came down to Omaha, Lincoln, Denver, or Kansas City. None of these cities was especially Democratic, but Kansas City stood out on two key dimensions: financial activity, and popularity with bankers. The city far outstripped its rivals in terms of financial business, and bankers preferred it overwhelmingly—even compared to St. Louis. As RBOC member Houston (1926, 103) noted in his memoirs, "I got a good many surprises. There was little enthusiasm for St. Louis anywhere." If we count votes only from those bankers in the states and regions ultimately assigned to the Kansas City district, Kansas City's popularity is even more pronounced. Just under half of those bankers designated Kansas City as their first choice; its closest competitor was Omaha, garnering only a quarter of the bankers' votes.

Some charged at the time that Missouri received two reserve banks because the Democratic speaker of the House, Champ Clark, hailed from Missouri and because Houston had served as president of Washington University in St. Louis. Yet we suspect that partisan connections at best smoothed the way for locating reserve banks in two Missouri cities. The choice more likely reflected the region's political economy (Kansas City was oriented to the West, and St. Louis to the East) and the desire to curry support of the most active banking communities (given St. Louis's status as a major financial center).

The results also offer some perspective on the RBOC's decision to place a bank in Richmond instead of Baltimore. Financial business in Baltimore was nearly twice that of Richmond. And bankers only marginally preferred Richmond to Baltimore. So why did the RBOC opt for Richmond over Baltimore? If the RBOC wanted to dilute the historic concentration of capital in the Northeast, selecting Richmond over Baltimore would have been a reasonable choice. Drawing a single reserve district to encompass Baltimore, Washington, and Richmond, and placing the reserve bank in Richmond, would have allowed the RBOC to push the center of financial activity beyond the Northeastern Seaboard and into the South. Of course, it is also possible that Richmond won out over Baltimore because Virginia was a more reliably Democratic state than Maryland; Wilson ran nearly twenty points better in Virginia in 1912 than in Maryland. Factor in the Virginia roots of Treasury secretary McAdoo, Representative Glass, and Wilson himself, and it seems plausible that the RBOC selected Richmond to reward a loyal Democratic city and state. For these reasons, we disagree with previous studies that find the RBOC "likely maximized" social welfare rather than its own (McAvoy 2006, 524). Even if we cannot know for sure whether regional diversity or partisan advantage motivated the RBOC, both accounts indicate that the selection of Richmond furthered the RBOC's agenda of looking beyond financial forces in locating the reserve banks.[25]

With twelve banks to dispense, the RBOC managed to place reserve banks in financially active cities and create new financial centers in regions historically deprived of reliable access to credit. In that light, it is not surprising that the RBOC refused to entertain any changes to the map, despite protests from city leaders in Baltimore, New Orleans, Denver, Pittsburgh, and elsewhere. Reopening the RBOC's decisions would have unraveled the committee's carefully knit plan. To be sure, partisan geography helped to shape the RBOC's map. If the RBOC sought regional balance in locating the reserve banks, southern reserve banks would be placed in Democratic hands. Nevertheless, concerns about regional balance were insufficient to secure a reserve bank in the vast and typically Republican expanse between Kansas City and San Francisco, even as Missouri received two district banks. Finally, given Democrats' interests in constraining the size of the New York district, the RBOC inevitably had to reward cities in the predominantly Republican Northeast (but not, it seems, in Progressive strongholds in the West or Midwest). Political geography helped to facilitate the RBOC's twin focus on financial and political priorities.

Conclusion

> The matter of locating regional banks is not primarily, nor even principally, a political question. Every governmental faculty, however, has a political element and every governmental agency a political phase. No system of banking will long succeed which does violence to a great fraction of the wishes of the people of this country. Such political considerations as affect this feature of the problem are therefore of an entirely proper character for consideration by this committee.
>
> —DALLAS RESERVE BANK ORGANIZATION COMMITTEE, "LOCATION OF RESERVE DISTRICTS IN THE UNITED STATES"

These observations by Dallas city leaders seeking a reserve bank capture the political nature of the RBOC's charge. Controlled by Democratic politicians, the RBOC had the latitude to build a financially viable and politically sustainable reserve bank system. The archival record supports such an interpretation of the RBOC's handiwork: the RBOC prioritized economic optimality tempered by a concern for the regional dispersion of access to credit. By looking beyond the financial claims of the cities desiring to host the new reserve banks, the RBOC exploited its unchallenged power to ensure that the reserve system would secure Democrats' goal of breaking up the Northeast's monopoly on the levers of credit. Top financial hubs, but not all of them, received a reserve bank. So too did some underdeveloped cities located in traditionally Democratic areas. The RBOC's balancing act drives home the political character of the Fed as an institution of monetary control.

Viewed more broadly, the genesis and organization of the Federal Reserve corroborates our political-economic logic of reform. In the wake of an epic financial crisis in 1907 that catalyzed electoral turnover, lawmakers and parties scrambled to avoid blame for the economic debacle as well as muster support for new measures to prevent a similar crisis from recurring. In 1913, a new governing majority broke decades of electoral and ideological resistance to central banking by bridging partisan and factional differences about the powers, organization, and governance of a new reserve system. As we demonstrated in this chapter, the price of enactment was a regional, federal system that mixed public and private control of reserve banks, and set them way beyond the exclusive reach of Wall Street and other dominant financial centers.

Compromises embedded in the Federal Reserve Act created an economically suboptimal but politically invaluable reserve system. Ironically, as we show in chapter 4, the Fed's federal architecture was partially to blame for the duration and severity of the Great Depression less than two decades later. As economists Friedman and Schwartz (1971, 193) characterized the early years of the Federal Reserve, there was "so much confusion about purpose and power, and so erratic an exercise of power." And when disagreements in 1929 surfaced between the reserve banks and Federal Reserve Board in Washington over how to rein in excessive market speculation, the dispute "paralyzed" monetary policy (ibid., 255). A decentralized Fed, Friedman and Schwartz (ibid., 298) concluded, "left a heritage of divided counsel and internal conflict for the years of trial that followed." Remarkably, the signature achievement of Wilson's administration proved incapable of generating effective monetary policy in the 1920s, contributing directly to the onset and severity of the Great Depression in the early 1930s.

Still, as we observe throughout the book, the choices made in 1913 baked political support for the Federal Reserve into its statutory skeleton. The compromises necessary to overcome a century of opposition to a central bank bolstered the Fed's institutional stickiness—an organizational backbone that has proven difficult to unravel. In particular, the quasi-public regional reserve system hardwired political support for the Fed in communities far from Wall Street and Washington. As we discuss in the next chapter, the Fed's stickiness emerged as early as the 1930s (when southern Democrats prevented reformers from fully centralizing control of monetary policy power in Washington) and recently as 2010 (when lawmakers failed to strip the reserve banks of their supervisory powers). To be sure, the Fed today after decades of reform is far more powerful and centralized than it was a century ago. But the institution's federal style persists today because it established a vast political network that central bankers can mobilize to protect the Fed when politicians put the institution in their cross hairs.

4

Opening the Act in the Wake of the Depression

Born of financial crisis and political compromise, the nascent Federal Reserve proved instrumental in helping to underwrite the nation's entry into World War I. But by 1920, its awkward structure contributed to a deep recession that hit agricultural states especially hard. The twelve regional reserve banks nonetheless deployed the Federal Reserve's original tools and new innovations to influence the flow of credit in the postrecession 1920s. The Fed emerged as a reliable lender of last resort for national and state banks in the system. Banks that failed were typically small, rural ones beyond the reach of the new federal network.

The stock market's spectacular 1929 crash—coupled with deflation and a slowdown in industrial production—marked the beginning of the Great Depression, and overshadowed the Fed's early challenges and successes (see figure 4.1). In the following years, almost 9,800 commercial banks in the United States closed their doors and unemployment reached 24.9 percent, leaving roughly 13 million out of work in 1933 alone.[1] The road out of the depths of the Depression was long: a stronger economy took root only after the enactment and implementation of President Roosevelt's New Deal

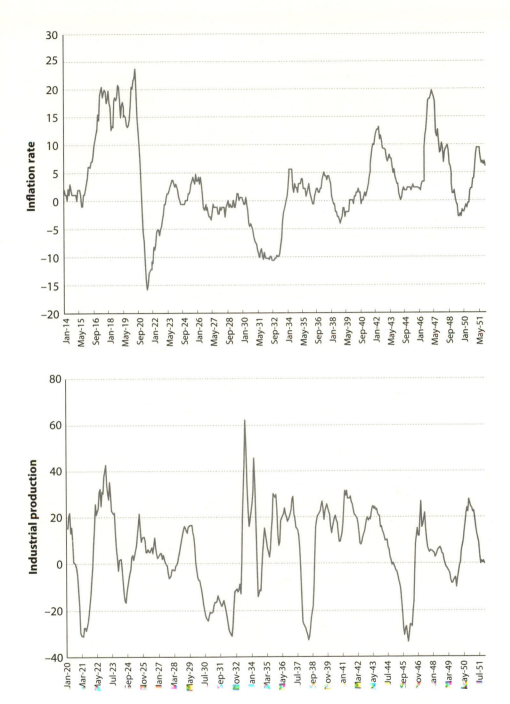

FIGURE 4.1. A. Economic conditions: annual inflation rate, 1914–51. US Bureau of Labor Statistics, n.d. B. Economic conditions: year over year change in industrial production, 1920–51. Board of Governors of the Federal Reserve System.

policies, including a de facto dollar devaluation and vast fiscal expansion in the run-up to World War II. Even so, the recovery was fragile; in 1937, the Fed imposed higher reserve requirements on banks, throwing the country back into recession. Years later, economists Friedman and Schwartz (1963) blamed the Federal Reserve for the Depression, arguing in *A Monetary History of the United States* that the Fed's decentralized structure and lack of leadership after the sudden death of Benjamin Strong (who was governor of the Federal Reserve Bank of New York) undermined the Fed's capacity to prevent financial crises and engineer economic recovery. Or as Federal Reserve governor Bernanke (2002) conceded on Friedman's ninetieth birthday, "You're right, we did it. We're very sorry. But thanks to you (Friedman and Schwartz), we won't do it again."[2]

Just as the Panic of 1907 catalyzed the genesis of the Federal Reserve, the Great Depression sparked a new blame and reform dynamic. Reacting to the Fed's abject failure to prevent financial and economic collapse, lawmakers exploited electoral change to reopen the Federal Reserve Act. In this chapter, we apply the political-economic perspective to explain why, when, and how Congress revamped the Fed during and after the Great Depression. In short, while blaming the Fed, Congress deepened its Depression-induced interdependence. In a series of existential legislation, Congress strengthened and centralized Fed power in Washington, but significantly curtailed its independent authority to conduct monetary policy, subordinating a revamped Washington-based Board of Governors to a mere agent of the Treasury Department until the Fed regained its effective independence in 1951.

As we explore in detail in this chapter, reform politics in the 1930s followed several of the original 1913 fault lines. Once again, no single party or branch of government could impose its ideal plan for allocating as well as structuring the power to conduct monetary policy. Fissures within the Democratic Party—reflecting regional, ideological divides over FDR's New Deal agenda—further complicated reform. A consolidation of power within the Board went only as far as the Democratic South would allow, cementing the Fed's decentralized, federal character even though the hybrid structure had been expressly blamed for the onset and severity of the Great Depression. We conclude by reviewing the consequences of the 1930s' reforms—changes that landed the Fed, willingly at times, under the thumb of the Treasury throughout the ensuing war years.

Early Evolution of the Fed

The Fed's conduct of monetary policy evolved considerably over its first two decades. As economic historian David Wheelock (1991, 13) has observed, these developments transformed the Fed's original "passive, self-regulating" monetary regime to an "activist policy strategy." These initial Fed experiences also highlight the limitations of the original compromise over Fed power and governance as well as lawmakers' willingness to periodically reconsider the law. First, the limited and decentralized reserve system hampered the new central bank's ability to formulate and coordinate national monetary policy. Second, legislators frequently revised the Federal Reserve Act, tweaking the law to address the nation's evolving financial needs and meet lawmakers' political objectives. And while the Fed and Treasury initiated requests for several of these changes, lawmakers took full ownership of other changes, including efforts to expand lending to farmers and rural commerce.

The Federal Reserve Act of 1913 was designed to create an elastic currency—a money supply that would rise and fall with changes in agricultural and business activity. This "real bills doctrine" that the Fed followed required that lender of last resort activity (that is, loans by a central bank to ensure liquidity of its member banks' balance sheets) occur primarily through separate discount windows operated by the twelve district banks. Member banks would bring commercial paper to the reserve banks that reflected their short-term credit needs, and the Fed would rediscount the paper—lending for agricultural and business purposes. Reflecting lawmakers' efforts to rival London's status as a world financial center, the act allowed the reserve banks to rediscount "banker acceptances"—but only for the import and export of foreign goods; rediscounting for domestic shipments was prohibited. More generally, the Federal

Reserve Act placed strict limits on the types of obligations acceptable for rediscounting, limiting borrowing to short-term, "self-
liquidating" collateral (Hackley 1973). As borrowers' commercial
paper was paid off, currency would return to the reserve banks,
allowing the amount of currency to vary closely with agricultural
and commercial needs (ibid.).

THE IMPACT OF WAR

The Federal Reserve Act's strict limits on legitimate lending did not
last long. In 1917, with the onset of World War I, Congress amended
the act to lower the nation's costs to finance the war. Specifically,
changes to the law allowed for rediscounting of banker acceptances
for domestic shipments and permitted reserve banks to lend to
member banks using the banks' holdings of government securities
as collateral. Perhaps as important, Congress enticed state banks to
join the Federal Reserve System by exempting them from supervision by the comptroller of the currency, leaving them subject to
examination only by state authorities. Expanding the number of par-
ticipating banks as well as the acceptable collateral moved the Fed
away from strict application of the real bills doctrine.

War reshaped the Fed: the central bank's key activity during the
war was selling Treasury bonds (Liberty Loans) at interest rates that
enabled the Treasury to finance its deficits at a low cost (Meltzer
2003, 89). To provide a cheap source of financing for the Treasury,
the Federal Reserve regional banks offered below market, prefer-
ential rates on Treasury securities—a potentially inflationary policy.
Selling Treasury bonds became a profit center for the reserve banks,
and Fed lending revolved primarily around Treasury debt. Such financing continued even after the war to help the Treasury pay off
its debts at low rates.

As agents for the Treasury's bond sales, the Fed's conduct of monetary policy was exceedingly intertwined with the government's financing needs. For example, Strong, the governor of the New York
Fed, found himself in effect working for the Treasury department
(Garbade 2012). Strong had two jobs in addition to formulating

monetary policy at the New York Fed: he headed the Liberty Loan Committee, and served as the Treasury's fiscal agent. As Lester Chandler (1958, 141) points out, Strong probably didn't know what job he was doing since "he would have been reluctant to insist on a monetary policy that would make much more difficult his job of raising great sums for Treasury." All told, the Fed's new role in service to the Treasury supplanted its original one of managing the currency to meet the needs of business and farming—foreshadowing pressures the Fed would again face twenty-five years later when the United States entered World War II.

The war did more than move the Fed's twelve reserve banks away from the real bills doctrine. It also made open market operations (that is, buying and selling government securities in the open market) a permanent feature of the Fed's monetary policy tool kit. Open market operations had originally been used by the reserve banks as an occasional means of securing interest-bearing assets to fund reserve bank costs. But after the 1920–21 discount rate hikes caused a brief but sharp recession, the reserve banks relied more aggressively on open market purchases to ease access to credit (Wheelock 1991, 13). Buying and selling government bonds enabled the Fed to inject or withdraw money from banks, influencing interest rates and the supply of credit. These open market operations soon exposed a fault in the system: the Board in Washington could not coordinate system-wide operations in pursuit of a national monetary policy— helping to contribute to the onset and severity of the Depression.

POWER STRUGGLES WITHIN THE FED

The political compromise of 1913 that demanded a decentralized reserve system generated two power struggles within the system during its first two decades. As Liaquat Ahamed (2009, 173) observes in *Lords of Finance*, jockeying for control within the system was to be expected: an ambiguous statute and "too many big egos" made the power struggle inevitable. One dilemma stemmed from disagreements over the discount rates charged by the regional reserve banks; the other emerged from differences of opinion about the conduct of open market operations. In some ways, these were simply coordination problems: How should discount rates be set, and how should open market operations be conducted across a diverse regional reserve system? These difficulties over policy were at root a struggle by the reserve banks, Federal Reserve Board, and Treasury to assert power within the hybrid, decentralized central bank. Complicating these conflicts were disagreements within the regional reserve system, as the New York and to a lesser extent Chicago reserve banks came to dominate decision making. New York was always first among equals, given its role as the fiscal agent for the Treasury's borrowing and the influence of its district's banks.

Conflict over Discount Rates

These struggles reveal how little the original act arbitrated and resolved inevitable conflicts within the system. Meltzer (2003, chapter 3) details the difficulties encountered over the use of the discount window and setting of rates. The Federal Reserve Act empowered the Board to approve discount rate requests from the regional reserve banks, though in practice the Treasury subordinated the Fed and the regional banks. Preferring to keep rates artificially low to defray the cost of financing the war, Treasury pressured the reserve banks to offer below market discount rates—stoking demand for credit and a sharp rise in inflation. When reserve banks sought the Board's approval to raise their discount rates, the Treasury pressured the Board to reject the rate increase requests.

After inflationary and deflationary policy mistakes by the regional banks in 1919–20, pressure arose to amend the act.[3] Indeed, after raising rates in 1920, the Fed came under attack from lawmakers for contributing to the recession that year; Congress even debated legislation that would have capped the Fed's power to raise discount rates without congressional consent. Farm failures during the recession increased congressional pressure to broaden the Fed's responsiveness to the credit needs of the agrarian South, including expanding the Federal Reserve Board to include a representative of agricultural interests.[4] Even after Congress and President Warren G. Harding also enacted the Agricultural Credits Act of 1923 to address the specific borrowing needs of farmers, disputes over the authority to raise or lower discount rates continued.

Conflict over Open Market Operations

Greater reliance on open market operations also generated a power struggle within the reserve system. As a supervisory body, the DC-based board lacked the explicit authority to initiate open market operations or direct the reserve banks to carry them out. After all, lawmakers in 1913 had explicitly created a decentralized reserve system: each regional reserve bank would operate its own discount window (albeit with its rate changes subject to approval by the Board in Washington). Caught between the Treasury and Congress, the nascent Fed struggled to coordinate and homogenize policy as the evolving economy and financial system created previously unforeseen pressures. It would be a generation or two before a more mature and centralized board began to assert more powerful monetary autonomy.

The governors of the reserve banks did not wait for Congress to authorize the creation of a committee to coordinate open market operations. In fact, the governors had been meeting since 1914 in a Governors' Conference, which excluded the members of the Federal Reserve Board, much to the members' consternation (Meltzer 2003, 142). In 1922, the New York Fed's Strong took the lead to create the Committee of Governors on Centralized Execution of Purchases and Sales of Government Securities to improve the coordination of open market operations and centralize decision making in a way that excluded the Washington board. As Meltzer notes, however, Strong's fellow reserve bank governors resisted any coordination that limited their own authority to conduct open market operations, suspicious of endowing the New York Fed with too much power. Strong's compromise was to create an executive committee that included the New York, Boston, Chicago, Philadelphia, and Cleveland heads. Moreover, the committee was limited to recommending and executing open market operations ordered by the regional reserve banks.

The governors' solution did not last; the Board attempted to revamp the committee one year later. Ultimately, the committee that replaced the governors' panel—the Open Market Investment

Committee (OMIC)—replicated the reserve banks' dominance by placing the same five bank governors on the committee and allowing the Board only supervisory authority over open market decisions. As US House Committee on Banking and Currency (1971) staff members remarked decades later in a review of the Fed's early performance, the OMIC soon took the initiative to both formulate policy and implement it. Frustrated with the New York Fed's dominance of the OMIC, other reserve banks also periodically challenged the committee's authority. The Boston Fed, for example, defied the committee's policy in 1924 by purchasing government securities to bolster its earnings, counter to the open market rules promulgated by the New York–led committee (ibid., 136).

Conflicts in the committee and with the Board continued throughout the decade, before and after Strong's untimely death in 1928. In March 1930, the reserve bank governors acted in concert to replace the OMIC with a new Open Market Policy Conference (OMPC), modeling it on the original governors' conference. Once again, all twelve reserve bank governors were made members and the committee empowered itself to set its own agenda. As economic historians argue, though, the Fed had little interest in conducting open market operations as an instrument of countercyclical policy in the early 1930s—even with the restructured committee. Barry Eichengreen (1992) contends that the reserve banks were stymied by the Fed's strict adherence to the gold standard out of fear that other countries would doubt the United States' metallic commitment.[5] With little commercial activity against which to issue notes, the Federal Reserve Act required a hefty gold supply to back the issuance of currency. To hold onto its gold supply in 1930 and 1931, the Fed raised rates, tightening credit, increasing loan losses, and allowing deflation to set in (Ahamed 2009, 436).

Even when Congress passed the first Glass-Steagall Act of 1932 (allowing the reserve banks to back currency issues with government securities), increased open market operations were short-lived. As Chang-Tai Hsieh and Christina D. Romer (2006) document, the Chicago, Philadelphia, and Boston Feds were reluctant to continue to buy securities, with Chicago actually balking at additional purchases. Given an open market committee that allowed individual reserve banks to object to open market purchase plans, opposition from Chicago derailed further purchases after spring 1932. Moreover, as Friedman and Schwartz (1963, 362) note, the open market purchases that spring were largely conducted under pressure from Congress after enactment of Glass-Steagall; with Congress's adjournment in August, the deadlock over additional open market purchases resumed. Owen Young, deputy chair of the New York Fed's Board of Directors, remarked that July that "you may have two or three banks dictating the policy of the System at a critical time, just because of their ability to block a System program" (quoted in Hsieh and Romer 2006, 172).

Despite the stalemate that stemmed partially from the Fed's dysfunctional open market committee, Congress gave the OMPC a statutory basis when it wrote the 1933 Banking Act (signed into law by FDR in June 1933). Rather than find a way to centralize the design of open market operations, Congress ratified the regional structure of the OMPC, creating the Fed's new FOMC. We explore below why Congress opted to allow all twelve reserve bank heads a vote on setting monetary policy when it created the original FOMC in 1933. That decision would come under fire for perpetuating private banker influence over monetary policy when Eccles (FDR's pick from the Treasury to lead the Fed in 1935) turned his attention to increasing public control of the Fed in 1935.

We doubt the authors of the Federal Reserve Act—some of whom still served in Congress in the early 1930s—would have been surprised by the organizational difficulties encountered within the reserve system in this period. The Fed's framers knew that New York would wield unparalleled power within the system as it did under Strong's leadership. In 1913, New York's concentration of national banking capital guaranteed the outsized influence of the Wall Street–based New York Fed. Democrats' insistence on locating several reserve banks in the underdeveloped, agrarian South also contributed to the uneven stature and power of the twelve reserve banks. Almost by design, New York could dominate most of the other, smaller reserve banks.

The broader problem lay in the diffusion of authority and power across the reserve system. The Board in Washington retained authority for crafting monetary policy, but lacked the power to implement it. The open market committee of reserve bank governors lacked the ability to coordinate the execution of monetary policy; reserve bank governors retained the power to block the open market operations they opposed. The lack of coordination in the reserve system and clipped authority of the Reserve Board in Washington left a power void that the New York Fed easily filled.

CONGRESS'S SLUGGISH RESPONSE

Despite the Fed's policy-making challenges, Congress was slow to act. We list changes to the law enacted by Congress and presidents between 1914 and 1935 in table 4.1.[6] Just as a Republican Congress in 1908 took only incremental steps in the wake of a devastating banking panic in 1907, a GOP Congress after the Great Depression's onset made only minor changes to the Federal Reserve Act. With the exception of two emergency lending bills that were enacted into law during winter and summer 1932, major reform of the Federal Reserve System was not on the agenda when the 1932 elections delivered unified Democratic control.

Why was Congress so timid responding to the deepening economic and financial crises? Republicans' ideological commitment to fiscal austerity and letting weak firms fail likely stymied efforts at broader reform of the Fed. Landmark legislation was finally motivated by the collapse of the banking system and Democrats' success in blaming Republicans for the economic debacle. Like the shift in politics that helped drive the adoption of the Federal Reserve Act in 1913, broad rewriting of the Federal Reserve Act was conditional on the major electoral realignments of 1928 and 1932. FDR's landslide electoral win in 1932 and arrival of supersized Democratic majorities no doubt made possible the radical legislative moment of the New Deal.[7] As FDR and his Democratic majorities created dozens of new national institutions and programs to establish a social safety

TABLE 4.1. Major Changes to the Federal Reserve Act, 1914–35

Year	Changes to Federal Reserve Act
1917	Amendments to the Federal Reserve Act • Allowed Federal Reserve banks to issue currency against gold • Allowed nonmember banks to use Federal Reserve services • Allowed states to join Federal Reserve System without losing their state charters or regulator
1918	Third Liberty Bond Act • Allowed Federal Reserve banks to discount obligations of member banks backed by war bonds • Allowed Federal Reserve banks to issue currency against bonds
1922	Amendments to the Federal Reserve Act • Expanded Federal Reserve Board to six president-appointed members • Added reference to fair representation of agricultural interests to selection criteria for Board members
1923	Agricultural Credits Act • Provided additional credit facilities for agricultural interests • Extended credit for agricultural purposes from nine months to three years • Expanded the types of commercial paper and bills eligible for discount for agricultural purposes
1927	McFadden Act • Prohibited state banks with branch banking from joining the Federal Reserve System, unless branch banking was permissible under state law
1932	Glass-Steagall Act • Government bonds purchased by Federal Reserve Banks on open market can be used to issue currency • Collateral requirements relaxed (on a vote of the Federal Reserve Board) to particular borrowers in unusual circumstances (section 10b).
1932	Emergency Relief and Construction Act • Opened discount window to nonbanks in "unusual and exigent circumstances" by vote of the Board (section 13); authorized for individuals, partnerships, and corporations unable to secure adequate credit on the basis of notes, bills of exchange, or other eligible paper for discount
1933	Emergency Banking Act • Extended authority of Federal Reserve Banks to create currency and lend on basis of government securities held • Section 10b (lending to member banks without sufficient collateral for exigent and exceptional circumstances) extended and liberalized • Section 13 amended to authorize Federal Reserve Banks to lend to any individual, partnership, or cooperation on promissory notes secured by direct obligations of the United States • Authorized Federal Reserve with vote of Federal Reserve Board and support of president to increase or decrease reserve balances held by member banks in times of emergency

(*continued*)

TABLE 4.1. (*Continued*)

Year	Changes to Federal Reserve Act
1933	Agricultural Adjustment Act (Thomas Amendment) • Permitted Federal Reserve to purchase up to $3 billion of securities directly from Treasury on authorization of president • Gave president authority to issue $3 billion in currency if Fed refused to make direct purchases of securities • Permitted the president to devalue the dollar against gold and silver up to 50 percent of its value
1933	Banking Act • Ended the 90 percent franchise tax on Federal Reserve Bank earnings • Required Federal Reserve Banks to provide $139 million to charter a temporary federal deposit insurance program • Formalized the Federal Open Market Committee (section 12A); all reserve banks given voting power • Permitted Federal Reserve Banks to abstain from open market purchases with thirty-days' notice • Created Federal Deposit Insurance Corporation and deposit insurance • Expanded section 13 lending for longer periods • Separated commercial and investment banking • Bank holding companies placed under Board's supervision • Increased length of Board members' terms to twelve years • Prohibited interest payments on demand deposits • Gave Board power to set ceiling rates on time deposits
1934	Gold Reserve Act • Prohibited private ownership of gold and bullion by individual or institutions • Authorized president to set gold prices • Created Exchange Stabilization Fund for monetary policy operations in Treasury
1935	Banking Act • Replaced Federal Reserve Board with Board of Governors and expanded to seven governors • Expanded length of governors' terms to fourteen years • Removed secretary of Treasury and comptroller of the currency from the Board • Board of Governors given seats and voting rights on FOMC • Five Federal Reserve bank presidents given voting rights on FOMC • Board given power to alter reserve requirements • Federal Deposit Insurance Corporation made permanent

Source: We use lists of legislative changes recorded in the annual reports of the Federal Reserve Board (1913–34) and Board of Governors (1935–2014); see FRASER 2015.

net and restore the economy, they also sought to fix the financial system. Congress imposed currency inflation in 1933, overhauled the organization of the banking system in 1933, and rewrote the Federal Reserve Act in 1935. In the rest of this chapter, we explore the politics of each of these pivotal legislative moments for the Federal Reserve System.

Forces Shaping Depression Era Reform

Dynamics shaping reform of the Fed in the wake of the Depression bear a strong resemblance to the forces that influenced the adoption of the Federal Reserve Act in 1913. In the wake of financial crisis, electing Democratic majorities to Congress and regaining control of the White House empowered reformers to advance their political and economic priorities in rewiring the Federal Reserve System. Legislators in the 1930s inherited the original 1913 design, or what Strong called a "multi-headed hydra" of a privately owned reserve system appended to a publicly controlled Washington board. Despite Democrats' historic electoral sweep, political support for the status quo—powerful regional reserve banks with control of credit beyond the reach of Wall Street—constrained reformers seeking to centralize monetary policy making and revive the economy. Competition within and across the parties—as well as between the executive and legislative branches—ultimately limited the power of reformers to concentrate monetary power in Washington.

IMPACT OF THE CRISIS

Lawmakers typically respond to crises by trying to prevent a reoccurrence. In the midst of the Depression, the failures of the Fed were well known. No less than Republican president Herbert Hoover decried the Fed's inability to stem the financial crisis that followed the stock market crash or restore the banking sector. The Federal Reserve, as Hoover (1952, 212) later observed in his memoirs, was "a weak reed for a nation to lean on in a time of trouble." Naturally, reformers looked to remedy those deficiencies that enfeebled the Fed during the Depression.

The Fed's perceived problems were twofold. First, as monetary policy was increasingly implemented through open market operations, the Fed's decentralized organization exposed the Board's inability to fully coordinate and compel the regional reserve banks to buy and sell securities. Thus, some reformers—particularly those outside Congress—advocated centralizing monetary policy decision making in the Washington-based board by reducing or eliminating the powers of the twelve regional reserve banks. Second, as banks failed and access to credit dried up, the Fed had few means beyond the regional discount windows to serve as a true lender of last resort. Redressing these and other institutional weaknesses formed the backbone of Depression era proposals to revamp the Federal Reserve Act.

PARTISAN CLEAVAGES

Electoral waves that brought Democrats to power in the 1928 and 1932 elections shaped how Congress and the president responded to the failings of the Federal Reserve. At the White House, electoral change produced a president eager to claim credit for rescuing and restoring the national economy. We know that prior to his departure in 1933, President Hoover implored President-elect Roosevelt to join forces with his outgoing administration to regulate bank closures. Roosevelt refused (Hoover 1952, 213–15). According to his aides, FDR calculated that he would benefit politically by blaming Hoover and Republicans for the economic wasteland he inherited, and taking credit for swift action on taking office (ibid., 215). Lending support to Hoover's final initiatives would saddle Roosevelt with part of the blame for the financial collapse. Congressional Democrats likely felt similar electoral incentives to act swiftly after years of GOP foot-dragging as well as a hamstrung and decentralized Fed. Indeed, such electoral incentives in 1933 were often sufficient to compel partisans to support the president's proposals, even in cases where they favored other policy solutions.

IDEOLOGY AND ECONOMIC INTERESTS

The severity of the Depression—coupled with divisions within both political parties—helped to dilute partisan fighting over Democrats' proposals. Some Republicans, particularly Progressives representing hard-hit midwestern farming communities, crossed party lines to support Democratic policy initiatives when they addressed the needs of their constituents. Constituency interests—including manufacturing, agriculture, and banking—shaped lawmakers' votes on both sides of the aisle. Critically, the onset of deflation generated bipartisan support for inflationary measures to restore prices.

Ideological divisions within the Democratic Party—captured by the unique policy and political views of southern Democrats—also shaped the contours of reform. Given the size of southern congressional delegations, their support in the House and Senate was pivotal to the passage of each of the landmark measures enacted during FDR's first term. "Each of the era's milestone laws required their [southerners'] support," Ira Katznelson (2013, 252) observes, adding that "each would have been blocked without it." Indeed, two Fed-familiar southerners led the rescue of the banking system: conservative senator Glass, and loyal New Dealer representative Henry Steagall (D-Alabama) (ibid., 255).

Southern lawmakers brought regional priorities to the table in writing and supporting New Deal legislation (see ibid.). Southerners' overriding concern was typically to protect their region's racialized economy and southern culture from federal intervention. On issues such as reconstructing the banking system—where race did not play a central role in shaping southern lawmakers' views—southerners were willing to support strong federal regulatory solutions, so long as southern state banks and depositors were protected. Southerners' efforts to safeguard regional interests during the Great Depression should sound familiar. As we saw at the formation of the Fed two decades earlier, southerners had distinctive needs in constructing the original reserve system: they sought to make farmers less dependent on Wall Street bankers for access to credit and bring new economic institutions to their depressed region of the country.

In analyzing lawmakers' decisions regarding the Fed in the wake of the Depression, we keep a close eye on the regional interests of the South that might have helped to shape congressional votes and reform of the Fed.

Explaining Depression Era Reform

The economic-political framework outlined in chapter 1 helps to explain the dynamic changes to the Federal Reserve Act in the 1930s, including some existential sections of US banking law. We focus on four key laws enacted after FDR took office: the inflationary Thomas Amendment to the 1933 Agricultural Adjustment Act, 1933 Emergency Banking Act (passed within hours of FDR proposing the bill his first week in office), Gold Reserve Act of 1934 that handed new monetary policy powers to the Treasury, and 1935 Banking Act that markedly revamped the powers and governance of the Fed. For each episode of reform, we explore how economic and political forces shaped compromise over reform, even with FDR and newly empowered Democratic majorities at the helm.

Importantly, lawmakers neither delegated reform to the administration or Federal Reserve technocrats, nor washed their hands of responsibility for restructuring a failed institution. They instead pushed the Fed and president to pursue an inflationary course in 1933, and then resisted Eccles's plan to fully centralize Fed power in Washington in 1935. Notably, the philosophy of central bank independence played no role in these efforts. At each legislative juncture, Congress brought the Fed and its power to set monetary policy under greater public control. And yet on the eve of World War II, with more congressionally granted power than ever, the Fed still remained subordinate to the Treasury and White House.

THOMAS AMENDMENT OF 1933

The Thomas Amendment represents the most direct congressional intervention into reflationary monetary policy over the course of the Fed's first century. Sponsored by Senator Elmer Thomas

(D-Oklahoma), Congress added the Thomas Amendment to an agricultural bill that sought to raise prices for farm commodities. The amendment was inflationary and prescriptive: it authorized the president to request the Federal Reserve's open market committee to purchase up to $3 billion of federal securities from the Treasury. If such operations were insufficient to generate inflation, and thus produce higher commodity prices for farmers and lower real interest rates, the president was authorized to direct the Treasury to issue up to $3 billion dollars in currency, reduce the gold content of the dollar by as much as half, or accept silver at a reduced price from European nations paying off their World War I debts (thereby devaluing the dollar). If successful, the inflationary Thomas Amendment would reduce the size of the outstanding debt, devalue the dollar, and boost consumer demand.[8]

The adoption of the Thomas Amendment suggests lawmakers initially had little interest in fixing the institutional deficiencies of the Federal Reserve System. Instead, legislators took monetary policy into their own hands. If Fed actions proved insufficient, Congress directed the president to devalue the dollar to create inflation. In light of the Fed's aforementioned failures and a deep deflation gripping the country, particularly in the South and West, dictating policy was arguably the right course for Congress to take. Reversing deflation was essential to fix the economy. Taking the nation temporarily off the gold standard was fast and effective: it helped drive up inflation and industrial production (recall figure 4.1). But delegating power over monetary policy to the president did little to optimize the Fed's capacity to make monetary policy.

Thomas's proposal was hardly novel; various lawmakers had pushed for inflationary steps a year earlier during consideration of the first Glass-Steagall bill. That previous effort failed because hard-money Republicans, who favored maintaining the gold standard, controlled both branches of government in 1932 and opposed stoking inflation. Even after inflation-friendly Democrats took control of Congress in March 1933, their varied proposals (including gold, silver, and greenbacks) took time to coordinate. As the new chair of the Senate Finance Committee, Duncan Fletcher (D-Florida) noted that month, "Their views are so contradictory that he did not see at present how they could reach any agreement." The *New York Times* concluded, prematurely it turns out, "in this very diversity of opinion lies the great 'safeguard' against tampering with the currency."[9]

The severity of the Depression and arrival of new Democratic majorities ultimately generated political incentives in factions of both political parties to support the amendment. To be sure, Roosevelt surprised many of his economic advisers (let alone his Treasury secretary) when he revealed that he was likely to support congressional Democrats' move to devalue the currency. Indeed, FDR's support appears to have flowed almost entirely from political calculation. Once he judged a congressional majority would succeed, he not only jumped on the bandwagon but also led the way.

A member of FDR's brain trust, Raymond Moley (1939, 156), later provided an eyewitness account of those days in the White House:

> This certainly isn't to imply that Roosevelt himself was "sold" on the idea of inflation before or immediately after his inauguration. I can testify that he wasn't. But he was very consciously waiting to see whether the effort to preserve the monetary standard after March 13th wouldn't entail greater sacrifices in terms of sinking money incomes than the American people would bear, or should be expected to bear, and wouldn't be overwhelmed by the political forces demanding what would amount to uncontrolled inflation.

As Moley's recollection of the fight in the Senate over the Thomas Amendment reveals, once Roosevelt read the tea leaves in support of inflation, he pushed for changes to Thomas's amendment to make it more palatable. Specifically, he pushed Thomas to soften the amendment to empower rather than require him to inflate the currency in the face of Fed inaction (Wicker 1971, 876). "I doubt," Moley (1939, 157) observed years later, "that more than a handful of economists in the United States ever realized just how compelling the force of political circumstance was. . . . The cold fact is that the inflationary movement attained such formidable strength by April 18th that Roosevelt realized that he could not block it, that he could, at most, try to direct it."

TABLE 4.2. House Vote on the Agricultural Adjustment Act, March 1933

Variable	Coefficient (robust s. e.)
South	−0.108 (0.860)
State manufacturing value per capita	−0.014 (0.005)**
State's percent of US farmland in 1930	−0.166 (0.059)**
Party	−0.028 (0.005)***
Constant	7.464 (1.345)***
N	412
Prob > chi2	0.0000
Log pseudolikelihood	−148.74109

Notes: The dependent variable is House vote on the Agricultural Adjustment Act. Vote is House roll call vote no. 7, Seventy-Third Congress, March 22, 1933. Estimates calculated in Stata 14.2 *logit* command. Robust standard errors clustered by state in parentheses. One-tailed tests. ** p < 0.01; *** p < 0.001.

What made the passage of Thomas's amendment seem so inevitable to Roosevelt and his closest aides? The original version of the Agricultural Adjustment Act passed by the House on March 22, 1933, did not include the Thomas Amendment. Party lines were clear—though not lockstep—on the bill, which aimed to improve farmers' economic situation by taxing food processors to pay farmers to take certain croplands out of production. As one of the first bills of FDR's first hundred days' agenda, Democrats largely voted in support of the bill (275–25) while Republicans lined up against it (39–73). Still, legislators (regardless of party) from more agriculturally oriented states disproportionately favored the bill while those from stronger manufacturing states opposed it (see table 4.2).[10] Conservatives from both parties were also more likely to oppose the measure.[11]

Once the bill was received in the Senate, Thomas and his inflation coalition went to work. When reporters covered House passage of the farm bill, the *New York Times* noted that senators favoring stronger inflationary measures (termed "an expanded but controlled currency") intended to use the farm bill as a vehicle for their inflation proposals.[12] Thomas's original proposal authorized the Treasury to issue new currency, which Thomas called "Prosperity Notes," until commodity prices rose to levels experienced in the 1920s. With prices stabilized, the Treasury would stop issuing the greenbacks. Opponents—including those Democrats who favored

strict adherence to the gold standard—feared uncontrolled inflation. Yet opponents still believed that disorganization and diversity
of views among the inflationists would stall, if not derail, Thomas's
efforts. They also believed—erroneously, as Moley suggested in
his memoirs—that Roosevelt and his advisers would oppose any
schemes to devalue the currency.

The skeptics were wrong. Democrats such as Senator Glass opposed granting monetary policy power to the president, but party
lines soon coalesced behind Thomas's amendment. The *New York
Times* called the emerging opposition a "party attack on the Roosevelt Administration," showing a "natural emergence, a little sooner
than was expected, of a fundamental difference between Republican
conservatives and the administration."[13] That partisan movement—
tempered by Progressive Republicans willing to cast their lot with
the Democrats—appears to have rallied the Democrats. Democrats
were divided on whether it was a wise move to devalue the dollar's
gold content. But according to the *New York Times*, most of the
Democrats who were on the fence would "fall into the administration's camp." The *New York Times* concluded that the vote would
break along ideological lines, providing support for "people who
are fond of prophesying the day when a new alignment will put all
conservatives in one party and all non-conservatives in another."[14]

All but three Democrats in the Senate supported Thomas's
amendment, drawing the support of 40 percent of the thirty-one
Republicans who voted. In table 4.3, results from a model of the Senate vote on the Thomas Amendment point to the impact of partisan,
constituency, and institutional forces in shaping lawmakers' views
about empowering the president to set monetary policy. To ease
interpretation of the results, figure 4.2 shows the marginal impact
of each independent variable on the likelihood that a senator voted
for the Thomas Amendment.[15]

As expected, partisanship mattered. Holding other factors constant, a Democrat had a 95 percent likelihood of voting in favor
of the Thomas Amendment; a Republican, only 35 percent. To be
sure, some prominent Republican progressives crossed party lines,
including Wisconsin's Robert M. LaFollette Jr., Nebraska's George
Norris, and North Dakota's Gerald Nye. But on the Democratic side,

TABLE 4.3. Senate Vote on the Thomas Amendment, April 1933

Variable	Coefficient (robust s.e.)
South	−3.148 (1.658)*
State manufacturing value per capita	−0.010 (0.008)
State's percent of US farmland in 1930	1.079 (0.500)*
Party	−0.057 (0.017)**
Federal Reserve district bank in state	−2.401 (1.063)*
Constant	10.818 (2.973)***
N	85
Prob > chi2	0
Log pseudolikelihood	−19.980

Notes: The dependent variable is Senate vote on the Thomas Amendment. Vote is Senate roll call vote no. 26, Seventy-Third Congress, April 28, 1933. Estimates calculated in Stata 14.2 *logit* command. Robust standard errors clustered by state in parentheses. One-tailed tests. * p < 0.05; ** p < 0.01; *** p < 0.001.

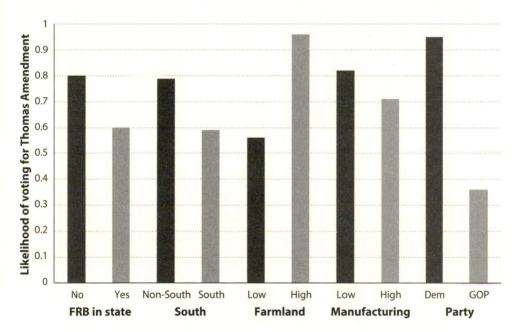

FIGURE 4.2. Likelihood of supporting the Thomas Amendment in the Senate. See notes for table 4.3.

partisans largely fell in line. Even after controlling for partisans' opposing views about the amendment, we still see a divide along agrarian lines: senators representing states more dependent on a farm economy disproportionately voted for the Thomas Amendment. Indeed, looking separately at the votes of Republican lawmakers, senators from more agricultural states were more likely to cross the aisle to side with the Democrats. Responsiveness to their constituents' economic needs—they sought higher prices for their goods and more inflation to reduce the value of their debts—shaped senators' votes about appropriate monetary policy.

The most prominent Democratic opponent of the amendment was none other than Senator Glass, who viewed the amendment as "immoral"—a direct affront to the integrity of the Federal Reserve System. Glass argued that debasing the currency "spelled the ruin for the country's credit and impotence of the Federal Reserve System."[16] Glass's opposition rallied a select group of his colleagues: senators who hailed from one of the eleven states that housed a Federal Reserve district bank disproportionately voted against the Thomas Amendment. Granted, those states in 1933 were disproportionately represented by Democratic senators, holding nearly three-quarters of the Senate seats in those eleven states. And most Democrats supported the amendment. But even after controlling for party and the state's agrarian or manufacturing bent, Republican senators from Federal Reserve System states disproportionately supported the Fed. Twenty years after the organization of the system, support for the Fed was hardwired into the states that secured regional reserve banks in 1914.

House members did not vote directly on the adoption of the Thomas Amendment. Rather, after the Senate passed its farm relief bill in April, House leaders devised a procedural vote to determine whether the House would call up the Senate-passed bill, with the Thomas Amendment now appended. Reports at the time considered the procedural vote paramount to a vote on the Thomas Amendment: House leaders "took advantage of every parliamentary rule to bring about prompt concurrence in the Senate's inflation amendment to the farm relief bill."[17] The procedural move worked, with the House favoring inclusion of the amendment by a vote of 307–86.

The proxy vote for the Thomas Amendment shows similar patterns to the Senate vote. As depicted in figure 4.3, state economies and legislators' partisanship again structured the vote. The more important farming was to a member's state, the more likely that

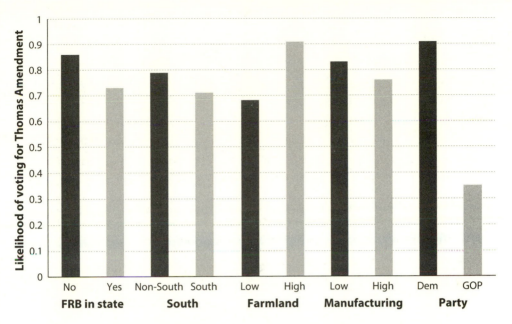

FIGURE 4.3. Likelihood of supporting the Thomas Amendment in the House. House roll call vote no. 26, Seventy-Third Congress, May 3, 1933.

member supported the Thomas Amendment; conversely, legislators from manufacturing-heavy states were less inclined to support the amendment. Lawmakers representing reserve bank states were again disposed against granting the president special monetary powers. Roughly 70 percent of Republicans opposed the Thomas Amendment, but more than 80 percent of Republicans from reserve bank states voted to kill the amendment. Because the amendment directed the Fed to issue greenbacks—and authorized the president to do so if the Fed declined—defenders of the Fed likely perceived the Thomas Amendment as a frontal attack on the powers of the Fed.

Congressional votes on the Thomas Amendment give us our first Depression era test of alternative ways to think about the legislative construction of monetary policy institutions. Most important, party positions mattered. Even in light of views within each party that the Thomas Amendment was more reckless than wise, party lines were drawn quickly. Still, parochial interests also mattered in shaping lawmakers' response to Thomas's proposal. Representatives from agrarian states coalesced around the proposal to raise farm incomes; those from manufacturing-heavy states tended to reject the inflationists' proposal. Remarkably, not even Roosevelt's brain trust of economists was able to convince FDR to oppose the Thomas Amendment; monetary politics—not theory—proved more persuasive. After Roosevelt sensed the emergence of a strong Democratic majority in favor of devaluing the currency, he jumped ahead to lead the way. As he said to reporters in a confidential press conference on April 17, "The whole problem before us is to raise commodity prices."[18] The Thomas Amendment—coupled with FDR's first steps that month to take the country off the gold standard—provided economically effective and politically safe monetary policy. It did little, however, to fix the Fed's institutional capacity to devise and execute monetary policy, or prevent future crises (Wicker 1971).

BANKING ACT OF 1933

One month later, Congress completed action on what would come to be known as the Glass-Steagall Act. (Technically, it was the second Glass-Steagall Act to be enacted during the Depression.) The new law aimed to improve the banking system in light of the Fed's failures as the lender of last resort. Most famously, the new law separated commercial and investment banking while creating the precursor to the Federal Deposit Insurance Corporation—a government institution that insured bank depositors. In 1913, lawmakers had rejected Senator Owen's proposal for deposit insurance in writing the Federal Reserve Act; those lawmakers representing states with healthier banking systems outnumbered supporters of deposit insurance who largely represented small, rural states. The dire state of the banking industry during the Depression weakened opposition to deposit insurance—an innovation intended to serve as a first line of defense against future bank panics.

Congress also addressed features of the Fed's organization that lawmakers believed contributed to the Depression. Some elements of the law were designed to preserve the Fed's decentralized structure. The new law formalized the Fed's open market committee, inaugurating the FOMC that remains in place today. In crafting the new FOMC, Congress only gave seats at the table to the twelve reserve bank heads; members of the Washington-appointed Federal Reserve Board were barred from voting on open market operations. Moreover, the act authorized reserve banks to break with open market operations decided on by the FOMC—a move intended to reduce the influence of the New York Fed over the other regional reserve banks. To some degree, Glass-Steagall simply ratified the status quo. Yet by formalizing these arrangements in statute, the Banking Act bolstered the authority of the reserve banks vis-à-vis the powers of the Board, thereby protecting Fed decentralization.

Other changes concentrated greater powers within the Fed's Washington board. Congress expanded the Fed's emergency lending authority (section 13), granting those powers explicitly to the Board. Congress also extended the terms of Board members to twelve years—slightly enhancing the Fed's autonomy from both Congress and the president. Some senators would have gone a step further to insulate the Board from political control: Senator Glass sought, but failed, to remove the secretary of the Treasury from the Board. As Glass argued on the floor early in 1933, the Treasury secretary had an "undue influence on the board" and the Treasury had made the Fed "a doormat of the United States Treasury." Glass, the dominant author of the original Federal Reserve Act, never designed a Treasury-controlled monetary authority.[19] Ultimately, the bill approved by the Senate Banking Committee removed the Treasury secretary from his ex officio Board position. But Glass agreed to reinstate the secretary as the price for securing the Democratic administration's support for the broader bill.[20] Glass would revisit the secretary's Board position in 1935 and prevail. Ironically, in the early 1940s, the Treasury would exert even more influence over monetary policy in the run-up to war.

Reform of the Federal Reserve in 1933 attracted relatively little attention at the time. Almost all of the reporting on the measure focused on conflict over deposit insurance. And neither the House nor Senate recorded votes on their own versions of the bill or the final conference report.[21] Lack of footprints makes it difficult to fully nail down the forces that drove the adoption of the changes. Instead, we interpret congressional motives by records left in floor debates and news coverage.

This approach yields several observations. First, lawmakers again avoided strong efforts to fix the deficiencies of the reserve system. Despite the governance and coordination issues that hampered open market operations during the Hoover administration, Democrats in 1933 failed to meaningfully endow the Board with more authority over bond market operations. Granted, Senator Glass headed the monetary policy subcommittee and was unlikely to fully centralize authority in Washington, at the expense of the power of the regional reserve banks. But even Glass had expressed interest during Senate Banking Committee hearings in 1931 for giving the Board greater supervision of open market operations (Meltzer 2003, 430). Glass's bill, however, made only incremental steps in that direction: reserve banks could conduct open market operations only with Board approval, but with thirty days' notice to the Board, they were also empowered to refuse to participate (ibid.). At the same time, the bill wrote the FOMC into law, granting all twelve reserve bank governors voting rights on FOMC decisions.

Second, competing objectives within the Democratic Party drove lawmakers' choices in writing the Banking Act. In giving up his quest to remove the Treasury secretary from the Federal Reserve Board, Glass noted that his subcommittee had unanimously endorsed the proposal. Moreover, the version of Glass-Steagall passed by the Senate in the previous Congress—but blocked by the House before enactment—had eliminated the Treasury's seat on the Board and been passed by the Senate, fifty-four to nine. As Glass explained on the Senate floor in calling up the banking bill on May 19, "That provision of the previous bill is not included in this bill only by reason of the fact that the Secretary of the Treasury seemed to regard it as a personal affront to him and as a curtailment of his power which ought not to be made at this particular time."[22] In avoiding a confrontation, Glass targeted the Treasury's influence over the decisions of the reserve system. Bemoaning that the reserve banks were perennially compelled to buy up the Treasury's bond issues, Glass contended that only in times of war should the Fed and Treasury coordinate their activities: "It was never intended that the Federal Reserve Banking System should be used as an adjunct of the Treasury Department."[23]

Why would Glass defer to Secretary William Woodin, when he had previously secured the Senate's consent to drop the Treasury secretary from the Board? Glass's decision was entirely strategic. The senator's top priority was securing separation of commercial and investment banking, as reflected in the *New York Times'* observation that spring that the bill was "designed chiefly to curb the use of Federal Reserve credit for speculation."[24] Glass no doubt judged that removing the Treasury secretary from the Board—particularly when the bill kept a seat for the comptroller of the currency (Clifford 1965, 126)—would put his primary goal in jeopardy. Indeed, we know that Glass also acquiesced to federal deposit insurance, even after he had led the opposition to it in writing the Federal Reserve Act some twenty years before. When the conference committee on the banking bill stymied over differences in the details of deposit insurance, Glass again prioritized separation of commercial and investment banks. Even given broad public support for insurance, Glass reportedly joined a majority of the Senate conferees voting to drop insurance lest the banking bill be lost.[25] That was a remarkable show of dedication to the securities provisions given reporting at the time that "Washington does not remember any issue on which the sentiment of the country has been so undivided or so emphatically expressed as upon this."[26]

Ultimately, the light touch Congress applied to the Fed in the banking law reflected both the lesser priority key lawmakers placed on redressing the institution's past failures and myriad prescriptions for how to fix the Fed. Representative Steagall cared primarily about creating deposit insurance; Senator Glass, segmenting the banking industry. Differing bicameral priorities led both lawmakers to use the banking bill as a common vehicle for securing their most important legislative goals. Centralizing monetary power in Washington and addressing the organizational dysfunction of the reserve system fell low on lawmakers' priorities. All that said, Congress the

month before had just empowered the president to take control of
monetary policy should the Fed fail to start buying sufficient sums
of government securities. In summer 1933, organizational reform of
the Fed was a pale substitute for handing the president the reins of
monetary policy.

GOLD RESERVE ACT OF 1934

The Gold Reserve Act of 1934 formalized the United States' departure from the gold standard. Following on the heels of FDR's 1933
executive order, the new law banned private ownership of gold
and transferred all monetary gold (including that owned by the
Federal Reserve) to the Treasury. The law also authorized the president to alter the price of gold by proclamation. FDR immediately
devalued the dollar by 40 percent.[27] The economic impact of the
Gold Act was substantial, especially in conjunction with the previous year's efforts to restore the banking system. As Ahamed (2009,
463) summed up, FDR's move in 1934 "broke the psychology of
deflation"—driving wholesale prices up 45 percent and doubling
stock prices. Most important, the real (inflation-adjusted) cost of
borrowing plummeted.

The Gold Reserve Act also created the Exchange Stabilization
Fund (ESF), which was stocked with the proceeds the government
accrued when it raised the price of gold. The Treasury was authorized to use the fund to buy or sell gold, securities, or other instruments, and conduct open market operations independent of the
Fed (Richardson, Komai, and Gou 2013). As FDR framed the ESF
to Congress in sending the bill to Capitol Hill in January 1934, the
provisions created a "permanent monetary policy," allowing the administration to usurp the Fed's power over currency.[28] What was to
become of the Fed once the Treasury secured the ESF? Secretary
Henry Morgenthau Jr. promised that the Fed would remain the "financial agent" for the Treasury. As we explore in the next chapter,
that promise came to fruition in 1942 when the Fed agreed to peg
interest rates to reduce the Treasury's borrowing costs in managing
the nation's war-driven debt.[29]

The initiative for the Gold Reserve Act appears to have come entirely from the administration. Early in January 1934, the *New York Times* reported a meeting of FDR and his advisers to discuss the contours of the administration's next move on monetary policy.[30] A consensus emerged to ask Congress for authorization to devalue the dollar and recoup the nation's gold reserves. Some wanted to go a step further to create a "central bank institution" within the administration, taking direct aim at the Federal Reserve. From Morgenthau's perspective, legislative action was needed to stabilize the price of gold—to relieve Roosevelt of setting the price of gold each day. Morgenthau also notes in his diaries that he was eager to create an exchange stabilization fund to counter a similar one available to the British government (Blum 1959, 120–25). Within days, Roosevelt sent a monetary message to Congress that proposed a "permanent monetary policy."[31]

Roosevelt encountered little opposition in the House. The bill was on the House floor within a week. House Democratic leaders appealed to their rank and file to stick together to back the president so as to "repair the wreckage of former Republican rule and restore to 'all the people' through their government, control over their own money."[32] If there were any lingering doubts among Democrats about the bill, the appeal sealed the deal. Just three Democrats voted against the bill, all from the South, and two from states that were home to a regional reserve bank. Republicans broke against passage: sixty-nine GOP opposed the bill, and thirty-seven defected to vote with the Democrats. Looking only at Republican votes, we detect a slight tendency for lawmakers from reserve bank states to oppose the bill.[33] As Representative John Hollister (R-Ohio) argued on the House floor, the bill would "emasculate" the Federal Reserve System by creating the ESF within the Treasury.[34] Until adoption of the Treasury-Fed Accord in 1951, Hollister's prediction turned out to be well founded.

The administration's bill faced tougher sledding in the Senate, but most observers seemed assured that the bill would pass intact. Not surprisingly, the bill's strongest Senate opponent was Glass, joined by former Treasury secretary McAdoo. Senate Banking Committee hearings on the bill provided a forum for Glass, McAdoo, and Fed officials to weigh in against the bill. Both the Boston and Philadelphia Federal Reserve bank heads strongly opposed the ESF's creation, asserting that the ESF would be the "beginning of the end" of the Fed.[35] The Fed's deputy chair, Young, took a middle course: he supported new authority for the president to stabilize the price of gold, but then condemned the transfer of the Fed's gold to the Treasury and the lack of limits on the new ESF. As Young argued before the committee, "When the influence of the credit volume of the country passes from the Federal Reserve System to the Treasury, then the Federal Reserve System is practically abolished. The result is that you have two great forces functioning in the credit market.... One may go in one direction and the other in another direction."[36]

Despite vociferous objections from Glass and several central bankers, the only amendment accepted by the administration was to sunset the ESF after three years (although it was subsequently extended and made permanent in 1945 in the Bretton Woods Agreement).[37] No lawmaker publicly opposed the bill's grant of authority to the president to devalue the dollar. Inflationary manipulation of the currency—beyond control of the Fed—attracted little, if any, dissent.

On the Senate floor, the bill's defenders faced two challenges. One, led by Senator Glass, would create a board of directors to run the ESF rather than entrusting it to the Treasury secretary. The other would authorize government purchases of silver, until the country secured a bimetallic standard. Glass's effort to alter the leadership of the ESF encountered a partisan wall: just six Democrats sided with him to dilute the leadership of the new exchange fund, and Republicans split twenty-nine to three. The silver amendment offered by Burton Wheeler (R-Montana) gave the administration a tougher scare, losing by just two votes. This time, party lines were not tightly drawn. Democrats split twenty-nine to twenty-eight in favor of Wheeler's amendment while Republicans split fourteen to seventeen.

As shown in figure 4.4, accounting for partisanship tells us little about senators' votes on Wheeler's inflationary amendment. But we see strong differences in the voting behavior of senators depending on their connection to the regional reserve system. Both Democratic and Republican defenders of the Fed were roughly twenty points less

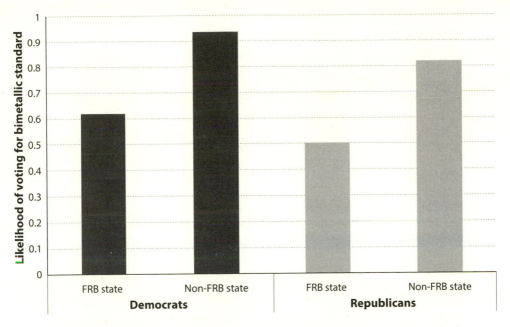

FIGURE 4.4. Likelihood of supporting Senate "prosilver" vote to establish a bimetallic standard, 1934. Senate roll call vote no. 106, Seventy-Third Congress, January 27, 1934.

likely to vote with the Silverites than their party colleagues without local connections to the Fed. Senators from strong manufacturing states were also far less likely to support inflationary silver policy, as were southern Democrats. After the silver coalition's narrow loss, the Senate moved to final passage. Party lines were tightly drawn on the Democratic side: only Glass opposed the president and defended the Fed. Republicans split ten to twenty-two, with farm state Republicans more likely than other Republicans to support FDR's inflationary bill. Partisan ties and home state interests shaped lawmakers' views about how to reform monetary policy, and who should hold the authority to make it.

BANKING ACT OF 1935

When Utah banker turned Treasury bureaucrat Eccles learned in 1934 that FDR would nominate him as the next Fed chair, he conditioned his acceptance on Roosevelt's support to overhaul the Federal

Reserve Act. As Eccles (1951, 166) noted in his memoirs, the public-private balance of the original act had become "unbalanced": private interests dominated decision making by the Fed and its reserve banks. Thus the impetus for even more Fed reform just two years after the 1933 changes stemmed from Eccles's conditional acceptance. Eccles met deep Senate resistance when he proposed in 1935 to fully centralize control of open market operations in the hands of the Federal Reserve Board. But he ultimately achieved much of what he sought: the 1935 Banking Act significantly increased the power of the Board over the reserve banks, more fully centralizing power within the Fed's federal system. Although the reserve banks retained some seats on the FOMC, the 1935 reforms brought forth a much more powerful Federal Reserve Board in the decades that followed.

A new Board of Governors in Washington was organized with seven governors, each of whom received a vote on a restructured FOMC. The heads of the twelve reserve banks, now called presidents, would rotate through the monetary policy committee; the Banking Act reserved just five seats for the district bank presidents (one of which in 1942 was permanently filled by the head of the New York Fed). For the first time, presidential appointees to the Board were empowered with real decision making and power to enforce open market operations, contingent on securing the support of a FOMC majority. Fed authority was further centralized by empowering the Board to set reserve requirements for member banks and strengthening its authority over the setting of the district banks' discount rates.

Centralization was accompanied at least on paper with greater independence from political overseers: Board governors were given fourteen-year terms, and the secretary of the Treasury and comptroller of the currency both were finally removed from the Board. Moreover, Congress authorized the Fed to move out of the Treasury building and construct its own office across town. As we examine in the next chapter, although Congress could grant the Fed physical autonomy from Treasury, it was much harder for the Fed to secure its operational autonomy—particularly once the onset of war increased the Treasury's leverage to demand that the Fed subordinate monetary policy to government's financing needs. The Fed remained tethered to the Treasury's policy dictates until pivotal lawmakers in 1951 lent their weight to freeing the Fed from Treasury's dominance.

The original bill Eccles sent to Congress proposed to revamp the Board of Governors in Washington as well as centralize power over open market operations, discount rates, and member bank reserve requirements with the Board. The bill kept the Board's eight members, including the Treasury secretary and comptroller of the currency. Seven Federal Reserve Board members would sit on the FOMC, but no reserve bank heads would have voting rights on it. Instead, a newly constituted advisory group of five district reserve banks could weigh in on open market operations and other matters, but decisions of the newly renamed Board of Governors would be binding on all twelve reserve banks.[38] Eccles also proposed improving public control of the Board by imposing a mandatory retirement age (thereby removing Board members out of sync with the New Deal).[39] Eccles (1951, 176) later wrote in his memoirs that he believed at the time that his legislative program "would stand or fall on the merits of the ideas it advanced," but as he soon discovered, "Senator Carter Glass of Virginia was to teach me that the contrary was the case."

Of the three titles of the bill, only Title 2 that revamped the organization and powers of the Federal Reserve Board proved controversial. The House and Senate considered the bill on parallel tracks in spring and summer 1935, with Eccles receiving a friendlier reception from Representative Steagall's House Banking Committee than from Senator Glass and his monetary subcommittee. Eccles was convinced that Glass opposed his proposals out of spite that FDR had not consulted with Glass over Eccles's (ibid., 178) appointment to chair the Federal Reserve Board. Although we cannot rule out Eccles's suspicions, more than political pique motivated Glass's opposition. To identify the forces that shaped the contending Eccles and Glass coalitions that spring, we analyze the handful of recorded votes that took place in the House and Senate on the competing proposals.

The bill brought to the House floor largely resembled Eccles's original proposal. It came under attack from House Republicans,

TABLE 4.4. House Vote to Strip Eccles's Proposals, May 1935

Variable	Coefficient (robust s.e.)
South	1.742 (0.818)*
State manufacturing value per capita	0.005 (0.004)
State's percent of US farmland in 1930	−0.156 (0.077)*
Party	0.051 (0.007)***
Federal Reserve district bank in state	1.128 (0.698)*
Constant	-9.202 (1.506)***
N	377
Prob > chi2	0.000
Log pseudolikelihood	−109.582

Notes: The dependent variable is vote is to recommit the House banking bill with instructions to strike Title 2 (the Eccles reforms). House roll call vote no. 46, Seventy-Fourth Congress, May 9, 1935.
Estimates calculated in Stata 14.2 *logit* command. Robust standard errors clustered by state in parentheses.
One-tailed tests. * p < 0.05; ** p < 0.01; *** p < 0.001.

who continued to represent the views of bankers who opposed centralizing control of monetary policy.[40] Republicans offered amendments to strip out the key elements of Title 2 that increased the power of the Board over the reserve banks, enhanced the power of the president over the Board, and augmented the power of both the Board and reserve banks to adjust member bank reserve requirements. Only one GOP amendment came to a recorded vote—a move to strip all of Title 2 from the bill. Democrats opposed the amendment, 248–24; Republicans supported it, 93–12. Of the 12 GOP opposing the bill, 6 were technically elected as Progressives from Wisconsin.

Voting alignments to protect Eccles's banking bill strongly resemble those seen two years earlier on the vote to adopt the Thomas Amendment (table 4.4). Partisanship and state interests shaped lawmakers' responses to a Republican proposal to reject Eccles's reforms. The clearest divide fell along party lines, with an 85 percent difference in the chance that a Democrat and Republican would vote in favor of the bill (figure 4.5). Lawmakers from agrarian states were also slightly more likely to support Eccles's changes. We suspect that lawmakers from rural areas might have been swayed by Representative Steagall's argument on the floor that the Eccles bill would

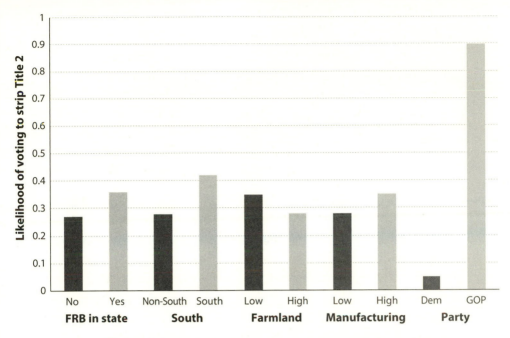

FIGURE 4.5. Likelihood of voting for the Eccles version of the House Banking Act of 1935. See table 4.4.

reduce the influence of the Federal Reserve Bank of New York on the making of monetary policy.[41] We also detect a regional effect, with southerners preferring to jettison Title 2. Nevertheless, that finding probably reflects the votes of a small handful of border-state Republican southerners, all of whom voted to strip Title 2. Democratic southerners generally voted with their northern colleagues against the amendment. Still, several defected—no doubt partially influenced by the objections of their southern colleague, Senator Glass.

Finally, lawmakers with a reserve bank (or two) in their states were slightly more likely to vote to protect the status quo from change. Locating the reserve banks in communities across the country again appears to have reaped benefits for the broader reserve system by hardwiring support for the district banks' monetary policy powers. Unfortunately for the reserve system, there were three times as many Democrats from reserve bank states than Republicans, and Democrats largely favored Eccles's reforms. Even so, a Democrat without a reserve bank in their state had a 6 percent chance of voting to strip Title 2 from the bill. That likelihood doubles to 12 percent for a Democrat representing a reserve bank state—even after controlling for the agrarian nature of his district. Small effects for sure, but the results suggest that local ties to the reserve banks continued to shape lawmakers' views about reforming the Fed.

The final House vote largely shows the same political dynamics. Just 21 House members—all but one a Democrat—voted to strip Title 2, but then switched positions to support the Eccles bill on final passage. Overall, Democrats were more likely to support the bill than were Republicans, and lawmakers from states with regional reserve banks again showed their loyalty to the reserve system by disproportionately opposing the bill. Ultimately, the bill secured votes from 113 southern Democrats, with just two southern Democrats defecting to join the Republicans. A majority of the House Democrats hailed from outside the South. But without the support of their southern brethren, Democrats from outside the South could not deliver reform since Republicans voted nearly lockstep against the bill. Despite comprising a minority of their party's congressional delegation, southerners were pivotal to securing enactment of Roosevelt's New Deal agenda.

In the Senate, Glass's subcommittee eliminated most of the new powers granted to the Federal Reserve Board that Eccles had persuaded the House to adopt. Most important, the Board in Glass's bill would be reduced from eight to seven members (and given longer, fourteen-year terms), the Treasury secretary and comptroller would be removed, and the FOMC would be comprised of seven members of the newly renamed Board of Governors and five of the twelve reserve bank heads (to be renamed reserve bank presidents). The Glass bill also mandated that two Board seats be reserved for bankers, and the whole Board be balanced along party lines, with four seats reserved for members of the president's party and three for the opposition.[42] Although Glass aimed his fire at Eccles's centralizing reforms, the new Board of Governors in Glass's bill would still get more authority to set credit and monetary authority. Glass, however, asked Eccles to pay a price: remove administration appointees from the Board and save a formal role for the reserve bank presidents in setting national monetary policy.

As Glass's version of the bill gained steam at the committee level, Eccles in a private memo to Roosevelt said that he was rethinking his intention of compromising with Glass (FRASER, n.d.). Eccles had suggested that spring that if the American Bankers Association would commit to supporting the bill, he would support giving back to the reserve banks their seats and votes on the FOMC. But even after Eccles signaled that he could support such a compromise, the association refused to accept the terms of the informal deal. Thus, Eccles upped the ante in July 1935, suggesting to FDR that the administration propose a five-member Federal Reserve Board and seven-member FOMC, with two reserve bank governors cycling on and off the monetary committee. Eccles's idea made little headway in the Senate, and the Glass bill was brought to the floor largely unchanged by the full committee.

Unfortunately, senators did not record their votes on the final passage of the Glass bill or any of the contested Title 2 provisions. Progressive senator LaFollette had planned to offer an amendment to restore Eccles's version of Title 2, but the *Wall Street Journal* reported that there was "a gentlemen's agreement to choke all efforts to amend the Banking Bill" (Huff 1935). As LaFollette lamented on the Senate floor, he was convinced that

> I would not get a real test of strength there in this body for this proposition. Therefore, in light of the fact that it has to go to conference, and that inevitably the conference committee will have to compromise upon this issue, I do not wish to jeopardize the possibility of a compromise more nearly in the direction of the position which I believe to be sound public policy.[43]

Senator Nye did offer a tangentially related amendment that would have created a true central bank by abolishing the reserve system. Senators defeated his amendment by a vote of ten to fifty-nine. His supporters were diverse, drawing from Progressives in the West and Midwest along with a smattering of southern senators. There is no clear pattern to the vote, however, other than the more conservative nature of Nye's Democratic supporters. The overwhelming rejection of the Nye amendment reminds us that despite Eccles's enthusiasm for greater centralization and public control of the reserve system, there was little congressional appetite for doing away with the hybrid, federal system of 1913. Support for the reserve system extended beyond lawmakers representing reserve bank states. With Nye's amendment rejected, the Senate by voice vote adopted Glass's version of the banking bill.

Because Eccles had all but agreed to restore the reserve bank presidents to the FOMC, a compromise was within reach when House and Senate conferees met to negotiate a final agreement on the bill. Eccles did suggest to the conferees that they place just four, rather than five, reserve bank heads on the FOMC to avoid a potential deadlock across the twelve FOMC members (seven Board members and five bank presidents).[44] But the agreement would have to be closer to Glass's model than to Eccles's if Eccles hoped to secure a final agreement. Ultimately, that agreement split the difference between the House and Senate bills. Eccles secured more authority for a seven-person Board of Governors over credit and monetary policy, but such powers were to be shared with five of the reserve bank presidents (with four serving in rotation, and one selected by the reserve bank presidents).[45] The new law removed the Treasury secretary and comptroller from the Board, and dropped Glass's requirements to require party balance on the Board and reserve two seats for bankers. Finally, as the price of centralizing more power within the Board, Congress also demanded greater transparency in the form of annual reports to Congress of the Board's and FOMC's votes and policy decisions. Establishing a trade-off that reappears each time lawmakers revisit the act, Congress coupled more power for the Fed with greater accountability to Congress.

Secretary Morgenthau speculated at the time that the sharing of Board and reserve bank authority on the revamped FOMC would likely stoke stalemate given their often-conflicting views about monetary policy. Morgenthau seemed to welcome the prospects of FOMC deadlock: "If the financial situation should go sour the chances are that the public will blame them rather than the

Treasury."[46] He supported removing the secretary and comptroller of the currency from the Board on similar grounds. As meeting notes from June 13 in his diary report, "He [Morgenthau] said they could then sit back and tell the Open Market Committee when it was wrong."[47]

House and Senate reactions in spring 1935 to Eccles's proposed reform of the Federal Reserve Systems drive home the intensely political character of congressional contests to shape the Fed. Partisan, electoral, and institutional interests each helped to mold the range of reforms considered as well as lawmakers' choices between contending visions for the Fed. Although much of the conflict was partisan, ideological and economic differences within the Democratic Party mattered as well: Democrats' views about how to remold the Fed were shaped in light of the party's Depression era failures. Just as in 1913, compromise over the fundamental question of who should control monetary policy was the price of successful reform.

Conclusions

Driven by economic calamity and partisan electoral change, politicians' competing priorities shaped congressional reform of the Fed and its power to make monetary policy in the wake of the Depression. Our analysis of roll call votes and news coverage of the period generates several conclusions. First, partisan considerations guided lawmakers' preferences regarding the appropriate governance and powers of the Fed. Appeals to party loyalty encouraged Democrats to blame the Depression on the failed policies of Hoover's Republican government, often bolstering Democratic support for measures to reform the Fed. Second, the dominant economic interests of the time—including agricultural and manufacturing sectors —influenced lawmakers' favored reforms. Third, political geography mattered: lawmakers who represented the home states for the regional Federal Reserve district banks were more protective of the status quo, resisting the drive to centralize power with the Board in Washington. Ultimately, no single legislative coalition in any of these conflicts secured an unalloyed win. Similar to the creation of the Fed some twenty years earlier, compromise was paramount and necessary—even after landslide elections in 1932 swept both FDR and supersized Democratic majorities into power.

Still, the Fed emerged far more centralized and powerful in 1935 than its 1913 design. Vestiges of its federal reserve system remained: the regional reserve banks retained a role in making national monetary and credit policies. But enactment of the 1935 Banking Act diminished their ability to resist policy decisions made by a reconstituted, reinvigorated Board. Moreover, the Fed gained additional means of pumping liquidity into the banking system, as new laws widened the types of collateral that could be used to issue currency and authorized emergency lending in exceptional circumstances on any asset. Eccles's visions of greater public control of monetary policy making were secured, at least on paper. Yet a newly empowered and more centralized Fed remained prone to making mistakes. In 1937, the Fed required its member banks to increase their reserves, tightening monetary policy when a sluggish economy demanded greater not lesser lending. The Fed threw the nation promptly back into a deep recession (Friedman and Schwartz 1963).

Even as lawmakers moved to centralize monetary policy decisions in Washington, the Fed did not become measurably more independent. True, presidential appointees lost their seats and votes on the new Board of Governors. But the Fed found itself under the thumb of the Treasury throughout the subsequent war years. First, Congress gave power to the president to inflate the money supply. Second, creation of the ESF gave the Treasury more power over monetary policy than it lost by giving up its secretary's seat on the Board. Conversations within the FOMC's executive committee in the late 1930s make plain that the ESF increased Treasury leverage over the Fed to compel its support for Treasury's bond sales. Indeed, Eccles reported to the executive committee in March 1937 that Morgenthau indicated "he would have to consider the use of every authority the Treasury has, including the use of the stabilization fund," if the Fed failed to sustain government bond price—leading FOMC members to observe that the ESF endowed the Treasury with "a large measure of responsibility for credit control."[48]

As we explore in the next chapter, nearly two decades would elapse before the Fed regained control over monetary policy from the Treasury via the Treasury-Fed Accord of 1951. It would take another war, a new congressional mandate for the Fed in the 1946 Employment Act, and a precipitous increase in inflation before the Fed could negotiate real separation from the Treasury and calibrate monetary authority on par with fiscal policy. Still, even after securing its operational policy independence, the Fed would remain dependent on the preferences and support of its legislative overseers.

5

Midcentury Modern Central Banking

Among the most widely held beliefs about the history of the Federal Reserve is that the 1951 Treasury–Federal Reserve Accord established the Fed's independence. An agreement negotiated by President Truman and senior Federal Reserve and Treasury officials at the outset of the Korean War, the Accord (as it is known) resolved an intensifying conflict over who controlled monetary policy in the postwar period. As the ultimate buyer of US government bonds, the Fed had been compelled to effectively monetize US debt at a low, fixed rate. The Accord ended this clear subordination of monetary policy to fiscal authorities and empowered the Fed to set interest rates unencumbered by the Treasury's postwar financing needs.

Historians and economists give the Accord foundational status, dating the Fed's modern independence to its adoption. We share scholars' appreciation for the existential impact of the Accord on the development of the Fed. Yet contrary to conventional accounts depicting the Accord as a mutual bilateral agreement devised by Treasury and Fed officials, Congress played a pivotal role in orchestrating and enforcing this institutional and political divorce. Midcentury archives suggest Congress was at the center of the 1951 dispute and reveal how key lawmakers empowered the Fed to reassert its control over monetary policy. First, we situate the Accord within the broader postwar economic and political relationships among the president, Congress, Treasury, and the Fed—a power structure in which the Fed initially (and willingly) cooperated with and then felt co-opted by the Treasury over the conduct of monetary policy. Second, we explore the politics of the 1946 Employment Act in which Congress stipulated a new mandate for the Federal Reserve and provided the ground on which pivotal legislators would later assert their authority to help resolve the Fed-Treasury conflict.

Reexamining the legislative dimensions of the Treasury-Fed divorce, we recast the nature of Fed independence that emerged by the end of the Fed's first half century. Importantly, the 1951 Accord did not create an independent central bank. Instead, it highlighted the interdependence of Congress and the Fed: the Accord unwound the Fed's Treasury dependence and reaffirmed its dependence on the legislature. Since the Fed's establishment in 1913, the Treasury relied on Federal Reserve (and district bank) support for government debt to finance World War I. And in the wake of the Depression, the onset of World War II revitalized the Fed's involvement in the US government bond market. It took another war, a politically weakened president, a steep rise in inflation, and the threat of legislative action to force the Treasury and Truman to drop their insistence that the Fed directly support government bond prices.

The political-economic perspective identified in chapter 1 drives the Fed's evolution at midcentury. This time, economic trouble and institutional competition to shape the economy motivated congressional intervention in the Treasury-Fed dispute, empowering the Fed to reassert control over monetary policy. The Fed emerged a more powerful institution in the wake of the Accord. Moreover, eliminating Treasury and presidential pressure on the Fed to monetize the debt—so that the Fed was no longer subsidizing the borrower by distorting the debt market—arguably increased congressional power over fiscal policy. In short, the Fed-Treasury divorce allowed Congress to rebalance legislative oversight over monetary and fiscal policy. Critically, the threat of congressional action on behalf of the Fed made plain that the Fed's monetary power depended on the strength of its congressional support. That support of course varied with the Fed's ability to design policy and deliver economic outcomes consistent with its statutory mandate as well as shifts in congressional partisanship. In this chapter, we explain why and when Congress challenged the administration by coming to the aid of the Fed in the early 1950s, and identify the consequences of the Fed's defiance for its relationship with both Congress and the administration.

The Puzzling Roots of the Accord

Despite its landmark significance, the terse Accord simply stated that an agreement had been reached: "The Treasury and the Federal Reserve System have reached full accord with respect to debt management and monetary policies to be pursued in furthering their common purpose to assure the successful financing of the Government's requirements and, at the same time, to minimize monetization of the public debt" (Federal Reserve Bank of Richmond, n.d.). Issued jointly by the secretary of the Treasury and chair of the Board of Governors of the Federal Reserve System, and released for publication on Sunday morning, March 4, 1951, the Accord suggested that the two parties had reached an agreement that would protect both sides' priorities, but was silent on the details of that Accord. Indeed, the text provides only a small hint of the agreement by specifying that the Accord extended to both "debt management" and "monetary policies."

During the period of rate pegging, the Fed's bond purchase program—directed by Treasury—was monetary policy. Separate mention of both debt management and monetary policy in the Accord suggests separation, and thus a new independence established by the agreement. Policy making in the wake of the Accord further indicates that the Fed reasserted its authority over monetary policy, while the Treasury retreated to its fiscal responsibility to manage the debt. Still, details of the Accord were never made public, rankling lawmakers who distrusted the Treasury's commitment to the deal given the Accord's informal status. In fact, days after the Accord's release, Senator Paul Douglas (D-Illinois) introduced a resolution with bipartisan backing that required the Treasury to manage the debt according to the Fed's monetary and credit policies. Congress did not act on the resolution. But no doubt it reminded the Treasury of Congress's capacity to legislate a solution should the Treasury insist that the Fed reinstate the peg.[1]

Although the Accord was negotiated at the highest level of government, most accounts of its genesis ignore the political dynamics that drove it. We find no account that even refers to the agreement as a "deal"; Fed historians seem to prefer the less contentious formal label of an "accord" to a term that connotes winners and losers in the conduct of monetary policy. Two Federal Reserve economic historians offer a typical account: "The Fed and Treasury were forced to compromise" (Carlson and Wheelock 2014, 15). Such versions leave unstated who secured the agreement, or how the Treasury or Fed was compelled to back down. Given that the Treasury acceded to the Fed's desire to end the peg, Treasury clearly was on the losing end of the Accord. Other accounts suggest that it was the Treasury that relented to the Fed's demands: "The Treasury granted the Fed its independence (Conti-Brown 2014, 48). Such versions of the Accord's history are ambiguous about why independence was the Treasury's to grant, and why the Treasury ultimately folded and reversed its decades-long domination of monetary policy.

Other explanations imply that adoption of the Accord reflected the government's commitment to the basic principles of central banking. As former Fed chair Bernanke (2012a, 2) noted during a lecture about the Federal Reserve's history, the Accord "was very important because it was the first clear acknowledgement by the government that the Federal Reserve should be allowed to operate on an independent basis." Granted, Bernanke does not argue that a normative commitment to central bank independence drove the players to negotiate the Accord. Instead, Bernanke's and other similar accounts imply that the Accord marked the genesis of the Fed's independence. Yet such accounts do not address the timing of the Accord: Why would the White House and Treasury have finally acknowledged this principle just when the onset of the Korean War had renewed the Treasury's interest in lowering its cost of funds?

Some historians recognize the broader political context in which the agreement was adopted, contending that lawmakers were watching from the wings as somewhat-innocent congressional bystanders in the Fed-Treasury feud. Others go a step further and admit that Congress could have played a role in tilting the political balance in the Fed's favor, but then conclude that Congress did little to settle the dispute. Bartholomew Sparrow (1996, 130), for example, argues that Congress could have resolved the conflict by using fiscal policy to lower the Treasury's need to issue more debt, but observes that Congress failed to do so. To be sure, Congress did not legislate to force resolution of the conflict. But as we suggest below, the absence of legislation belies clear signals over the postwar period from pivotal lawmakers who favored the Fed's position and credibly threatened that legislation could follow.

At least three prominent accounts offer more political context for adoption of the Accord (see Clifford 1965; Hetzel and Leach 2001; Meltzer 2003). Meltzer's (2003, 582) nuanced treatment, for instance, pinpoints a change in the political balance in favor of the Fed; he notes the importance of Senator Douglas's 1950 monetary policy report and the concurrent onset of inflation with the outbreak of the Korean War. Similarly, Robert L. Hetzel and Ralph F. Leach suggest that President Truman's diminished political support in Congress bolstered Fed leaders' ability to challenge the administration at the war's onset. Hetzel and Leach (2001, 49) ultimately attribute resolution of the conflict to decisive moves by the Fed that forced the Treasury to back down: "The Fed then forced resolution of the dispute. It informed the Treasury that . . . it was no longer willing to maintain the existing situation in the Government security market." Left unanswered in such accounts is why the Fed would have felt comfortable challenging the president at that precarious moment with the nation again at war.

We draw on these more politically attuned accounts to reconstruct Congress's role in helping to negotiate the Fed's divorce from the Treasury, and going forward, the Fed's accountability to

Congress. In highlighting the legislative dimensions of the conflict, we resolve several unanswered questions about the Fed's political evolution. First, how did shifting partisan and political alignments during and after the war shape congressional views about the government's role in managing the economy, and the respective roles of the Treasury and Fed in setting monetary policy? Second, how and why did the Fed ultimately prevail over the Truman administration after more than a decade of subordinating monetary policy to the Treasury's financial demands? The onset of inflation in 1950 might have made a difference, demonstrating to lawmakers the consequences of allowing the Treasury to direct monetary policy. But while shifting economic conditions might have been necessary to bolster the Fed's resolve, the arrival of inflation was arguably not sufficient to compel Truman and the Treasury to back down. The enactment of the 1946 Employment Act—as well as subsequent congressional threats to clarify the act's ambiguities—set the stage for a more centralized and institutionalized Fed to successfully reassert power at midcentury over the Treasury.

Monetary Politics in Wartime

The Fed emerged from the Great Depression with its authority over monetary policy severely curtailed by the executive branch. To adopt Meltzer's (2003) apt phrase, by the early 1940s, the Fed was "in the back seat," with FDR's administration at the wheel. A series of congressional and executive actions in the early to mid-1930s effectively undermined the Fed's control of monetary policy: the adoption of the inflationary Thomas Amendment in 1933, creation of the Treasury's ESF in 1934, and abandoning the gold standard in 1934. Each of these endowed the executive branch with new levers to influence the price and availability of credit, challenging the Fed's policy-making autonomy. As Congress concluded negotiations on the 1935 Banking Act, Treasury secretary Morgenthau boasted, "Our power has been the Stabilization Fund plus the many other funds that I have at my disposal and this power has kept the open-market committee in line and afraid of me."[2]

No doubt the Fed's 1937–38 policy mistakes—which doubled reserve requirements for member banks prematurely, tightened monetary policy, and threw the country back into recession—diminished the Fed's standing with Roosevelt and his Treasury secretary. Morgenthau had already blamed the Fed's increase in reserve requirements in 1936 for prematurely tightening credit. As Morgenthau's diaries reveal, Eccles, Morgenthau, and FDR strongly disagreed about whether, when, and how the Fed might support the bond market in a rising rate environment. The conflict came to a head in March 1937 when Eccles refused to accede to the Treasury's demands that the Fed begin open market purchases to buoy the price of government securities. The FOMC eventually relented only under intense pressure from the Treasury: Morgenthau leaned on his control of the ESF to threaten to infringe on the Fed's power to conduct open market operations.

Evidence of Morgenthau's tactics appears in both his diaries and FOMC meeting minutes. As Eccles reported to the FOMC on March 13, 1937, Morgenthau had "asked what the Federal Reserve System proposed to do to meet the situation and indicated that, in the event the System's action was not effective, he would have to consider the use of every authority the Treasury has, including the use of the stabilization fund and the discontinuance of the sterilization of gold imports."[3] The FOMC only agreed to consider bond purchases—a decision derided by the Treasury as insufficient (Blum 1959, 369–71).

By early April, with bond prices tumbling and rising interest rates threatening to affect corporate financing, Morgenthau delivered another ultimatum, this time formulated by President Roosevelt in a White House meeting. Morgenthau recounted FDR's threat in a meeting of Treasury and Fed staff on April 3:

You have been given by Congress this responsibility to look after the money market to keep an orderly market. You haven't done it. You have muffed it. Now I, Henry Morgenthau, Jr. speaking for the United States Government, serve notice on you that we expect you to do this, and we are going to give you one more chance.

If you don't do it, then the United States Government, through the Treasury, will take over the entire responsibility. We are going to put this on to you now and give you one more chance.[4]

Within days, the FOMC opposition—led by George Harrison, the president of the Federal Reserve Bank of New York—folded, and the Fed agreed to buy long-term bonds for its portfolio for the first time since 1933. Morgenthau might have overstated the leverage that control of the ESF conferred on the Treasury (Bordo, Humpage, and Schwartz 2015, 398n43). After all, unlike the Fed, the Treasury lacked authority to print money. Thus, Treasury purchases of government debt would not create new reserves in the banking system (unlike open market operations conducted by the Fed), and thus would not have directly loosened monetary conditions. Still, the episode is suggestive of the Treasury's willingness to encroach on the Fed's congressionally authorized power to conduct open market operations.

Given Morgenthau's threats, Eccles largely—although not entirely—acceded to Treasury's demands in the prewar period. Alarmed by increases in banks' excess reserves late in 1940 and the potential inflationary consequences, Eccles lobbied Congress early in 1941 to restore the Fed's autonomy to set and conduct monetary policy (Murphy 1950, 27). Submitting a unanimous report from the Board, the twelve district reserve banks, and the Fed's advisory council, Eccles urged Congress to take steps to reduce excess reserves held by the banks that fueled the Fed's fears of inflation. "While the Congress has not deprived the [Federal Reserve] system of responsibilities or of powers, but in fact has granted it new powers," Eccles observed in the report, "nevertheless due to extraordinary world conditions, its authority is now inadequate to cope with the present and potential excess reserve problem" (Barkley 1941). The report included calls to terminate the president's power to issue greenbacks under the Thomas Amendment, require the Treasury to secure the Fed's consent before using the ESF, and empower the FOMC to raise reserve requirements across the banking system.

Eccles made it clear that Congress had not purposefully reduced the Fed's institutional powers. In fact, the report recalled the broader powers endowed to the Fed by Congress in the wake of the Depression (presumably referring to the adoption of the 1935 Banking Act). Morgenthau, however, held a press conference the following week that preempted any serious congressional consideration of the Fed's report. He charged that the Fed's mere mention of recouping its monetary policy authority had caused the price of Treasury bonds to plummet, driving up interest rates. "It is a fact, not an opinion," Morgenthau stated. "Notice the date when he [Eccles] gave out his plan and notice what happened. From the day the statement came out money started to go up."[5] Fingering Eccles and the Fed for the increase in interest rates, Morgenthau upended Eccles's campaign to recoup the power to set monetary policy and fight inflation. Morgenthau's unequivocal response to Eccles's proposal no doubt reflected the Treasury's strongly held view that large amounts of excess reserves were essential for keeping interest rates low on both short- and long term government securities (Murphy 1950, 29). Making it easier for the FOMC to impose higher reserve requirements would undermine the Treasury's efforts to sustain higher levels of excess reserves in the banking system.

Months later, in December 1941, the Japanese attack on Pearl Harbor ended discussion of raising rates to stem inflation. The Fed's decisions in 1942 to demur to the Treasury's insistence on stabilizing low short- and long-term rates cemented the Fed's subordination to the Treasury and administration. Next we examine the mechanics and politics of these Fed's decisions to acquiesce to the Treasury's rate demands in the wake of the United States' entry into the war, and explore Congress's role in facilitating and supporting the arrangement between the Treasury and Fed.

ESTABLISHING AND MAINTAINING THE RATE PEG

The relationship between the Fed, Treasury, and administration was indelibly shaped by the changing nature of the nation's fiscal obligations before but especially during and after the war. In 1939, Treasury debt hit an all-time high of nearly $40 billion, which was just over half the nation's gross domestic product (GDP) that year.[6]

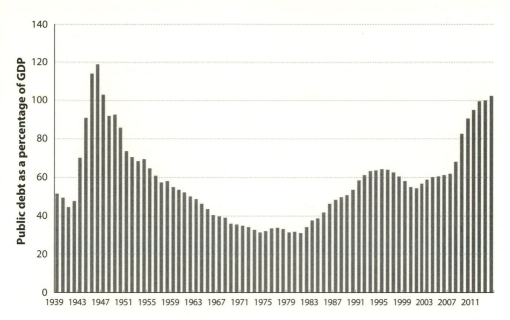

FIGURE 5.1. Total public debt as a percentage of GDP, 1939–2014. Federal Reserve Bank of St. Louis 2016c.

The total public debt as a percentage of GDP had roughly tripled over the previous decade (Congressional Budget Office (2010), and then increased exponentially once the United States entered the war in Europe (see figure 5.1). In 1941, the total debt relative to GDP was 44 percent; after the liberation of Europe five years later, it hit a record peak of nearly 120 percent. Naturally, the Treasury wanted to finance the heavy debt load cheaply. The Treasury's insistence on low rates and high bond prices left the Fed little room to maneuver once inflationary pressures set in. So long as the Fed was willing or felt compelled to accommodate the Treasury, the Fed targeted its monetary policy tools to buy government bonds, thereby keeping interest rates low. In short, the Fed capped the yield on government bonds, disintermediating a market that might have driven rates higher. The Fed's monetary policy during wartime was reduced to helping to manage the government's debt. Representative Patman, one of the Fed's fiercest Hill critics over his congressional career, would later put it best: "Who is master? The Federal Reserve or the

Treasury? You know, the Treasury came here first" (US Congress 1951, 173).

The mechanism for sustaining bond prices and dampening interest rates was known as the "peg," an arrangement in which the Fed would commit to stabilizing interest rates for short- and long-term government issues at predetermined, low levels. In other words, during the war, rather than let market forces determine the prevailing rates, the Fed would step in as needed to deploy its open market operations to sustain predetermined rates. We can see efforts within the FOMC's executive committee to reach consensus over the Fed's position in pegging rates after the war had begun in 1939, but before the Japanese attack on Pearl Harbor. For example, in June 1941, the FOMC debated a proposal it could pitch to the Treasury about the setting of long-term rates. The FOMC staff report suggested that

> a definite rate be established for long term Treasury offerings, with the understanding that it is the policy of the Government not to advance this rate during the emergency. The rate suggested is 2½ per cent. When the public is assured that the rate will not rise, prospective investors will realize that there is nothing to gain by waiting, and a flow into Government securities of funds that have been and will become available for investment may be confidently expected.[7]

Note first that the FOMC considered rate pegging as a feature of wartime policy, suggesting that a policy of fixed rates would be sustained "during the emergency." Also note that the staff proposal addressed only long-term rates. By September 1941, FOMC minutes indicate that the Fed had settled on a strategy for dealing with the Treasury: the Fed would agree to fix the long-term rate (given that it was already the prevailing one), and then push the Treasury for flexibility on the short-term rate.[8]

Before the United States was formally drawn into the war, the Treasury and Fed disagreed over how the peg would be sustained. The Fed preferred to publicly announce the pegged rates, allowing the market to push down the yield until it hit the peg. According to

Henry C. Murphy (1950, 92), the Treasury doubted the Fed's ability to use its open mouth operations to fine-tune interest rates, and worried about the consequences if the price of bonds faltered and interest rates rose. Instead, Treasury preferred that the Fed create reserves to facilitate the ability of banks to sell securities to the Fed. (Banks' reserve accounts at their district reserve bank would be credited by the Fed for the cost of securities bought by the Fed from the banks.) Disagreements between the Treasury and Fed about the mechanism of pegging proved especially acute over the setting of short-term rates. According to a Treasury official at the time, the Treasury did not see a cause-and-effect relationship between the level of rates and inflation (ibid., 96). Instead, the Treasury preferred a fixed, near-zero rate for short-term securities—a move Treasury staff believed would also help to stabilize the long-term interest rate at 2½ percent. In contrast, the Fed—always more confident of its ability to fine-tune the bond market than was the Treasury—believed it could maintain slightly higher short-term rates without undermining long-term rates.

The gravity and shock of the attack on Pearl Harbor bolstered the Fed's decision to both announce a short-term rate peg and compromise with the Treasury in setting the rate. On April 30, 1942, the FOMC announced a "posted" rate of ⅜ percent on short-term Treasury bills (ibid., 98)—lower than what the Fed might have preferred but higher than the Treasury's lower rate. Four months later, the FOMC announced that bills sold to the Fed at the posted rate could be repurchased at any time. As Murphy notes, "Treasury bills became excess reserves in everything except name" (99). With the Fed's summer move, both short- and long-term rates had been pegged. Ultimately, the Treasury's refusal to ever publicly announce the rate peg was immaterial; the FOMC had already managed to make the pegged rate clear to the market. As A. Jerome Clifford (1965, 165) concludes about the Fed's role in wartime monetary policy, the Fed was now creating reserves not in response to the commercial needs of business but rather to meet the government's war financing needs. The Fed had become an agent, coordinating and subordinating policy to fiscal objectives—arguably inevitable once the Fed was drawn into the business of managing the federal debt.

Kenneth D. Garbade (2012, 340) argues that the peg resolved a problem the Treasury had faced during World War I: How could the government convince investors to buy long-term debt during the war if investors believed that a lengthy war would produce higher bond yields in the future? The Fed's willingness to peg rates throughout the war removed the prospects for higher yields as the war wore on. Moreover, by setting the short-term rate so low, investors willingly sold their short-term bills to the Fed and exchanged them for higher-yielding long-term bonds. As a result, the Fed ended up buying—first on the market and then directly from the Treasury after 1942—most of the short-term war debt. In other words, the Fed monetized the country's debt: it printed money (that is, created bank reserves) to buy up Treasuries. As Garbade (ibid., 344) contends, monetizing the debt "laid the foundation for a sharp postwar spike in prices," creating the rift between the Treasury and Fed over whether and when to pull the peg. Whenever the Fed sought to secure the Treasury's consent to raise short-term rates after the war to stem inflation, the Treasury balked. As we explore below, that disagreement lasted nearly a decade until lawmakers stepped in and sided with the Fed in its postwar dispute with the Treasury.

Pressures on the FOMC to cooperate with the Treasury during the war likely emerged from several sources. First, the Fed arguably expected the peg to end with the war. FOMC minutes throughout the war period suggest that the Fed intended rate pegging only as an emergency wartime measure. Even in the week after the attack on Pearl Harbor, members of the FOMC reiterated that capping rates should be considered an emergency financing measure. References to maintaining a pattern of rates are typically qualified by stipulating that the rates would be in place "during the war period."[9] Second, having failed to get Congress to rein in the executive's monetary policy tools before the war, Eccles understood that the Treasury still held the reins of the ESF. The Treasury's undisputed control of the ESF likely motivated Fed officials to negotiate with them over the choice of rates and mechanics of the peg.

Third, congressional pressure no doubt limited Eccles's ardor for seeking permission to raise rates during the war (Meltzer 2003, 597). If the Fed had made such a move, Meltzer asserts, populists in Congress (including Patman) would surely have objected. More generally, outsized (though shrinking) Democratic majorities in the House and Senate during the period remained supportive of the government's wartime agenda. Katznelson (2013, 337–43) details the several war-related measures passed by Congress after 1939, including a war powers act that expanded the president's authority to command economic resources in service of the war effort—an emergency price control act intended to prevent wartime inflation, and an economic stabilization act that empowered the president to adjust wages and prices in prosecution of the war. With such enactments—in particular, wage and price controls—Congress continued its Depression era tendency of endowing the executive branch with key monetary policy tools. As one economist observed about the legislative activity in the war years, "No greater economic power was ever delegated by Congress to the President."[10] Katznelson (ibid., 345) argues that it was Congress that put the US economy on a "war footing": empowered through several legislative enactments before and after the nation's formal entry into the war in 1941, the administration "froze prices, capped profits and rationed commodities, crops, and commercial goods." The Fed was likely to encounter legislative resistance if it had tried to undermine the Treasury's efforts to finance the war. These forces collectively encouraged the Fed to continue capping rates throughout the war.

UNDERWRITING THE DEBT

In winter 1942 at the Fed's request, Congress amended the Federal Reserve Act to allow the Fed to underwrite debt issued by the Treasury during the war period. In writing the Second War Powers Act, Congress authorized the regional reserve banks to purchase government securities directly from the Treasury (as opposed to buying them from banks on the open market). The original Federal

Reserve Act allowed for such direct monetization. Congress revoked the authority when it amended the act in 1935 believing that its elimination would prevent excessive government spending. Hoping to monopolize dealings in government securities (Garbade 2014, 7), bond dealers also pressured Congress to disallow direct purchases. Without an escape clause that allowed the Fed to step in to purchase directly, the Treasury would only be able to issue as much debt and at such rates as the market would bear (ibid., 6). By lifting the ban on direct purchases in 1942, the Fed could finance the war even if the market balked at buying government debt—a situation that the Fed and Treasury had briefly feared just the month before when the markets opened after the attack on Pearl Harbor.

In testimony before the House Judiciary Committee in January 1942, Eccles pitched direct purchasing power as a temporary source of emergency financing. "It is designed to assure the Treasury of its needed financing without any hampering, without the Treasury being dictated to, in a sense, by the market," Eccles argued in executive session before the House Judiciary Committee. "In a war economy the markets for practically everything are controlled. . . . It certainly would seem to us that the Treasury with the assistance of the Federal Reserve System should be in a position, likewise, to exercise some control in the money market situation" (US Congress 1942b, 48). The Fed's request for this additional power is consistent with its general approach to monetary policy during the war period: Eccles saw the Fed's role as assisting in the management of the debt to ensure a stable source of low-cost financing.

Eccles rejected charges from Republicans in both chambers that direct purchase power subordinated the Fed to the Treasury. Senate Republican leader Robert Taft of Ohio, for example, pulled an alarm about direct purchases: direct purchases would disrupt the market for government securities, empower the Treasury to force the Fed to purchase the debt, and undermine the soundness of the currency.[11] More histrionically, academic economists wrote the House Judiciary panel echoing Republican concerns about the impact of direct purchases, contending that "the grant of this power to the Reserve Banks removes all obstructions to a rapid and direct monetization of the

Federal debt by the banks, and that this is precisely the path taken by Germany which led her to runaway inflation and the collapse of 1932."[12] Eccles countered his critics, holding that the Fed would retain its discretionary power to purchase securities and that the Treasury could not compel the Fed to buy them. That said, in testifying before the House Judiciary panel, Eccles called direct purchases an avenue for underwriting government debt if market participants ever failed to buy up new Treasury issuance (Garbade 2014, 9).

The Senate took up the bill in late January 1942. Among other provisions, the bill authorized unlimited purchases of government debt directly from the Treasury, restoring the provision of the Federal Reserve Act that had been dropped by Congress in the 1935 Banking Act. Taft initially introduced an amendment banning direct purchases, but then amended his own proposal on the Senate floor to cap the Fed's total amount of direct purchases from the Treasury at $2 billion. When Senator Glass came to the floor to defend unlimited direct purchases, Taft noted that Glass had authored the original ban on direct purchases adopted in 1935. Glass easily defended his new position in favor of unlimited purchases, disagreeing with Taft that the Treasury would now be able to compel the Fed to monetize the debt: "I think the Senator from Ohio is totally mistaken in his supposition that the Government now can force the Federal Reserve banks to buy its bonds" (US Congress 1942a, 764). Direct purchases, Glass countered, were unlikely to fuel inflation if the reserve banks could not be compelled to buy new issues from the Treasury. Moreover, Glass argued that Congress should view the powers of the Fed differently in times of peace and war. "What I said in 1935 in ordinary times is good logic now," remarked Glass in response to Taft. "But we were not . . . threatened by war then. This is merely a temporary device proposed by the Federal Reserve for the existing emergency situation now" (ibid., 765).

The only recorded roll call vote on the Second War Powers measure occurred on Taft's amendment to limit the amount of direct purchases. Taft's amendment was defeated twenty-five to fifty-one. Democrats largely opposed the amendment, splitting forty-seven to eight; Republicans split in favor, seventeen to four. Two dimensions

TABLE 5.1. Senate Vote to Limit Federal Reserve's Direct Bond Purchases from the Treasury, January 1942

Independent variable	Coefficient (robust s. e.)
Party	0.022* (0.009)
Ideology	5.266* (2.325)
Banking assets in state (in thousands of dollars, logged)	0.752* (0.383)
Number of national banks in state (logged)	−0.504 (0.504)
South	−0.465 (0.810)
Constant	−11.243** (3.921)
N	76
Log pseudolikelihood	−29.469
Wald chi2	24.10**

Notes: The dependent variable is the Senate vote on an amendment by Senator Robert Taft to impose a $2 billion limit on the amount of bond purchases that Federal Reserve banks could buy directly from the Treasury (January 28, 1942). Roll call vote no. 110, Seventy-Seventh Congress, second session. Banking data from US Commerce 1942; ideology measured with DW-NOMINATE (http://www.voteview.com). Estimates calculated in Stata 14.2 *logit* command. Robust standard errors clustered by state in parentheses. * p < .05; ** p < .01 (one-tailed tests).

of conflict on the vote stand out (table 5.1). First, senators voted largely along party and ideological lines. Democrats and more liberal senators tended to vote against limiting the Fed's power; Republicans and conservatives voted in favor.[13] Second, controlling for lawmakers' partisanship and ideology, banking interests back home still made a difference in shaping senators' votes. The more important the state's financial sector, the more likely its senator was to favor limits on direct purchases.[14] Direct purchases from the Treasury boxed banks out of the lucrative business of underwriting Treasury issuance, undermining support for direct purchases in some states. Senators representing states with a large banking sector disproportionately sided with Taft to oppose what they perceived as an inflationary policy change.

The two panels of figure 5.2 illustrate the forces that shaped senators' views about reinstating direct purchasing power.[15] First, the strength of the banking sector back home shaped the reaction of partisans to reinstating direct bond purchases (figure 5.2a). In states with less developed banking sectors (such as Nevada and

New Mexico), neither Democrats nor Republicans were especially likely to support curtailing Fed purchases of Treasury debt. But even with moderately sized banking sectors (such as that established in Minnesota or Virginia at that time), Republicans were far more likely to favor limits on direct purchases. Notably, even after controlling for senators' ideological views, both Democratic and Republican senators representing states with the most vibrant financial sectors (e.g., New York or Illinois) favored limits on direct purchases. As the strength of a state's banking sector grows, economic interests trumped ideology and partisan identity.

Second, senators' ideological commitments shaped their views about the powers of the Fed. Liberals—regardless of party—opposed limiting the power of the Fed to buy bonds directly from the Treasury (figure 5.2b). For instance, when the House considered the conference report on the bill, Democratic populist Representative Patman deemed the limit on purchases the "high-interest amendment," arguing that curtailing such purchases would permit "the big banks of this country to control our credit to the extent that the Government itself must pay a brokerage, a service fee, upon its own money that it creates itself" (US Congress 1942a, 2505). Similarly, LaFollette argued on the Senate floor that he would oppose his fellow Republican's amendment because he felt that raising taxes would be insufficient to secure enough funds to prosecute the war; the Treasury's need for a stable supply of low-cost financing, he maintained, necessitated direct purchases of government debt (ibid., 769). Among more conservative senators, Republicans were more likely to support limits on direct purchases than similarly situated Democrats. Still, regardless of party, the most conservative senators favored limits on direct purchases.

The House did not record roll call votes on the question of direct purchases. Opponents of the direct purchase provision made headway during House consideration of the bill, however. When the Senate bill came to the House floor, Representative Howard Smith of Virginia—a leader of southern conservative Democrats—convinced his colleagues to adopt a $5 billion limit on direct purchases. The tenor of the floor debate suggests that liberals (such as

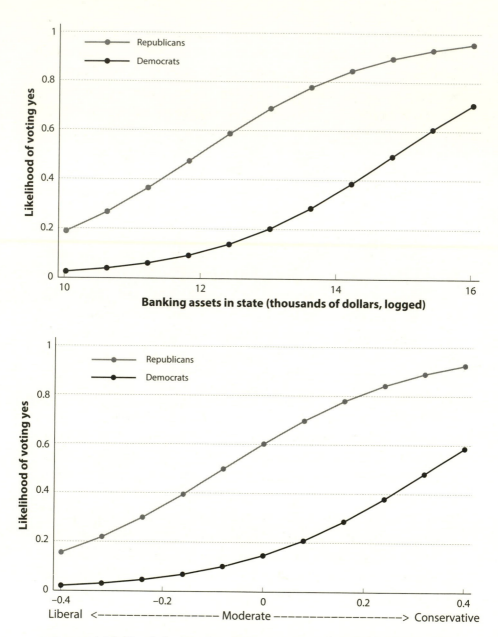

FIGURE 5.2. A. Likelihood of voting to limit direct purchases as a function of banking interests. Senate roll call vote no. 110, Seventy-Seventh Congress, second session Predicted support generated with *prgen* routine in Stata 14.2. For the parameter estimates of the underlying model, see table 5.1. B. Likelihood of voting to limit direct purchases as a function of ideology. Senate roll call vote no. 110, Seventy-Seventh Congress, second session. Predicted support generated with *prgen* routine in Stata 14.2. For the parameter estimates of the underlying model, see table 5.1.

Patman) tended to oppose the Smith amendment, while Smith's conservative allies favored it. House and Senate conferees retained the House-adopted Smith amendment and sent back to each chamber a bill that curtailed direct purchases.[16] Supporters contended that direct purchase authority was a temporary war measure, but the provision proved tough to dislodge. The Fed retained the power until the provision was repealed in 1980, long after its wartime rationale had become moot (Garbade 2014).[17]

Lawmakers' disagreements about direct purchases shed light on the relationship of the Fed, Congress, and the Treasury during the war. First, no matter the monetary consequence of direct purchases, lawmakers' differences over this power of the Fed remind us that Congress was central to resolving disputes about the Fed's institutional powers during the war. Even during a period in which the Treasury was said to dominate monetary policy, Congress retained and exercised its overarching authority to set the boundaries of the Fed's powers. Second, coalitional politics—shaped by lawmakers' electoral, partisan, and ideological commitments—influenced congressional decisions about the Fed's mandate and authority. As the vote and debates on direct purchases reveal, midcentury decisions about Fed powers were neither purely partisan nor entirely ideological: the strength of the banking sector at home conditioned lawmakers' views about the appropriate powers of the Fed. Finally, the episode highlights the limits on the Fed's autonomy that prevailed before and during the war period. Lawmakers dickered over the extent of direct purchases, and Republicans and conservatives fretted about the inflationary effects of such close collaboration between the Treasury and Fed. But large Democratic majorities in this period did not challenge the state of affairs between the Fed and Treasury; the Fed's conduct of monetary policy remained subordinated to the Treasury's fiscal demands throughout the war. As we discuss below, Congress would continue to play a central role in defining the mandate and powers of the Fed at midcentury in the wake of war, ultimately supporting the Fed in its battle with the Treasury a decade later.

Politics of 1946 Employment Act

After the war, President Truman and Congress managed the challenging transition to a peacetime economy. Innumerable statutes had given Truman congressional authorization to operate the civilian economy to mobilize for and win the war. The government controlled prices, converted plants to war production, modernized the steel industry, restricted strikes, and more. By the end of the war, the federal government owned some 40 percent of the nation's capital assets (Katznelson 2013, 345). A massive fiscal expansion mobilized for war production was critical to victory—and reversing the Great Depression. Between 1930 and 1940, unemployment averaged 18 percent; by the war's end in 1945, unemployment had dipped below 2 percent.[18] Lawmakers' immediate challenge was to prevent the return of unemployment when the government reduced its footprint in the economy.

When lawmakers turned their attention to Truman's postwar agenda and the role of the Federal Reserve, three broad factors shaped Congress's policy choices. First, Democrats remained in control of both the House and Senate, albeit with much smaller majorities than the party had enjoyed at the height of the New Deal. In fact, Republicans picked up what proved to be short-lived control of both chambers in the 1946 elections, losing control in the following ones. Even with nominal Democratic control, lawmakers were unlikely to reverse the major of programs of the New Deal—programs that had inaugurated a central role for the federal government in regulating and managing the economy. Second, Keynesian economic thinking—which had begun to take root with the 1936 publication of *The General Theory of Employment, Interest, and Money*—reinforced Democrats' commitment to New Deal innovations. The Republicans' adherence to classic laissez-faire principles (which assumed free markets would generate full employment after economic downturns) was replaced by John Maynard Keynes's theory that countercyclical macroeconomic interventions were essential for rebuilding and sustaining a robust economy.

Third, as Katznelson (2013, chapter 10) argues, the emergence of a bipartisan congressional conservative alliance of southern

Democrats and conservative Republicans shaped lawmakers' policy choices in the wake of the war. Southern Democrats endorsed the party's emphasis on budgetary planning and the use of fiscal policy to manage the economy. They drew the line, though, at any new federal programs that would directly intervene in their region's economic arrangements, and by implication, the racial order that sustained it. One key presidential priority in 1946, for example—a proposal to make permanent a wartime fair employment committee—was successfully filibustered by southern Democrats; they opposed the bill on the grounds that it would nationalize the relationship between employers and workers, thereby threatening discriminatory employment practices that were long embedded in southern practice and law (Farhang and Katznelson 2005). Conservative Democrats constrained their party leaders in responding to labor and employment issues arising as the war wound down.

These three forces collectively shaped Congress's consideration of President Truman's other key postwar priority: enactment of a full employment program that would guarantee citizens the right to a job. The 1946 Employment Act that emerged from the legislative process revealed Congress's pro-Keynesian attitudes about economic policy. Yet the final law bore limited resemblance to Truman's initial proposal: southern Democrats and conservative Republicans allied against a right to employment, and any new policy or institution devised to guarantee it. Most important from our perspective, the new law did not expressly create new powers for the Fed. Nevertheless, in assigning new responsibilities of macroeconomic management to the federal government in the wake of the war, the 1946 Employment Act implicitly gave the Fed a new and broader mandate. Standard accounts of Fed history attribute the Fed's dual mandate and enhanced accountability to the reforms enacted in 1977. But as we argue below, the provenance of the dual mandate and Fed's broader responsibilities rests in the 1946 law.

President Truman cut short Congress's summer recess in September 1945, calling the Congress into special session to consider his "21-Point Program for the Reconversion Period." Truman (1945) built his program on FDR's 1944 proposal for an economic bill of rights, urging Congress to "make the attainment of those rights the essence of postwar American economic life." Central to achieving the goals of Roosevelt's economic bill of rights, Truman argued, was the establishment of full employment in a peacetime economy. Truman (ibid.) called on Congress to pass the employment bill that was already under consideration in the Senate:

> A national reassertion of the right to work for every American citizen able and willing to work—a declaration of the ultimate duty of Government to use its own resources if all other methods should fail to prevent prolonged unemployment—these will help to avert fear and establish full employment. The prompt and firm acceptance of this bedrock public responsibility will reduce the need for its exercise.

The president's proposal required increases in government spending (or as Truman contended, possibly just a commitment to do so) when the private sector failed to generate sufficient jobs. The bill was received warmly by Senate Democrats that month, but was amended slightly in the Banking Committee in response to pressures from a range of moderate and conservative senators. The panel rejected an amendment from the Republican leader Taft that would have raised taxes whenever spending to create jobs would add to the public debt. But a slightly modified amendment was adopted that replaced citizens' "right" to work with the statement that citizens were "entitled" to work.[19]

The committee-passed bill faced some weakening amendments on the floor. First, amendments from Bourke Hickenlooper (R-Iowa) sought to prevent government competition with private enterprise and limit government intervention in labor markets; both were rejected largely along party lines.[20] Second, the full Senate revisited the issue of how government finances might be affected given the open-ended commitment to full employment. Senator Carl Hatch (D–New Mexico) secured adoption of an amendment stipulating that the government's investments to secure full employment would have to be "consistent with the needs and obligations of the Federal Government" (Bailey 1950, 122). Taft's revised amendment to require a program of taxation to pay for spending in pursuit of full employment was adopted unanimously after the bill's sponsors secured language that guaranteed the government's commitment to full employment (Bailey 1950, 122–23). With those changes—indicative of the rougher road ahead for the bill in the House—the Senate adopted the bill, seventy-one to ten. GOP critics of the bill largely folded, leaving just a handful of Senate conservatives from both parties on record against the bill.[21]

Two months later, House Democrats were plotting ways to kill or drastically amend the Senate bill that had been referred to the House Expenditures Committee—a panel headed by southern Democrat Carter Manasco of Alabama. The *Washington Post* reported in late November that Manasco had proposed to combine the full employment bill with a bill to make permanent the Fair Employment Practices Committee—the employment commission that was ultimately felled by a Senate filibuster.[22] As Stephen Bailey (1950, chapter 7) suggests, House opposition reflected a more rigorous and coordinated campaign against the bill spearheaded by the National Association of Manufacturers, and joined by various state chambers of commerce. Perhaps most critical in undermining southern Democrats' support for the Senate bill was the opposition of the American Farm Bureau (ibid., 146–48). Members of the bureau came late to lobbying against the Senate bill, but turned out in full force against the House bill. They asserted that government spending on public works programs would create higher-paying jobs than those offered to farm employees, leading southern farm business to fear the loss of cheap labor.

The House committee eventually reported an amended employment bill in December—a slowdown that prompted one of the bill's supporters to charge the committee with staging "a little bit of a filibuster here" (Barkley 1945). In place of "full employment," the committee-passed bill called for a "high level of employment," abandoning both the president's call for a right to a job and the Senate's formulation of an entitlement to one. Instead, the House bill called for "the maximum opportunity for employment . . . production and purchasing power." Federal spending on job creation was required to be "consistent with a financially sound fiscal policy" in the event of a lack of privately created jobs (Bailey 1950, chapter 7).

The watered-down House version carried the day on the floor, passing 255–126. Democrats split 195–21, and Republicans voted 58–105.[23] Divisions on the bill reflected both partisan and ideological commitments. Controlling for Democrats' proclivity to support the bill, more conservative House lawmakers disproportionately opposed it, finding the promise of countercyclical government spending fiscally imprudent. Racial conservatives also disproportionately voted against the bill, even in its diluted form—likely reflecting rising concerns about federal interventions into labor markets. Supporters of the Senate's stronger version looked to a bicameral conference to restore the heart of the bill, while journalists conjectured that the House was unlikely to reverse itself even with Truman lobbying hard for conferees to adopt the Senate's version (Belair 1945).

The conference stretched long past the president's Christmas deadline, coming to an agreement in early February. The Senate's full employment and House's high level of employment were reconciled in a new version of the bill that declared the government's commitment to maximum employment, production, and purchasing power. The *New York Times* deemed the compromise a "masterpiece of semantics, embodying to a large degree the ideology contained in the 'full employment' form but expressing itself in the terminology already adopted by the House of Representatives" (Tower 1946). Others suggested that the final agreement essentially endorsed the principle underlying Truman's original full employment proposal: the bicameral compromise declared that it was the policy and responsibility of the federal government to maintain conditions that would promote maximum employment, production, and price stability. For this reason, the sponsor of the original Senate bill, Senator James Murray (D-Montana), claimed victory, holding that the bill contained "all the essentials of a full employment program" (Trussell 1946). In contrast, Senator Taft alleged that the conference agreement bore no resemblance to the plan for compensatory spending to generate jobs in an economic downturn. In short, the bill spelled out a new objective for the federal government's economic policy, even as Congress left the means for achieving it ambiguous.

Both chambers approved the compromise agreement. The Senate had to first suspend a southern Democrat-led filibuster against Truman's fair employment practices bill. After the filibuster was paused, Democrats called up and passed the employment compromise before southern Democrats resumed their filibuster. It is noteworthy that southern Democrats did not oppose the employment bill; they could have prevented its consideration by refusing to suspend their filibuster. Instead, whatever tweaking had been done to the Senate bill was sufficient to bring most of their cohort on board. The House passed the compromise agreement with majorities of both parties. Nine Democrats switched their votes to support the compromise, as did thirty-nine Republicans who had previously voted against the original, weaker version of the House bill. The switchers were predominantly conservative Republicans whose votes were likely secured by removing the assurance of jobs for all who sought them.

The Employment Act of 1946 did not directly amend the Federal Reserve Act to create an explicit new mandate for the Fed. Indeed, Senator Douglas in congressional hearings in 1952 called on Congress to write a more explicit mandate for the Fed (Timberlake 1993, 326). But as Meltzer (2003, 742) observes, the bill's emphases on employment and production required countercyclical policies—in essence requiring the Fed to become an active partner in the government's effort to manage the economy. Even though the enacted bill was watered down, J. Bradford De Long (1996, 49) argues that it signaled a new federal commitment to foster maximum employment—a shift in the "concerns and missions of economic policymakers ... [that] continues to hold." Moreover, as De Long notes, by creating the Council of Economic Advisers and placing it in the White House, the law empowered a set of economists—subject to the advice and consent of the Senate—to help centralize macroeconomic policy planning in the White House.

Most important, the bill reasserted Congress's authority over economic policy in the wake of the war. As Senator Joseph O'Mahoney (D-Wyoming) contended on the floor during the

Senate's consideration of the 1945 bill, "This is a bill to vest in Congress the power and the responsibility of meeting the issue, instead of continually delegating the power to the executive branch of the government."[24] His appeal to congressional power likely contributed to the Senate's strong bipartisan vote in favor of the contested bill—aided by the bill's ambiguity about how the new mandate would be pursued or achieved. Moreover, the 1946 Employment Act marked a shift in congressional preferences about the Federal Reserve and the goals of monetary policy. Congress rejected the passive and reactive Fed that had emerged over the course of its first three decades, instead directing the Fed to foster and sustain economic conditions conducive to maximum employment, production, and purchasing power of the dollar. As we assert below, the Fed's capacity to take the reins of monetary policy would require Congress to help break the Fed's subordination to the Treasury.

Standard Account of the 1951 Accord

Historians and economists give the Accord formative status as a cornerstone of the Fed's independence. Most accounts portray it as a mutual agreement between Treasury and the Fed (e.g., Hetzel and Leach 2001; Conti-Brown 2016). We offer an important political perspective: heavy-handed tactics by President Truman, coupled with White House fears of a Fed-friendly legislative solution, tipped the balance of power between Congress and Truman toward the legislative branch. Far from reflecting a new, mutual modus operandi between the Treasury and Fed, the Accord marked the Fed's political divorce from the executive made possible by legislative intervention on behalf of the Fed.

The congressional perspective resolves several puzzles about the Accord. First, if the Fed had originally agreed to peg rates only on an emergency, temporary basis during the war, why did it take so long for it to end the peg and recoup its operational authority to set interest rates after the war ended in 1945? Second, given the Treasury's success in compelling the Fed's cooperation to cap bond yields for so long, why did the Treasury finally fold in 1951? Standard

FIGURE 5.3. Annual inflation rate, 1940–60. Federal Reserve Bank of St. Louis 2016b.

accounts do not explain why the Fed was ultimately able to prevail over the objections of President Truman and Treasury secretary John Snyder. In fact, uncertainty about the severity and duration of the Korean War—accompanied by a new threat of war with China late in 1950—should have bolstered the Treasury's resolve to stand firm. But the Treasury and president caved precisely when the Fed's cooperative bond buying would have been particularly valuable given the onset of a new war.

The standard narrative—offered by Hetzel and Leach (2001), and more recently Peter Conti-Brown (2016)—highlights clashes of institutions and personalities after the war ended. According to Conti-Brown (2016), Eccles's and Truman's relationship frayed when a rise in postwar inflation converted Eccles into an inflation hawk. As shown in figure 5.3, the rate of inflation by 1946 had reached 18 percent, and spiked again at 9 percent before the Accord's adoption in 1951. Indeed in January 1951, Eccles charged that the Treasury's pressure on the Fed to cap bond yields had converted the banking system—aided by the regional reserve banks—into an "engine of inflation (US Congress 1951). Because the Treasury assumed that the Fed would continue to keep a floor under government bond prices, the FOMC had little choice but to continue to create bank reserves to facilitate bankers' purchases of government securities. Eccles's arguments against the peg in this period gained him little and cost him much: Truman replaced Eccles as chair in 1948, appointing Thomas McCabe in his stead. Eccles refused to leave the Fed, however; he settled into the vice chair's position and became even more assertive in challenging the peg, joined by Allan Sproul, the president of the New York Federal Reserve Bank.

By the end of 1950, the conflict between Eccles and Truman had intensified, and expanded to include both Sproul and Snyder. Seeking to end the Fed's newfound resistance to the Treasury's debt management policy, Truman summoned the FOMC to the Oval Office for, in Conti-Brown's (2016) terms, an unprecedented "presidential lecture."[25] Afterward, Truman went public, releasing a statement that claimed Fed officials had assured the president that they would "fully support the Treasury defense financing program" (Belair 1951d). Armed with the Board's memo summarizing what was actually said in the Oval Office and encouraged by the *New York Times* reporter covering the events (see Hetzel and Leach 2001, 45), Eccles leaked an account to the press that challenged the president's version of events (Belair 1951d). As Eccles (1951, 496) put it in his memoir, "The fat was in the fire." It proved explosive.

With the unprecedented dispute between the president and Fed splashed on the front pages of the *New York Times*, *Washington Post*, and *Washington Evening Star* (Hetzel and Leach 2001, 46), the FOMC threatened to take unilateral action to end the pegging of long-term rates if the Treasury refused to negotiate. From Hetzel and Leach's (2001, 49–50) perspective, the Fed's threat "forced resolution of the dispute" since the Treasury now "believed it had no choice but to end the public dispute" to ease uncertainty in the markets. Conti-Brown (2016) notes that at that point, cooler heads prevailed on both the Treasury and Fed staffs. Probably aided by Snyder's two-week absence while he recovered from eye surgery,

Fed and Treasury negotiators (now led by assistant Treasury secretary William McChesney Martin) shook hands on an informal agreement in early March that they dubbed "the Accord."[26] The short paragraph of the Accord would thereafter be treated as the critical junction in creating an independent Fed.

A Political Account of the Accord

Why would the Treasury abandon the architecture underpinning the nation's finances when the nation was once again on the brink of war? As Secretary Snyder maintained years later in an oral history, the Fed's push for higher interest rates in 1950 was particularly ill timed: "I had seen a lesser incident than the invasion of South Korea cause two world wars" (Hess 1969). The spike in inflation in 1950 and early 1951 noted by economic historians surely played a role in bolstering the Fed's claims that debt monetization undermined the health of the economy. But economics alone cannot explain why the Fed was able to secure its separation from the Treasury. If adverse economic conditions were sufficient to compel the Treasury to back down, the Accord would arguably have been written after the first postwar spike in inflation in 1946.

Recent accounts of the Accord cannot answer these questions. To explain the Fed's break with the Treasury in 1951, we broaden our focus to highlight the legislative and political context in which the Fed fought to regain control over monetary policy. First, we explore lawmakers' incentives to contest the Treasury's domination of the Fed, contending that Congress's ability to set fiscal policy would be enhanced by stripping the Treasury of influence over monetary policy. Second, we examine Senator Douglas's campaign to legislate a solution to the Treasury-Fed stalemate. Some Democrats sided with the Treasury. But Douglas's marshaling of bipartisan support for the Fed in a period of narrow Democratic majorities arguably mattered in reaching the Accord. Finally, we look at Truman's precarious political position early in 1951 when his ham-fisted tactics against Fed officials backfired, undermining the Treasury's position. In short, Congress's credible threat to intervene on the Fed's behalf—coupled with Truman's weak public standing and political overreach early in 1951—compelled the Treasury to back down, ceding authority to the Fed. Far from reflecting a mutual agreement to end the peg, the Accord sealed the Treasury's loss of fiscal dominance over monetary policy, and paved the way for Congress to rebalance legislative and executive control over fiscal policy.

CONGRESSIONAL INCENTIVES

Many accounts of the Accord treat Congress as an innocent bystander in the contest to end the postwar price fixing of government bonds. Granted, no votes were cast on the House and Senate floors pertaining to the dispute. Nor were Democrats united in their support for the Fed against the Treasury. But the lack of congressional floor footprints masks lawmakers' institutional and political motivations to intervene in the debt management dispute.

Consider legislators' institutional interests. In writing the 1946 Employment Act, Congress established a central role for the Federal Reserve in managing the economy. To be sure, the new law neither detailed the Fed's particular responsibilities nor established an explicit mandate for the central bank. Still, by outlining the goals of maximum employment, production, and maintenance of the purchasing power of the dollar, Congress signaled that it expected the Fed to play a central role in sustaining the economy—including managing inflation. Yet so long as the Treasury compelled the Fed to buy the debt, the Fed's ability to conduct effective monetary policy suffered. Moreover, subordinating the Fed to the Treasury undermined Congress's power to make effective fiscal policy; the burden of fighting inflation shifted to lawmakers, complicating their ability to target the government's other fiscal objectives (Stein 1996, 218). Breaking the grip of the Treasury over the Fed promised to bolster the institutional power of both Congress and the Federal Reserve.

Many legislators' political interests also have steered them to support the Fed in its dispute with the executive branch. Republicans in particular had little reason to side with the Truman administration. GOP banking and business constituencies tended to favor

FIGURE 5.4. Public approval of Harry S. Truman, 1945–52. American Presidency Project, "Job Approval: Harry S. Truman." Presidential Job Approval." Accessed August 4, 2016, http:// www.presidency.ucsb.edu/data/popularity.php?pres=33&sort=time&direct=DESC&Submit =DISPLAY.

more aggressive action to fight inflation (Kirshner 2007, chapter 5), limiting GOP support for the Treasury over the rate peg. Republican electoral gains during the postwar period likely further diminished any GOP inclination to support the administration. Republicans held both the House and Senate after the 1946 elections (although they lost control to Democrats when Truman pulled in Democratic majorities in 1948). Steep Democratic losses in the 1950 elections again put control of Congress within reach for Republicans, especially in the Senate, where Democrats held just a two-seat margin over the GOP. Tight electoral competition—coupled with a growing Democratic North-South divide—generated few incentives for Republican lawmakers to lend a hand to the White House in its battle against the Fed.

Finally, Truman's public standing had been declining steadily since 1949—likely reflecting the public's negative reactions to a 1949 recession, rising inflation in 1950, and Truman's public disputes with General Douglas MacArthur over the onset, scope, and conduct of the Korean War (see figure 5.4). By February 1951, only

25 percent of the public approved of the president. Truman's collapsing popularity—stemming in part from a sliding economy—made it easier for Democrats to side with the Fed over Truman's objections and encouraged Republicans to forcefully support the Fed in its breakup with the administration.

THE DOUGLAS REPORT

The Senate in 1949 passed a concurrent resolution directing the Joint Committee on the Economic Report to investigate "certain economic and fiscal matters including the problem of the effectiveness and coordination of monetary, credit, and fiscal policies in dealing with general economic policy."[27] At the direction of Senator O'Mahoney, chair of the Joint Committee, Senator Douglas headed a bipartisan panel to investigate the relationship between Treasury and the Federal Reserve, and evaluate the impact of the Fed's bond-buying commitment on the state of the economy. In eleven days of hearings late in 1949, Douglas drew out the contending arguments surrounding the division of monetary authority between the Treasury and Federal Reserve.

Proponents of the Treasury's position charged that the market for government bonds was too weak to sustain the consequences of ending the peg. Government financing would be subject to the instability of the bond market, and higher rates would be the inevitable result if the Fed no longer committed to capping yields on government securities. Defenders of the Fed asserted that the market could stand on its own and survive the absence of directed price controls. Most important, Fed proponents stressed the role that Congress should play in resolving the dispute between the Treasury and Fed. The president of the Federal Reserve Bank of New York, Sproul, contended that "Congress, as final arbiter, might be able to provide a mandate which would charge debt management as well as monetary management with some responsibility for the objectives specified in the Employment Act of 1946."[28] Moreover, Eccles suggested that an expression of support from Congress would stiffen the Fed's own resolve to assert its power to independently set monetary policy: "If Congress would, as a result of hearings of this sort, make it apparent that this support policy [i.e., the rate peg] on the part of the Open Market Committee was not desirable, I think you would find, maybe, a greater independence on the part of the Open Market Committee."[29]

The Douglas panel made front-page news in national papers when it issued its unanimous report in January 1950, urging Congress to (among other steps) take action to "restore the supremacy of the Federal Reserve System over the nation's credit structure" (Belair 1950a). Remarkably, Representative Patman, the Fed's sharpest critic and most reliable defender of the Treasury, signed the report along with the subcommittee's two Republicans and two other Democrats. (Patman would later claim that he hadn't signed the report: "Somehow or other my name got on it, but I didn't put it there.")[30] The report is worth quoting at length. It demonstrates the panel's unambiguous endorsement of the Fed in its dispute with the Treasury. And it links support for the Fed back to the goals written into the Employment Act of 1946:

> We recommend that Congress by joint resolution issue general instructions to the Federal Reserve and the Treasury regarding the objectives of monetary and debt-management policies and the division of authority over these policies. These instructions need not, and in our judgment should not, be detailed; they should accomplish their purpose if they provide, in effect, that, *(a)* in determining and administering policies relative to money, credit, and management of the Federal debt, the Treasury and the Federal Reserve shall be guided primarily by considerations relating to their effects on employment, production, purchasing power, and price levels, and such policies shall be consistent with and shall promote the purposes of the Employment Act of 1946; and *(b)* it is the will of Congress that the primary power and responsibility for regulating the supply, availability, and cost of credit in general shall be vested in the duly constituted authorities of the Federal Reserve System, and that Treasury action relative to money, credit, and transactions in the Federal debt shall be made consistent with the policies of the Federal Reserve.[31]

Keep in mind that the Joint Economic Committee under House and Senate rules lacked authority to write or report a bill; its powers were to study and advocate. Nor did the full committee endorse the panel's findings. Instead, it reported later in the year that it lacked "sufficient data on the subject to pass judgment on the merits of the case" and called for additional study (Belair 1950b, 1). The Douglas hearings, furthermore, were insufficient to compel an early resolution to the impasse; on the advice of Douglas's GOP colleague on the panel (Senator Ralph Flanders of Vermont), Douglas brought together Eccles, Snyder, McCabe, and fellow panel member Frank Buchanan (D-Pennsylvania) to try to forge a resolution behind closed doors in December 1949. The effort failed.[32]

Still, public hearings, the report, and a February 1951 Douglas floor speech propelled Douglas's campaign to resolve the impasse in the Fed's favor. Three dimensions of Douglas's efforts appear to have been consequential. First, the panel's report signaled bipartisan congressional support for the Fed in its disagreements with the Treasury. Endorsement of the report by both of the panel's Republican members was deemed "noteworthy" when the *Washington Post* covered the release of the Douglas report (Friendly 1950). Douglas's ability to attract support from Republicans is hardly surprising given Republican abhorrence of inflationary policy. Indeed, when the Senate banking panel chair opted not to intervene publicly in the Fed-Treasury dispute in February 1951, Senate Republican leader Taft indicated that he would take up the issue.[33] Bipartisan support for Douglas's aims remained intact in the aftermath of the Accord when the senator finally introduced his resolution: three Republicans and two Democrats joined Douglas on March 5 to introduce a Senate resolution to force the Treasury to manage the debt according to the policies set by the Federal Reserve (Belair 1951b). In a Congress with a narrow majority and divided Democratic Party, bipartisan support for the Fed's position surely signaled to the White House the fragility of siding with the Treasury.

Second, the Douglas report and his threat to legislate signaled to top Fed officials that they could count on some congressional support. As Douglas confirmed in 1952 hearings commissioned to examine debt management in the wake of the Accord, "I have heard that it [my threat to legislate] was very helpful to the Federal Reserve, enabling it to assert its independence and to reach an accord with the Treasury." When Fed chair Martin demurred, Douglas pressed on: "It sometimes helps . . . to have a little legislative protection."[34] Explicit backing from pivotal lawmakers likely encouraged the Fed to be more aggressive in seeking separation from the Treasury.

We see one glimpse of this in summer 1950 when the Federal Reserve Board in August raised the New York Fed's discount rate from 1½ to 1¾ percent. At the same time, the Treasury issued two new loans at 1¼ percent.[35] The Board publicly noted that it was "prepared to use all of the means at [its] command to restrain further expansion of bank credit."[36] Observers at the time forecast that the practical effect of the rise in short-term rates would not be too great. But ten days later, the *Wall Street Journal* noted that the public dispute between the Board and Treasury had rattled the market, creating an "erratic market" in government securities.[37] Board members refused to go on the record about the next steps in their battle with Treasury over the control of bond prices, but one official argued that "the effect is psychological. It is a clue of what is to come."[38] Officials made it clear that the Board was prepared to turn to Congress to secure additional credit-curbing powers if needed.[39] Congress's capacity to tilt the dispute in the Fed's favor seemed obvious at the time to Fed officials, and it appears to have bolstered the Fed's resolve to challenge the Treasury.

Third, Douglas's efforts shaped expectations in Washington about how the dispute was likely to be resolved; inevitably, only Congress held the authority to resolve the deadlock. This view infused news coverage of the institutional impasse, including an October 1950 *Times* observation that "even if President Truman should throw his weight behind Secretary Snyder in the controversy it is difficult to foresee how the Treasury could win in the end. Members of the Reserve Board owe their fifteen year appointments to the President, but, as an agency, they are responsible only to Congress and are independent of the Executive Branch" (Belair 1950b, 93). No less than Walter Lippmann (1951) concluded just before the Accord was reached that the impasse was "an issue which Congress alone can decide." Fed officials spread a similar message, especially as the impasse heightened in winter 1951. Sproul, for example, noted in a letter to the chair of the American Bankers Association that "it looks like there is going to have to be a determination, probably by the Congress, as to whether we are to have a central banking system . . . or whether it is to become a bureau of the Treasury."[40] Similarly, years later, Sproul would recap the events of 1951, arguing that Congress "was the only place the dispute could be decided."[41]

Bipartisanship notwithstanding, one might wonder whether a divided Congress would ever have succeeded in legislating a solution to the impasse. Actual prospects for legislation arguably mattered little: pivotal Truman staff believed the Fed would act, and that belief appears to have helped persuade the Treasury and White House to back down. This dialogue from a 1985 oral history with Grover Ensley, executive director of the Joint Economic Committee in 1951, suggests the credibility of Douglas's threat to legislate:

> I got a call one evening from Dave Bell, assistant to President Truman. He asked me: "Grover, do you think that the Douglas bill will move?" I said, "I think it will." Three days later, the administration announced the Treasury–Federal Reserve Accord. Which did substantially what Douglas's bill called for, making legislation unnecessary.[42]

White House staffers were nervous enough about the depth of Douglas's congressional support that they reached out to the Hill for legislative intelligence. Committee staff exploited the opportunity to signal the bill was likely to move (perhaps overstating its prospects). But so long as the threat to legislate was credible, no further action was necessary. As Lippmann (1951) observed to his readers just before the release of the Accord , "Sen. Douglas has a resolution which would decide it, and it should be brought forward—*far enough forward at least to offset the heavy pressure which is being exercised . . . by the White House*" (emphasis added). As became clear the next day, Douglas's bipartisan efforts went just far enough to help shift the balance of power away from the Treasury and into the hands of the Fed.

EXECUTIVE OVERREACH

Douglas's leverage was enhanced in the final weeks before the Accord by Truman's public stumbles. We recounted earlier that Truman summoned the FOMC to the Oval Office in early February 1951 and then lied publicly about what had transpired at the meeting—claiming falsely that the Fed was still committed to monetizing the debt. On February 26, Truman (1951), somewhat desperately, established an emergency committee to suggest ways to resolve the conflict between a stable government debt market and rising inflation—but on the condition that interest rates would remain unchanged. Truman appointed Snyder, McCabe, Charles E. Wilson (the head of the Office of Defense Mobilization), and Leon Keyserling (head of Truman's Council on Economic Advisors) to the committee, and directed them to report back by March 15 with a list of policy solutions that Truman could approve.

The committee was doomed. Its chair expressed skepticism about the task the panel had been assigned. Speaking with Sproul and McCabe on the evening after their visit to the Oval Office, Wilson "expressed doubts as to whether the problem could be resolved by this committee setup; in fact, it looked as if he might be caught in the middle of an irreconcilable dispute and one which he would not have time to study in all of its many aspects because of the many other more direct demands on his time" (Sproul 1951). As head of the defense office charged with wage and price controls to combat inflation, Wilson had good reason to support strong measures to reduce inflationary pressures (Lippmann 1951). Yet as a Truman appointee, he could not side with the Fed without publicly disagreeing with the president who appointed him—leading to Wilson's "irreconcilable dispute."

Had Truman let the committee generate its own solutions, the group might have made headway. But Truman proposed a set of policy options for the committee's review. Some were not especially noteworthy: voluntary lending controls by bankers and expanded power for the Fed to raise reserve requirements. One solution, though—impose government controls on bank lending—raised

hackles. The *New York Times* observed that Truman had "admin-
istered the shock-treatment when he disclosed that direct Government controls on bank lending were in store." Even his Treasury
secretary was reported to have opposed "the drastic form of direct
control suggested in the President's recent memorandum" (Belair
1951a)." And lest the nation's bankers not fully recognize the implications of Truman's directive, Sproul dashed off a letter to James
Shelton, head of the American Bankers Association, on February 28:
"I haven't mentioned the more arbitrary controls over bank lending,
which some are suggesting, as a way to restrict credit and peg interest rates at the same time. I assume we would all abhor this kind of
Government control. If you are afraid of state socialism, this would
be it."[43] Fortunately for the committee, within days of the memorandum, Martin and McCabe reached their deal on the Accord, making
the panel moot. In establishing the committee, Truman had finally
acknowledged that the Fed's constant creation of bank reserves to
facilitate bond buying fueled inflation. Yet the Fed, with bipartisan
congressional backing, had already moved to end its subordination
to the Treasury and Truman.

Conclusion

A pivotal development in the Fed's evolution, the Accord broke the
inflationary subordination of monetary policy to fiscal authorities.
The divorce enabled the Fed to set interest rates independent of the
Treasury, unconstrained by the administration's financing needs. To
be sure, the Fed had to learn how to use its monetary independence.
Christina D. Romer and David H. Romer (2002) suggest that it took
an evolution of policy makers' economic beliefs to stabilize inflation
in the 1950s. Still, the long-term impact of the Accord is visible in
figure 5.5, which charts inflation volatility from the late nineteenth
century (before the founding of the Fed) until the present. By the
end of the 1950s, inflation volatility is sharply diminished and stabilized. Once the Fed stopped monetizing the debt, it could pursue
its new congressionally mandated goal of stable prices as set by the
Employment Act of 1946. The Accord also benefited the Treasury.

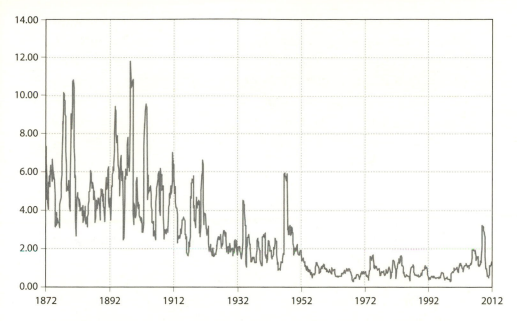

FIGURE 5.5. Inflation volatility, 1872–2014. "Online data Robert Shiller." Accessed January 30, 2017, http://www.econ.yale.edu/~shiller/data.htm. Data revised and updated in Shiller 1989, chapter 26. Inflation volatility measured as annualized standard deviation of monthly changes in the Consumer Price Index (rolling 12 month window).

Freed from the explicit price fixing before the Accord, private under-writers of US government debt helped to create a larger and much more liquid market for the Treasury's financing needs. Had the Fed's rate capping continued, the supply of credit would certainly have been smaller.

The Accord cemented the interdependence of Congress and the Fed. Lawmakers' willingness to side with the Fed over the Treasury made it plain that Fed autonomy was contingent on the strength of its political support in Congress. As our political-economic framework suggests, the postcrisis, postwar environment set the table for Congress to act and the Fed to finally push back to establish operational independence from the executive. Only when backed by bipartisan congressional support in a period of rising inflation, divided majorities, and a deeply unpopular president could and would the Fed assert its power. At the same time, the Accord reinforced congressional dependence on the Fed. Forceful and effective fiscal policy required steady demand for US government debt, which remained quite high in the postwar years relative to GDP (recall figure 5.1). As the Fed improved its capacity to control inflation, fiscal policy no longer had to shoulder the extra weight of an economy unduly burdened by monetary concerns. Counterintuitively, more potent fiscal policy was conditional on ending the Fed's subordination to the Treasury, a free market setting of interest rates, and a growing appetite for US debt (Garbade 2012).

Midcentury separation from the Treasury granted the Fed operational independence, contingent on its accountability to Congress. Lawmakers positioned themselves to escape blame for future Fed mistakes, and Congress began to rebalance executive and legislative influence over fiscal policy—a necessary move for a legislature eager to recoup power delegated to the executive during economic and military crises. As we explore in the coming chapter, the Fed's disastrous performance in the 1970s sparked another cycle of blame and reform, leading Congress to tighten its Fed leash and find new ways of holding the Fed accountable to its legislative boss.

6

The Great Inflation and
the Limits of Independence

William McChesney Martin's and the Fed's newfound freedom helped usher in a booming postwar recovery. Having moved from the Treasury to the Fed after the 1951 Accord, Martin led the Fed during two decades of strong economic growth, earning a reputation in his first ten years for effective countercyclical monetary policy: "Our purpose is to lean against the winds of deflation or inflation, whichever way they are blowing." By the end of the 1960s, however, policy makers enabled both highly expansionary fiscal policy and easy monetary policy. New economic beliefs, diminished confidence in the power of monetary policy to combat inflation, and recurring, geopolitically induced oil price shocks accompanied unbridled inflation, indelibly defining the decade's economy. With Martin retired, rumors also spread that President Richard Nixon pressured his successor, Arthur Burns, to kick-start the economy before Nixon's 1972 reelection campaign (Rose 1974). Whatever the causes, the result was stagflation, as it came to be known: high inflation paired with stagnant economic growth and high unemployment. Caught up in politics at both ends of Pennsylvania Avenue, the Burns Fed proved

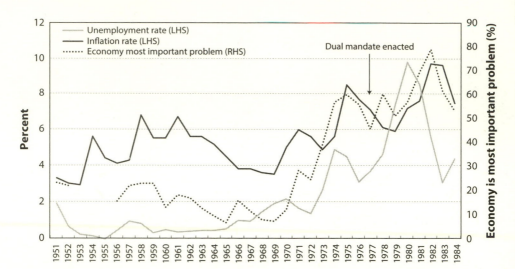

FIGURE 6.1. Public views of the economy after the Accord, 1951–84. For the unemployment rate, see Federal Reserve Bank of St. Louis 2016a. For the inflation rate, see US Bureau of Labor Statistics, n.d. On the economy's most important problem, see Policy Agendas Project, http:// www.policyagendas.org/page/datasetscodebooks#gallups_most_important_problem.

unable to combat stagflation, the macroeconomic and political challenge of the decade.

Gallup polls show that a rising share of the public cited the poor state of the economy as the "most important problem" facing the nation (figure 6.1).[2] The public held the Fed responsible for the economic downturn: Only 15 percent of the respondents to a Cambridge Reports survey in 1978 absolved the Fed for the late 1970s' stagflation.[3] Lawmakers blamed the Fed as well. The Burns Fed's tightening of monetary policy in the mid-1970s, at the cost of rising unemployment, frustrated many legislators, especially Democrats. In November 1977, warning President Jimmy Carter not to reappoint Burns for a third term, Senator Hubert Humphrey (D-Minnesota) summed up many Democrats' concerns: "If the Federal Reserve tightens up on credit and raises interest rates whenever purchasing power expands," he argued, "it can frustrate any attempt by the President and Congress to stimulate economic growth and reduce unemployment."[4]

In this chapter, we use congressional and Federal Reserve archival materials to examine economic and political developments that drove a new cycle of blame and reform during the 1970s and early 1980s. Unlike previous cycles that largely endowed the Fed with more centralized power, an emboldened Congress imposed an explicit macroeconomic mandate on the Fed, and required far more transparency and accountability—enduring reforms that continue to shape Congress and Fed interdependence. Similar to previous cycles of blame and reform, hard-nosed partisan politics—not the pursuit of economically optimal change—reshaped the Fed's statutory contract with Congress.

More broadly, we investigate why the Fed's autonomy seems so limited in this period, given historians' claims that the 1951 Accord freed the Fed to make monetary policy independent of political constraints. In fact, under pressure from the Nixon White House to keep interest rates low even as stagflation took root, the Burns Fed failed to marshal and sustain a politically unpopular attack on the distressed economy. It took a severe downturn in the economy—coupled with the Democrats' loss of the White House and Senate in the 1980 elections—to generate sufficient political support for the Fed (under Fed chair Volcker's leadership) to finally tackle inflation in the early 1980s. Volcker's brilliant political radar finally identified cover for his hawkish, inflation-taming policy. Even at the Fed's most celebrated instance of independent policy making, Volcker's operational autonomy was conditional on the strength of the Fed's political support.

The Political Economy of Stagflation

Figure 6.1 shows the onset of stagflation: sharp, roughly tandem increases in unemployment and inflation starting in the early 1970s. Unemployment ebbs slightly by the end of the decade before rising sharply again in the early 1980s. Focusing on inflation trends in figure 6.2, inflation peaks several times in the period after the Accord: the years 1969, 1974, and 1980. Economists disagree about the causes of the decade of stagflation, why it took root, and why it lasted so long. Some point to the impact of faulty economic theory. Romer (2005) argues that both monetary and fiscal policy makers

FIGURE 6.2. Inflation rate, 1951–84. US Bureau of Labor Statistics, n.d.

were prone to adopt misguided economic frameworks in the 1960s with the arrival of the Kennedy and Johnson administrations (and their new appointments to the Fed's Board of Governors). Belief in the Phillips curve early in the 1960s led policy makers to assert that increases in inflation were simply the price to be paid for securing a permanently lower level of unemployment.[5]

By the 1970s, Friedman (1968) had debunked the notion of a permanent trade-off between inflation and unemployment. Instead, policy makers assumed that there was a natural rate of unemployment below which expansionary monetary policy would fuel inflation. Measuring the natural rate has always been particularly tricky (Staiger, Stock, and Watson 1997), and policy makers in this period likely underestimated it (Meltzer 2005), given that studies now show that the natural rate was steadily increasingly throughout the period (Orphanides and Williams 2002). Incorrectly thinking that unemployment had further to fall before it would stoke inflation (Romer and Romer 2004), central bankers kept monetary policy too accommodative for too long. Moreover, when inflation was slow to ebb even as unemployment rose, Burns argued early in his term that monetary policy was ill suited in this context for controlling inflation (Wells 1994, chapter 4; De Long 1997). Instead, Burns championed wage and price controls during the Nixon administration to remedy rising inflation directly. Such unconventional, often-misguided economic theorizing, Romer and Romer (2004, 140) contend, "made policymakers unwilling to tolerate even modest unemployment." As a result, the Fed's expansionary monetary policy in the 1970s fueled inflation that was only rarely checked.

In contrast, several economic historians offer a political explanation for the Fed's struggle to control inflation over the course of the 1960s and 1970s.[6] Meltzer, for example, recognizes that policy makers adopted misguided economic theory in this period. And he notes the inflationary impact of mid-1970s' oil price shocks that also induced a steep recession from 1973 through 1975. The slowdown led the Fed to loosen monetary policy, fueling even more inflation. Still, Meltzer places stronger weight on central bankers' political incentives to coordinate monetary policy with fiscal policy makers. Some of the coordination had been regularized in the Fed's "even keel" policy in the 1960s—an arrangement that led the Fed to aid Treasury bond sales by supplying reserves to maintain the Treasury's intended interest rates (Meltzer 2005, 153). The advent of government bond auctions in the 1970s obviated the need for the Fed to directly support Treasury debt.

Starting in 1961, policy coordination was further institutionalized with a regular meeting of the chair of the Federal Reserve Board, Treasury secretary, budget director, and chair of the Council of Economic Advisers, sometimes joined by the president (Kettl 1986, chapter 4). The *New York Times* dubbed this "Quadriad," the "first semi-formal machinery ever devised for bringing the Federal Reserve into direct contact with the Chief of State."[7] According to White House meeting logs, the Quadriad (including Martin as Fed chair) met with the president on average six times per year in the 1960s, or roughly double the degree of interaction between Martin and Dwight D. Eisenhower in the 1950s (Kettl 1986, 94). Granted, counts of meetings are hard to interpret. We know, for instance, that

Martin at times resisted pressure from the White House to keep rates low, even after being famously summoned to Lyndon B. Johnson's ranch in December 1965 and given LBJ's famous "treatment" (Bremner 2004, 209). Despite pressure from the Johnson administration to continue easing, Martin's Fed tightened twice, first in 1966 and then in 1969. Both rounds of tightening generated criticism from the Hill for driving interest rates too high (Kettl 1986, 109).

Viewed more broadly, the expansionary fiscal policy of the Great Society (and later, an expensive war in Southeast Asia) re-created age-old pressure for the Fed to help finance growing deficits—incentives that once again subordinated monetary policy and undermined the Fed's post-1951 independence. Burton A. Abrams (2006), relying on Nixon's tapes of Oval Office conversations, documents that Nixon pressured Burns to keep policy easy beginning late in 1971 and lasting through spring 1972; Nixon clearly worried that Burns might lead the Fed to tighten the money supply, risking Nixon's 1972 reelection. Moreover, using FOMC transcripts from the 1970s to document Fed officials' concerns about political pressure on FOMC decision making, Charles L. Weise (2012) demonstrates that such pressures—along with economic conditions—led to an overly easy monetary stance with rare exception during the decade. Despite Burns's academic, economic brilliance, the Fed under his leadership proved unable to sustain an attack on inflation and succumbed to political pressure to ease.

After leaving office, Burns (1979) termed this dilemma "the anguish of central banking." Burns himself partially blamed political pressure for the Fed's inability to sufficiently tighten policy. The central bank, Burns observed, "would be frustrating the will of Congress to which it was responsible—a Congress that was intent on providing additional services to the electorate and on assuring that jobs and incomes were maintained." As Meltzer (2005) put it, central bankers lacked political support from the president and Congress for taking steps that would have imposed job losses as the price for breaking inflation. In sum, long after the adoption of the Employment Act of 1946, reducing unemployment remained the overriding economic goal of Democratic majorities in Congress. Lawmakers always remembered the Keynesian lesson of the Great Depression: government has an obligation to use its powers to maximize employment for its citizens. Consistent with this political imperative, successive Fed chairs allowed inflation to take root, ultimately raising unemployment by the end of the 1970s. Flawed economic theory mixed with Keynesian pressure from the administration and Congress no doubt undermined the economy in the 1970s.

Humphrey-Hawkins and the Dual Mandate

The 1974 recession provoked sharp attacks on the Fed from Capitol Hill. A Democratic Congress did little to address the economic downturn, passing few of President Gerald Ford's "Whip Inflation Now" proposals.[8] Instead, the burden of fighting the recession fell on the Fed, whose litany of policy mistakes made it an easy scapegoat for lawmakers seeking to distance themselves from measures that would impose hardship on voters back home. Early in 1975, the Fed tightened the money supply, bringing steep increases in interest rates and leading Burns's critics to deem him the "architect of the worst recession in 40 years" (*Business Week*, April 21, 1975, cited in Kettl 1986, 134). Concurrent increases in unemployment in 1975—reaching its highest level since the Accord 's adoption—emboldened lawmakers to intervene (figure 6.3).

The 1976 elections returned Democratic majorities to the House and Senate, and put a Democrat, President Carter, in the White House. With the economy still suffering from high inflation and unemployment, the return of unified Democratic control increased the prospects for major changes to the Federal Reserve Act. Over the course of the Ninety-Fifth Congress (1977–78), the House and Senate adopted amendments to the act that provided Congress with several, more overt avenues of influence over monetary policy.

Rather than grant the Fed more power and responsibility, Congress rewrote the law to make the Fed more accountable to Congress for its policy choices. Congress gave the Fed an explicit "dual mandate" to "promote effectively the goals of maximum employment, stable prices, and moderate long-term interest rates," and imposed

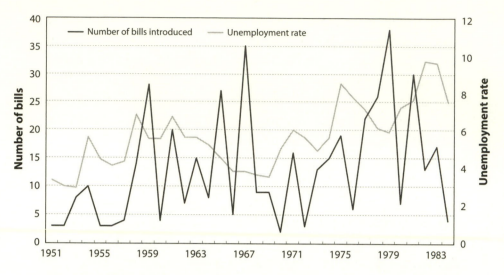

FIGURE 6.3. Legislative attention to the Fed, 1951–84. Bills determined from Adler and Wilkerson n.d. For details on coding, see chapter 2.

new requirements for greater transparency.[9] These changes in the wake of the 1970s' stagflation institutionalized a new relationship between Congress and the Fed. We begin by examining the 1977 Federal Reserve Act Amendments and 1978 Humphrey-Hawkins Full Employment Act that gave the Fed its first explicit, statutory mandate.

Fighting inflation and bolstering employment were not explicit priorities in the original Federal Reserve Act.[10] In the wake of the Panic of 1907, Congress and bankers cared primarily about financial stability along with revamping the nation's system of credit. Specifically, the original act was designed to "provide for the establishment of the Federal Reserve banks, to furnish an elastic currency, to afford means of rediscounting commercial paper, to establish a more effective supervision of banking in the United States, and for other purposes."[11] Congressional goals for the Fed were closely attuned to the macroprudential challenges of the period: preventing future banking panics and rebuilding a functional credit system for the country. As Fed chair Eccles testified to Congress some two decades later, the Fed's mandate was simply to "supply the credit needs of commerce, agriculture, and industry."[12]

Despite early efforts by lawmakers to revamp the Fed's mandate, congressional goals for the Fed remained essentially unchanged—even with major changes to the act in 1933 and 1935. In both instances in the 1930s, with the country mired in a deflationary depression, Congress remained focused on rebuilding the financial system as a means to get Americans back to work. Given the prevailing economic context, limited congressional attention to price stability is not surprising; high inflation was rare at the time. Even when lawmakers advocated requiring the Fed to stabilize price levels, the idea was considered in the context of raising rather than lowering them. Eccles made plain during congressional hearings in winter 1935 that the Fed's mandate should be jobs not inflation. "I don't say that prices are not part of the consideration," Eccles argued in a House Banking Committee hearing. "I think that every effort should be made to maintain stable prices," he added, "but stable prices should not be the sole and paramount objective, so that the Board would be directed to maintain stable prices and not to consider total production and employment at all."[13] Eccles continued to prioritize employment and production before the onset of World War II, consistent with congressional objectives.

As we explored in chapter 5, Congress's more singular concerns about growth drove the formulation of the 1946 Employment Act. Congress was primarily concerned with converting a wartime economy to a peacetime footing. Because the key economic challenge was employment not inflation, Congress directed the federal government in 1946 to pursue economic policies that would maximize job creation and—at the insistence of mostly GOP critics—bolster the purchasing power of the dollar. Granted, the 1946 act did not specifically direct the Federal Reserve to comply with these macroeconomic goals. But Congress considered the Federal Reserve an integral part of economic policy making within the government in the aftermath of World War II, and expected the Fed to support the goals of the 1946 act as the country transitioned to a peacetime economy. To be sure, fighting inflation became a key concern of Fed officials and pivotal lawmakers by the end of the 1940s, when the Treasury and Fed disagreed about ending the inflationary, wartime interest rate peg. Yet the longer history of the Federal Reserve's mandate suggests economic and employment growth, more than inflation, shaped Congress's expectations about monetary policy over the Fed's first half century.

By the 1960s, Federal Reserve officials were expressing concern about the difficulty of securing a dual mandate that would include the pursuit of both price stability and unemployment. As the president of the New York Fed, Sproul summed up the Fed's dilemma in 1964, "Certainly the Federal Reserve System must have its own objectives in the field of monetary policy and realize its capacities and limitations, but I do not believe that it is possible in the light of the Employment Act, and what it reflects of national purpose, for the central bank to be completely free" (Ritter 1980, 84). Sproul's argument that the Fed could ever have been "completely free"—but for the Employment Act—is curious. His broader point, though, highlights the import of the Fed's employment mandate: it reflected the "national purpose" as legislated by Congress over the course of the twentieth century.

Viewing the dual mandate in historical context changes the received wisdom about Congress's 1977 legislative approach. First, the dual mandate was not created *de novo* in 1977. Congress simply made explicit the Fed's operational mandate that had been suggested in the 1946 Employment Act. Second, the Fed's dual mandate is especially notable because most national legislatures give their central banks a single (or priority) price stability mandate (Bank of International Settlements 2009). But the United States' brief history of the dual mandate indicates that Congress's inclusion of an employment dimension was not especially controversial in the 1970s. Instead, conflict over the dual mandate was focused on whether and how to balance employment and price stability in revamping Congress's somewhat-competing objectives for the Fed.

The language of the dual mandate adopted in 1977 technically directs the Fed to pursue *three* goals: "maximum employment, stable prices, and moderate long-term interest rates."[14] In 1977, the mandate was included in the Federal Reserve Act Amendments of 1977; the following year, Congress wrote more specific details about the mandate into the 1978 Full Employment and Balanced Growth Act (commonly known as the Humphrey-Hawkins Act, after its Democratic sponsors Senator Humphrey and Representative Augustus Hawkins of California). Formalizing the dual mandate language in 1977 seems not to have sparked conflict: *New York Times* and *Washington Post* coverage of the 1977 amendments instead focused on the mechanism for selecting the Board of Governors' chair and vice chair, the chair's testimony before Congress, and GAO audits of the Fed—issues we discuss below. But little debate occurred, and no floor votes were cast specifically on the dual mandate in 1977. The House adopted the amendments 395–3, and the Senate adopted them by voice.

In contrast, the adoption of Humphrey-Hawkins sparked controversy. The 1978 negotiations came on the heels of failed legislative efforts in 1975 and 1976. The original 1975 legislative proposal had been targeted to reduce persistently high levels of unemployment, particularly among African Americans. The 1975 bill set a single employment goal for the federal government and established the government as the employer of last resort: Americans were granted the "right to a job" (Pine 1977). The bill called for the government to tailor job programs, tax proposals, and monetary policy to achieve the unemployment target, and expressly forbade the government from trading the pursuit of full employment for price stability (Cowan 1977). The bill was a nonstarter for a Republican White House, and the Democrats folded.

In summer 1977, congressional Democrats (mainly liberals and the sixteen-member Congressional Black Caucus) entered talks with the Carter White House over a new employment bill. The Carter White House, however, proved equally reluctant to support a full employment act. To make progress on the measure, Democrats in late 1977 granted several concessions to the White House. First, "reasonable price stability" was added as a government commitment. Second, with unemployment then hovering near 7 percent, the level of full employment was set at 3 percent for adults, and 4 percent overall (to capture higher jobless rates for teens). Third, the administration was given five versus four years to hit its employment targets. Fourth, the president was allowed to modify the employment goal if the pursuit of the goal was driving up inflation (Cowan 1977). Importantly, unlike the 1946 employment measure, the proposal explicitly directed the Federal Reserve to commit to the same goals as the administration and Congress (Pine 1977).

Many supporters of a robust employment bill argued that the compromises reduced the bill to "a nullity." They charged that the new proposal only required the president to report their administration's plans for achieving the employment goal, allowed the next president to revise that goal, and gave the White House flexibility to decide how much fiscal stimulus the economy could absorb without sparking too much inflation (Cowan 1977). Defenders of the compromise justified the concessions as inevitable and necessary: "We knew we needed the President's support to get the measure passed" (Pine 1977). But in December, Senator Humphrey (1977), who would pass away in the middle of January 1978, defended the compromise in the *Washington Post*—highlighting that the measure for the first time would "require the close coordination of all national economic policies, including the policies of the Federal Reserve System, directed toward achieving the goals established as national policy." The measure, Humphrey contended, would "recognize, in law, that unemployment and inflation feed upon each other and that, as a result, methods must be used to reach our goals that reinforce their achievement and do not sacrifice progress on one in the name of achieving the other."

Even though critics decried the measure as toothless, House floor consideration of it in March 1978 proved contentious. Opponents, mostly Republicans, argued that the measure was inflationary: they noted that while the bill included a specific employment target of 4 percent, the measure lacked a specific numerical inflation goal. For "the sake of equity," numerous Republicans tried to amend the measure to quantify a specific inflation goal (Shabecoff 1978). Republican Jim Jeffords of Vermont offered an amendment to require the president within three years to include in the annual Economic Report of the President a goal of "reasonable price stability"—defining price stability as reduction of inflation to 3 percent within five years of enactment. The amendment failed, 198–223.

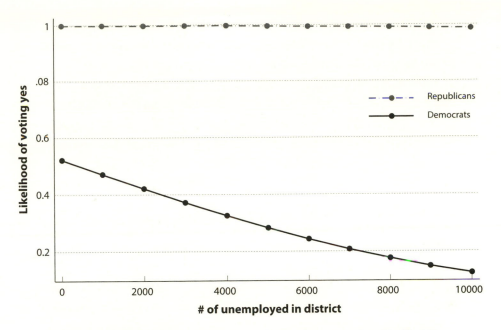

FIGURE 6.4. Likelihood of voting to add price stability mandate to Humphrey-Hawkins bill. Ninety-Fifth Congress, House of Representatives, vote 806, March 9, 1978, accessed August 8, 2016, http://voteview.com/HOUSE95.htm. For details on the model, see text. Predicted support calculated via *prgen* routine in Stata 11.2.

Just 2 of 144 Republicans abandoned their party to oppose the amendment; both were liberal Republicans, from Ohio and Massachusetts.[15] In contrast, Democrats split on the amendment: roughly 20 percent of House Democrats joined Republicans to write a specific inflation target into the bill. Democratic votes on the Jeffords amendment varied directly with the unemployment rate in their district, controlling for the district strength of unions and the finance industry (figure 6.4).[16] Democrats from districts hit hard by the recession voted against the amendment; Democrats from districts with higher employment were more likely to vote in favor.[17] On the failure of the Jeffords amendment, Majority Leader Jim Wright (D-Texas) offered a successful amendment that required the president to include in the annual economic report goals for reasonable though undefined targets for price stability. Several days later, with Humphrey's widow, Senator Muriel Humphrey (recently appointed to fill her deceased husband's seat), present on the House floor, the chamber adopted the Humphrey-Hawkins bill with an uneven dual mandate: the bill specified only an employment target.

Observers expected the Senate to pass the measure quickly; the bill was seen as a "legislative memorial" to the late Senator Humphrey (Russell 1978). Supporters were wrong. Two Senate committees reported versions of the bill: the Human Resources Committee sent the House-passed version of the bill to the Senate floor, and the Banking Committee added an inflation target, requiring a 3 percent inflation target by 1983 that would ratchet down to zero by 1988. On top of the committees' inability to resolve their differences, Senator Orrin Hatch (R-Utah) threatened to filibuster the bill on the Senate floor unless it included a tough inflation target. Despite a Democratic Caucus of sixty-one senators, Humphrey-Hawkins advocates' stalled four votes shy of the sixty required to end debate on the bill (Jarrett 1978). Conservative southern Democrats joined Republicans in refusing to commit to cloture unless the measure included an inflation target. Senate majority leader Robert Byrd (D–West Virginia) assigned a group of proponents and opponents of the bill the task to negotiate an agreement before the bill would be called up on the Senate floor.[18] The bill that eventually went to the floor adopted the 3 percent inflation target (lowering to zero by 1983), but also included language prioritizing the unemployment goal over the inflation target. Democratic supporters of the bill argued to the bill's advocates that the choice had come down to accepting an inflation target or giving up the bill altogether (Kaiser 1978).

The Senate took up the bill in mid-October. Only the inflation target attracted an amendment. If adopted, the amendment offered by Senators Muriel Humphrey and Edmund Muskie (D-Maine) would have replaced the inflation target with a goal of reducing inflation to 3 percent "at the earliest possible date"—in essence removing the target dates from the bill. In short, Humphrey and Muskie's amendment would neuter the inflation target, leaving only the employment goal. The amendment failed, forty-one to forty-five; almost 90 percent of Republicans voted against the amendment, while two-thirds of Democrats supported it.[19] The split among Senate Democrats reflected both ideology and strategy. Liberal Democrats (who opposed placing limits on government stimulus to fight inflation) from highly unionized states voted to dilute the inflation target; conservative Democrats (opponents of an employment mandate they saw as inflationary) sought to treat the inflation and unemployment targets equally.[20] Yet some strong supporters of the employment bill also opposed the amendment, fearful that its adoption would spur conservative Republicans to filibuster the bill (Schantz and Schmidt 1979). With the amendment defeated, the Senate moved to adopt the bill; most Democrats and just over half the Republicans supported final passage.

From today's perspective, the dual mandate seems anomalous. Most central banks worldwide have a single goal of price stability. And those with more than a single mandate, such as the European Central Bank, are often directed to prioritize stable prices over employment, financial stability, or other goals.[21] Viewed in its historical context, however, the Federal Reserve's dual mandate reflects a half century of congressional concern about the Fed's role in sustaining full employment. Given the benign inflationary history since founding the Federal Reserve and the employment debacle of the Great Depression, Congress was always unlikely to have instructed the Fed to care equally about fighting inflation and sustaining employment before the onset of inflation in the 1970s. To be sure, compromises in writing the 1946 Employment Act led to the law's instructions that the government pursue maximum employment, production, and purchasing power. But the appearance of stagflation in the 1970s made the trade-off between growth and inflation more palpable to politicians.

Given the mandate's roots in the Employment Act, it seems inevitable that in 1977, Congress would direct the Fed to devise policies to maximize employment. In contrast, supporters of prioritizing inflation—a minority of both chambers at the time—exploited congressional rules to advance the inflation side of the dual mandate, particularly given that Democrats held both Congress and the White House at the time. Only by holding the employment side hostage could Republicans and conservative lawmakers in 1978 write both

sides of the mandate into law. With the majority party divided ideologically in this period, both parties' preferences shaped Congress's
priorities for the Fed.

Making the Fed More Accountable

Efforts to require greater monetary transparency began with tentative
congressional steps in 1975. With Republican president Ford in the
White House, Democratic lawmakers Representative Henry Reuss
(D-Wisconsin) and Representative Thomas Rees (D-California)
found little support for writing new requirements into the law. Instead, they advanced a concurrent (nonbinding) resolution that
declared Congress's view of the policies the Fed should pursue.[22]
H. Con. Res. 133, as it was known, declared that it was the "sense
of Congress" that the Federal Reserve should pursue policies in the
first half of 1975 that would secure lower long-term interest rates, and
would "promote the goals of maximum employment, stable prices
and moderate long-term rates." The resolution directed the Fed to
lower interest rates and report to Congress quarterly on the Fed's
progress. As a "concurrent resolution," the measure lacked the force
of law: it would not be presented to the president for his signature,
and the Fed would not be legally bound to comply with Congress's
call for lower interest rates.[23]

The final House vote on the House-Senate conference report affords
a glimpse of congressional divisions over monetary policy. Majorities
of both parties favored adoption: 96 percent of Democrats joined
73 percent of Republicans voting in favor. Although the nonbinding
measure lacked teeth—a GOP lawmaker called it "a stump speech by
the Congress—no more, no less"—a quarter of the GOP conference
still voted against the resolution.[24] Lawmakers' partisanship and economic dislocation back home shaped their votes.[25] As shown in the
simulations in figure 6.5, Democrats—regardless of the job situation
in their district—were predisposed to support Reuss's resolution; the
likelihood of Democrats voting yes varied from roughly 80 percent to
just under 100 percent. Republican proclivity for directing the Fed to
lower rates, though, varied with the impact of the economic downturn

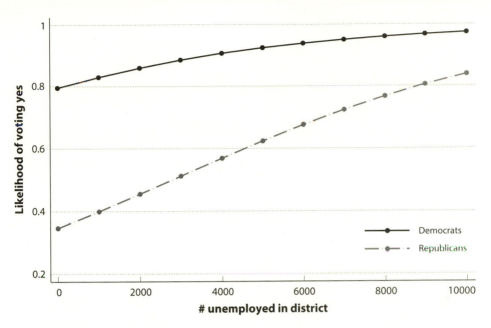

FIGURE 6.5. Likelihood of voting in support of greater Fed transparency. Ninety-Fourth Congress, House of Representatives, vote 24, March 4, 1975, accessed August 8, 2016, http://voteview.com/HOUSE94.htm. For details on the model, see text. Predicted support calculated via *prgen* routine in Stata 11.2.

at home. In economically robust districts, Republicans were unlikely to vote for the measure; as district unemployment increased, the likelihood of a yes vote increased steadily as well. Still, even at the highest observed levels of job dislocation, Democrats were still more likely support the measure than were Republicans.

Political scientist John Woolley (1984, 147) calls Congress's effort in 1975 "toothless," "compromised," and "flawed." Even quarterly testimony before Congress, Woolley argues, was nothing more than "an opportunity for fruitful exchange." Moreover, as Donald Kettl (1986, 146–47) reports, a confidential, internal Fed staff memo in April 1975 laid out a strategy for the FOMC to guide the Fed through its first congressional hearing under H. Con. Res. 133. The strategy was to obfuscate by supplying Congress with multiple monetary targets (to make it more likely that the Fed would hit one of them), a wide range for each monetary target (making them easier to reach), and a "roll the base" tactic in which the Fed would provide new annual targets at each quarterly congressional testimony to diminish lawmakers' ability to hold the Fed accountable for previously announced targets. Such tactics surely complicated lawmakers' efforts to use H. Con. Res. 133 to hold the Fed accountable for its policy performance.

But adoption of the sense of Congress resolution mattered in several ways. First, the resolution laid the groundwork for subsequent legislative efforts in that Congress to enact binding changes to the Federal Reserve Act. In spring 1976, the House passed a much more comprehensive set of proposed changes to the act, including new statutory provisions requiring regular congressional testimony by the Fed chair, authorizing the GAO to conduct an audit of FOMC monetary policy making, and aligning the terms of presidents and Fed chairs. Democrats rallied to vote nearly lockstep for the bill, with roughly 60 percent of the Republican conference supporting the measure. Although the Senate ignored the bill, the broader language became the basis for legislative efforts in the next Congress once the 1976 elections returned control of both Congress and the White House into Democratic hands.

Second, Burns recognized the danger of failing to pay heed in some way to Congress's call for greater transparency. Burns warned his FOMC colleagues in summer 1977 that the money supply targets to be announced at the chair's upcoming semiannual testimony before the banking panels could be politically problematic for the Fed:

> We have very troublesome legislation in the Congress, and what we do and the way our testimony goes on the 29th, when these targets will be announced, may have some effect on the course of the legislation in the Congress. I think to the extent that there is a political factor here, it's really legislative—legislation involving or affecting the Federal Reserve.[26]

Even if H. Con. Res. 133 was purely advisory and strongly opposed by Burns, Fed officials understood the potential for tougher sanctions from Congress in response to the Fed's failure to stem stagflation. As we explore below, with Burns no longer able to rely on a Republican White House to support the Fed in its confrontations with Congress, Burns understood that Congress's nonbinding call for greater accountability would likely soon gain teeth.

After the expiration of H. Con. Res. 133 at the end of the Ninety-Fourth Congress in 1976, Democrats proposed making permanent the requirement that the Federal Reserve chair testify regularly before Congress. Aiming to strengthen the Fed's accountability to Congress, Reuss advocated additional changes to the Federal Reserve Act to make the Fed chair more responsive to the president and Congress. One set of proposals targeted the appointment process. The terms of the president and Fed chair and vice chair would be synchronized: one year into a president's term, the president would be assured the opportunity to appoint a new Fed chair. For the first time, the bill also required Senate confirmation of the Board of Governors chair and reduced the role of bankers in selecting the boards of directors for the district reserve banks. Another set of proposals imposed greater transparency on the Fed. During semiannual testimony before each of the chamber's banking panels, the Fed would be required to forecast interest rates, money supply growth, and the composition of the Fed's balance sheet—moving beyond the 1975 requirement that the Fed provide estimates of money supply growth. As examined later in the chapter, the bill also required an audit of the Federal Reserve by the GAO.

Renewing the requirement for regular appearances of the Fed chair before Congress's banking panels elicited objections from the Fed. Burns did not object to placing the semiannual testimony requirement into statute. He drew the line, however, at requiring the Fed chair to include the FOMC's forecast for future levels of interest rates in the semiannual testimony. Burns argued in House hearings in July 1977 before the House Committee on Banking, Finance, and Urban Affairs that "public reports each quarter on the interest rate expectations of the Board of the FOMC could rock financial markets."[27] Given that expectations could change or be mistaken, Burns warned lawmakers about market reactions to incorrect information: "The capacity for mischief inherent in the interest rate provision is so apparent that I find its inclusion in the bill inexplicable." Semiannual testimony was written into statute, absent the interest rate provision that was dropped before the House banking panel reported the bill to the floor.[28]

Burns's opposition to aligning the terms of the president and Fed chair did not break House support for the change. In September 1977, the House nearly unanimously adopted the bill to reform the Federal Reserve Act, including the new requirement that presidents appoint a Fed chair during the second year of a president's term. Under the House version, the change in appointment practices would have been delayed until 1982—kicking in only after the presidential election of 1980. The bill also made minor changes to the boards of directors of the reserve banks, banning discrimination in the selection of directors, and expanding the range of economic interests embraced in the selection of Class B (nonbanker) and Class C (so-called public) directors of each reserve bank.

In November 1977, Reuss's move to align presidential and Fed chair terms failed in the Senate.[29] Proponents of the provision in the House had asserted that the change would promote coordination of monetary and fiscal policies—as well as continuity of policy through election seasons. In the Senate, no one defended the provision during the chamber's quick consideration of the bill. Senator John Tower (R-Texas)—speaking for the absent ranking member on the Senate banking panel, Senator Edward Brooke (R-Massachusetts)—objected on the grounds that giving the president "his own man" as chair of the Fed would undermine Fed independence. As Tower contended, "I still think the drive of many of us to maintain the independence of the Fed is strong enough that we do not feel this would be a wise move. We feel the present system has worked successfully."[30] Tower, on behalf of Senator Brooke, offered an amendment to strike the change to the appointment process, leaving in place the requirement for Senate confirmation of future Fed chairs.

Notably, the Senate banking panel chair, William Proxmire (D-Wisconsin), accepted the Tower-Brooke amendment with no recorded vote. But Proxmire and the GOP senators offered different reasons for opposing the alignment of terms. Proxmire argued that the Reuss provision would have given future presidents too much potential influence over future Fed chairs:

> I have long favored the independence of the Federal Reserve Board from the executive branch. It is a creature of the Congress. It is clearly, under the Constitution, our creature. We can abolish it. We can modify it. It is our responsibility. We have the money power, and we delegate it to the Federal Reserve Board. I have opposed making the term of the chairman coterminus [*sic*] for a long time because I felt this would make the Reserve subject to the power of the President directly and explicitly.[31]

As a Democrat, Proxmire clearly viewed the problem of accountability through a different prism than his GOP colleagues. Republicans saw the proposal as a move that would have rebalanced the trade-off between accountability and independence; GOP senators preferred to keep the balance unchanged. A Fed chair pushing to tighten—in face of Democratic efforts to push for more growth (employment)—surely appealed to traditional hard-money Republicans. Particularly with a Democrat in the White House, the prospect of making future Fed chairs more responsive to the president likely had little appeal to the GOP. In contrast, Proxmire's concern was unrelated to the balance between accountability and independence. More at issue was the existential question, Accountability to whom? For Proxmire, aligning the Fed more closely with the president would weaken the Fed's accountability to Congress. As Proxmire reminded his colleagues, the Constitution gave Congress the "money power": the power to coin money and regulate its value. With both parties opposed, the Senate struck the key provision and passed the rest of Reuss's bill. Not willing to risk the rest of the reforms, Reuss moved for the House to adopt the revised version of the bill, placing into statute new requirements for transparency, accountability, and the newly explicit dual mandate for the Fed.[32]

The Original Audit the Fed

In 2009, House Republicans reacted to the most recent financial crisis by calling for new government powers to audit the Fed. As we explored in chapter 2, Representative Paul was the most vocal proponent of the idea, leading the House several times in the wake of the crisis to vote to allow the GAO to audit the FOMC's deliberations and decisions.[33] Ironically, that movement had its roots in Democrats' efforts in the 1970s to impose greater transparency on the Federal Reserve—the original Audit the Fed movement. In fact, a compromise in 1977 that exempted monetary policy from the eyes of GAO auditors ultimately gave rise to Paul's later campaign to remove the exemption.

Representative Patman's campaign in 1973, and Reuss's and Proxmire's proposal in 1975, would have allowed the GAO to audit all aspects of the FOMC and Board of Governors' activities, including monetary policy decisions and FOMC open market operations. The Burns Fed quickly grasped the political momentum behind Patman's and others' efforts; the *New York Times*, for instance, endorsed Patman's proposal in 1973. In the wake of the recession that lawmakers (naturally) blamed on the Fed, Reuss's 1975 proposal gathered considerable steam. And in what would reappear years later as a nationwide support network for a different Fed chair under attack, the Burns Fed orchestrated an aggressive lobbying campaign against each of these legislative efforts, calling on reserve bank directors, friendly members of Congress, past Treasury secretaries, and former Board members to rally to the Fed's defense (Kettl 1986, 156).[34] Kettl unearthed details of the Burns Fed's campaign in Burns's papers; the "Outline of Contacts and Projects on GAO Audit Issue" in 1973, for instance, detailed the Fed press office's efforts to place "horror stories" about potential audits in the *Wall Street Journal, Washington Post*, and other prominent news and business papers.

Burns's efforts paid off. In 1973, 1975, and 1976, sympathetic House members succeeded in weakening the audit bill to keep auditors out of FOMC meetings, and the Senate failed to act each time. In 1977, with a Democratic Congress and White House willing to consider reform of the Fed, Reuss and Proxmire succeeded in passing the audit bill through Congress. Once again, the Fed's supporters in the House weakened the bill, precluding GAO review of FOMC open market and district reserve bank discount window operations. Now a safe vote allowing lawmakers to cast a cost-free vote in favor of transparency, nearly every Democrat voted in favor, joined by roughly 80 percent of their GOP colleagues. The two-dozen Republican opponents were markedly more conservative than the supporters, and they drew the line at supporting a bill originally intended to challenge the Fed's decision-making autonomy.[35] As the ranking member on the House Ways and Means Committee, Barber Conable (R-New York) explained his vote: "I don't see why one should support a bill simply because it does only a little harm" (Farnsworth 1977, D5). With the GAO banned from auditing monetary policy decisions, the limited audit has survived nearly four decades since its creation in the wake of the Fed's 1970s' failures.

The Politics of Beating Inflation

Burns delivered a valedictory "Anguish of Central Banking" speech in September 1979, declaring that the Federal Reserve was captive to "philosophic and political currents" that had brought on secular inflation (Burns 1979, 15). "It is illusory," Burns (1979, 21) warned, "to expect central banks to put an end to the inflation that now afflicts the industrial democracies." And yet Volcker, appointed Fed chair by President Carter just one month before Burns's lecture, was already laying the groundwork to launch a sustained fight against inflation.

At Volcker's first FOMC meeting in October, annualized inflation had reached 7 percent, with an unemployment rate of 6 percent (figure 6.1). From the October 1979 meeting until October 1982, the Volcker Fed conducted a concerted attack on inflation by tightening the money supply, trying a new approach by targeting the level of bank reserves rather than the Federal funds rate (the Fed's customary target). When Volcker ended the Fed's anti-inflation program in fall 1982, inflation was trending downward—having peaked in February 1980 at over 14 percent. By the end of 1982, inflation would fall below 4 percent. The cost of Volcker's success was the country's worst recession since the Great Depression. The monthly unemployment rate peaked at nearly 11 percent when the Fed finally began to ease policy.[36] By the November elections in 1984, the economy was booming; it was "morning again in America."[37]

Why did Volcker succeed when Burns had failed? We entertain three hypotheses. First, conventional accounts credit the effects of the 1951 Accord: the framers of the Accord secured the Fed's independence from the Treasury precisely for the purpose of securing price stability (Conti-Brown 2016). Combine Volcker's ability to manage dissent within the FOMC and his willingness to raise interest rates sharply even in face of intense political opposition from Capitol Hill, and the result was a course of monetary policy that slayed inflation after a decade of previous failures under Burns.[38] Volcker finally achieved what the Accord allegedly made possible: an independent Fed that could tighten credit policy, thereby prioritizing stable prices, at the cost of a deeply unpopular recession. The received wisdom begs two questions. First, why would the Accord— that cemented the Fed's independence from Treasury—also free the Fed from congressional and therefore political influence? Second, why wasn't Burns able to exploit the Fed's "independence" after the Accord to tame inflation with tighter policy?

A second hypothesis emphasizes the limitations of economic theory during Burns's tenure at the head of the Fed (Romer 2005). Improvements in economic theory over the course of the 1970s might have ultimately aided Volcker in his drive to finally control inflation (Romer and Romer 2002). Volcker's monetarist policy solution in October 1979 did indeed initially change the course of policy by focusing on the amount of money in the system rather than fluctuations in the federal funds rate. So it is certainly possible that economic learning—perhaps in addition to Volcker's assertion of central bank independence—drove the Fed's improved performance by the end of Volcker's first term as head of the Fed. Still, the FOMC's abandonment of monetarist policy tools soon thereafter raises doubts about whether we can attribute the difference in Burns's and Volcker's records to their choice of policy tools.

We favor a third hypothesis. Given Burns's claim that political currents derailed the Fed from pursuing an optimal monetary policy, an alternative explanation for Volcker's success points to changes in the economic and political context during his two terms leading the Fed. Many argue that the dire state of the economy had reached crisis proportions, lowering politicians' resistance to a tough and sustained anti-inflation program. In other words, rather than attributing the Fed's success to Volcker's assertion of policy independence following the Accord, we contend that the Volcker Fed remained deeply dependent on strong support from within the political system to embark on its anti-inflation policy. With the risks of challenge from Congress and the White House subdued in light of the dire nature of the economic crisis, Volcker could persuade the FOMC to pursue a hawkish policy path even at the cost of inducing a recession. Once signals of political support weakened with the onset of a deep recession late in 1982, Volcker eased policy to help stimulate the economy.

We find moderate evidence for the third hypothesis. Certainly the state of the economy had markedly worsened since its recovery after the oil price shocks of 1974 and the 1973–75 recession. When Carter moved short-lived Fed chair William Miller to the Treasury Department and appointed Volcker in August 1979, the prime lending and federal funds rates had returned to their record heights of the mid-1970s, having doubled over the three previous years (figure 6.6). In that same period, inflation had nearly tripled (figure 6.1). Volcker took the reins at a particularly opportune time for undertaking a tough anti-inflation program. And given that Carter had just appointed Miller as his new Treasury secretary, Volcker might even have found a sympathetic ear in the administration for the challenges that the Fed faced. With stagflation getting worse, the economic context fueled the urgency of combating inflation. Put simply, "this time was different" (Samuelson 2008, 112).

Both inside and outside the FOMC, Volcker expressed confidence that a broader political agreement favored tough action in fall 1979. We use the transcripts from FOMC meetings in this period to establish participants' views about the degree of political support for an aggressive program against inflation. Importantly, many members of the FOMC understood that its meetings in this period were tape-recorded. But according to Ellen E. Meade and David Stasavage (2008) and others, most members of the FOMC at this time believed that the tapes were recorded over after they were used to prepare

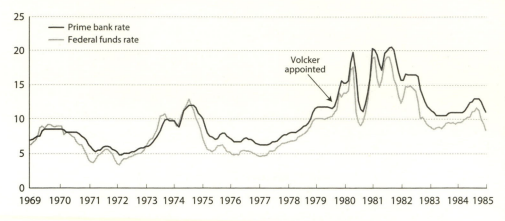

FIGURE 6.6. Interest rates, 1969–84. Federal Reserve Bank of St. Louis 2015a, 2015b.

meeting minutes. In other words, "meeting participants did not know that their deliberations would be made public" (Meade and Stasavage 2008, 697).[39] The assumption of privacy helps to account for what appear to be candid views from Volcker and his colleagues about the political implications of their policy choices.[40]

Chairing his first meeting of the FOMC, Volcker stressed that a political consensus would sustain the Fed through a tough round of tightening: "I have also told you that [the administration] is ready for a strong program. I think it's clear that the decision is one that is within our province and we have to make it today. We need a program that's as convincing as we can make it."[41] Whereas Burns claimed soon after leaving the Fed that the political current made sustained Fed action against inflation impossible, Volcker argued that political winds had shifted sufficiently to empower the Fed to act. Five months later, Volcker reiterated that the political environment continued to support a tough plan to break inflation:

> The worst thing we could do is to indicate some backing off at this point when we have an announced anti-inflation program. We have political support and understanding for what we have been doing. People don't expect it to be too easy. There is an understanding that a lot of burden has been placed on credit policy, and there's a willingness to be supportive for the moment in that connection.[42]

Remarkably, Volcker's appeals continued even as unemployment and interest rates continued to rise during the Fed's first two years of aggressive action to tighten the money supply.

When the FOMC met in July 1981, J. Roger Guffey (in his fifth year as president of the Federal Reserve Bank of Kansas City) summed up the Fed's political challenge:

> Historically, the Federal Reserve has always come up to the hitching post and then backed off simply because the Administration and the Congress have thrown bricks at us or have not been supportive of a policy of restraint. Through the course of recent history at least, we've backed off and we've made a mistake each time. I think we have an opportunity this time to carry forward what we should have done before because for the first time ever we do have, for whatever length of time, the support of the Administration at least. So, we ought to take advantage of that opportunity.[43]

Such a view dilutes the robustness of Fed "independence." In theory, a truly independent central bank would tack against the wind: central bankers would vote to tighten monetary policy when the risk of inflation proved too costly for a growing economy. But looking backward, Guffey questioned whether the Fed had "historically" been able to sustain tough policy choices in the face of political critics. Even more striking, Guffey did not then call for the Fed to stiffen its backbone and go against the grain; he suggested the FOMC capitalize on changing political winds that generated cover to tighten policy. We have no doubt that Volcker's political acumen—and independent mindedness—contributed to the Fed's resolve. Yet the FOMC's clear reliance on outside political support drives home the limited capacity of the institution for true independent action.

Notably, members of the FOMC did not take public support for granted. Policy makers disagreed about the depth of political support and whether it might wane if the economy failed to improve. Lawrence Roos, president of the St. Louis Fed, for instance, warned in October 1981—two years into the monetarist program targeting bank reserves—that the Fed's reputation would depend on the institution's ability to turn the economy around. "It seems to me," Roos noted at the October 6, 1981, FOMC meeting, "that we have to think of our vulnerability from a public opinion point of view if the economy remains soft, as it probably will, to the end of the year."[44]

As public temperatures rose, Volcker persevered within the FOMC with a tight monetary stance. In October 1981, he responded to his colleagues who urged easier monetary policy, arguing that looser policy would be premature:

> Let me tell you just from a public relations standpoint that there is great restiveness and anger, as I said before, growing out there. That would be relieved, obviously, by some decline in interest rates. But in some way the worst thing that could happen to us is to have a great sense of relief and not policy—and then have them racing up again. I think the public patience for climbing up the hill very rapidly again may be extremely limited.[45]

Volcker recognized that the public would give the Fed only one chance to fix the economy. The public's patience might be wearing thin, Volcker acknowledged. But he also maintained that the public was unlikely to swallow tough medicine if the Fed relaxed its efforts and the economy worsened. Senior White House staff and several Reagan top appointees began to pressure the Fed to start easing early in 1982 (Meltzer 2009, chapter 8; Kettl 1986, 180). Volcker, though, continued to push the FOMC to keep policy tight until summer 1982. Support from President Reagan—both privately and in public—no doubt helped to sustain Volcker's persistence, even as Reagan's approval ratings began to sink in the 1982 election year (Samuelson 2008, chapter 4). As Reagan's secretary of state, George Shultz (2002), noted many years later, "Well, to do something difficult, even if you are the independent Federal Reserve, it makes a huge difference if the president is on your side and is strong and understands the problem, and when things get tough he doesn't go the other way and denounce you, but holds in there." Viewed in this vein, Volcker's capacity to sustain a vigorous anti-inflation campaign rested directly on FOMC members' perceptions of support from the president and his administration.

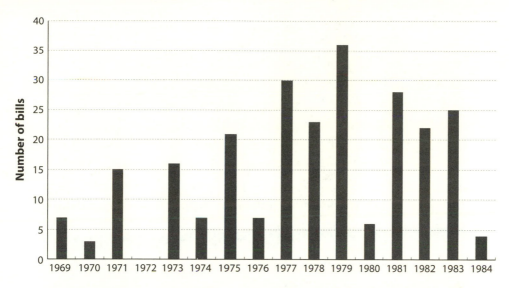

FIGURE 6.7. Total bills targeting the Fed, 1969–84. Bills determined from Adler and Wilkerson n.d. For details on the coding, see chapter 2.

What about Congress? In some ways, lawmakers reacted no differently to the Volcker Fed than they did to the Burns one. With the economy in the tank and oversized Democratic majorities in both chambers, electorally motivated lawmakers continued to blame the Fed. As shown in figure 6.7, with the exception of the anomalous lull in 1980, lawmakers targeted the Fed for reforms at similar levels before and after Volcker became Fed chair. It is conceivable that in 1980, lawmakers' were willing to give the Fed a chance to test out its monetarist policy tools. Given the sharp, albeit temporary, drop that year in the prime bank rate, forbearance might have limited legislative activism during that first full year of the Fed's tightening.

Congress and the president in 1980 enacted the Monetary Control Act—a measure that both deregulated portions of the banking sector and expanded the powers of the Fed. Commercial banks had been leaving the Federal Reserve System over the previous decade—draining the amount of reserves left in the system. To stem the loss of reserves the new law required all depository institutions—regardless of whether they belonged to the Fed—to comply with the reserve requirements established by the Board of Governors.[46] Coupled with provisions that eliminated interest rate ceilings and authorized banks to offer interest on checking deposits, the Monetary Control Act markedly expanded the reach of the Fed over the banking industry. As such, the bill was important economically and politically for the Fed. For monetary policy, expanding the number and type of institutions maintaining reserves at the Fed broadened the Fed's ability to shape the money supply by targeting bank reserves.[47] Politically, the new law reinforced the power of the Fed by removing banks' ability to threaten to leave the reserve system (Woolley 1984, 79). Moreover, by increasing the number and type of depository institutions subject to the Fed's reserve requirements, the new law likely created new political allies for the Fed. The *New York Times* at least predicted as much on the law's enactment: "More Clout for the Fed," it declared (Farnsworth 1980).

Congressional restraint proved temporary. Lawmakers continued to vent their anger toward the Fed when the economy worsened in 1981 and 1982 (figure 6.8). In early 1979, months before Volcker was appointed Fed chair, one Republican lawmaker revived the idea of auditing the Fed. Two years later, well into the interest rate roller coaster of the Fed's tightening period, lawmakers advocated much tougher political solutions for the economic mess. One Democratic member, Representative Byron Dorgan of North Dakota, sponsored a bill to allow three-fifths of both chambers to impeach the Fed chair; Henry Gonzales (D-Texas), head of the House banking panel, introduced a measure to abolish the Federal Reserve System. A year later, Representative John Dingell (D-Michigan) advocated statutory limits on interest rates, while Representative Thomas Corcoran (R-Illinois) proposed returning the Treasury secretary to the Board of Governors.

A majority of congressional attacks on the Fed came from Democrats. Nevertheless, loss of the Senate and White House in the 1980 elections blunted their political and legislative leverage. Republicans continued to oppose tampering with monetary policy—not surprising given the GOP's creditor-based constituency, whose assets were devalued by unbridled inflation. In control of the White House and Senate, Republicans had little incentive to block Volcker's tough

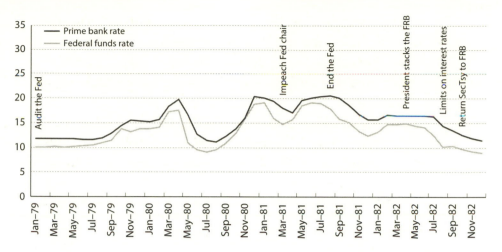

FIGURE 6.8. Interest rates and reform proposals, 1979–82. For interest rate sources, see figure 6.6. Figure also shows selected bills to amend the Federal Reserve Act. For bill source, see figure 6.7.

monetary policies. There were few recorded roll call votes on matters related to the Fed during Reagan's first term, but we can find glimpses of the partisan reaction to Democrats' efforts to intervene in setting monetary policy. One such vote defeated a Democratic amendment that would have directed the president to intervene in the FOMC's policy making process to lower interest rates, falling largely along partisan lines. Republicans voted lockstep to kill the amendment, thus protecting the Fed's autonomy. Three-quarters of the Democrats voted in favor of monetary intervention, protesting ever-rising interest rates that accompanied the Fed's tightening of the money supply. A combination of liberal supporters of Volcker and conservative southern Democrats bolted to vote with all the Republicans.

Divisions within the Democrats limited their capacity to legislate. When House and Senate Democrats tried to write a "sense of the Congress" resolution in 1982 to push the Fed to abandon its monetarist policy tools, they failed to coordinate on a solution. "It was a disaster," one Democratic aide acknowledged.[48] Senate Democrats in particular were divided over whether to support Volcker's approach. Their party leader, Byrd, spoke for those Democrats frustrated by

high interest rates, and eager for Congress or the president to intervene in monetary policy making. But the ranking member of the
Senate Banking Committee—Proxmire, a decidedly liberal member
of the Senate Democratic Caucus—came repeatedly to Volcker's and
the Fed's defense.

When the FOMC first moved to tighten policy in October 1979,
Proxmire immediately both defended the Fed and obliquely ad-
monished Minority Leader Byrd for warning the Fed that Congress
would have little patience if policy proved too tight. On the Senate
floor, Proxmire explained to his colleagues why the Fed had to first
curtail inflation if it sought to rein in interest rates. He emphasized
that any such policy would "cause pain":

> Anybody who says we can do it without more unemployment or
> more recession is just either deceiving you, Mr. President, or is
> deceiving himself, because there is no way you can do it without
> more unemployment, without some business failures you would
> not otherwise have, without serious farm losses and, for millions
> of Americans who will be affected by it, as Paul Volcker has said,
> who has been attacked for it but he is speaking the truth, a lower
> standard of living. . . . This policy has been attacked by many, but
> nobody offers a different course. I wish there were a different
> course. If there were, we should follow it immediately.[49]

Proxmire's defense of the Fed lasted throughout the FOMC's tightening campaign. Even in fall 1982, when the country faced the deep-
est recession since the Great Depression, Proxmire joined with a
handful of fellow Democrats to vote with Republicans to protect the
Fed's autonomy. Divided Democrats both protected the Fed from
legislative action and lent credence to Volcker's claims of strong political support for the Fed's program.

Was political support for the Fed's anti-inflation policy as deep
and broad as Volcker suggested to his colleagues within the FOMC?
Surely there was a change in attitudes within the White House, particularly in the Oval Office; Reagan both in public and behind closed
doors continued to support Volcker's decision to stay the tightening
course for so long. Congressional support was probably never as

strong as Volcker suggested, although most Republicans consistently voted against efforts to curtail the Fed's anti-inflation program. But the emergence of a divided Congress and divided party control of government after 1980 probably helped the Fed: intraparty divisions among Democrats and disagreements between the two parties undermined lawmakers' capacity to limit the Fed's autonomy. With both divided party control of government and split party control of Congress, Democrats' threats to intervene with legislation were not credible.

The perception of political support allowed Volcker to embark on an anti-inflation program from which Burns had backed away. Such perceptions also shaped the timing of the FOMC's decision to ease policy. When Volcker was finally ready to end the Fed's tight monetary policy, he seemed acutely aware of the political costs of getting the policy right. He highlighted to his FOMC colleagues the "risk to the institution" in the committee's policy decision: "If we get this one wrong, we are going to have legislation next year without a doubt. We may get it anyway. It's a matter of judgment as to how that might come out and where the risks are, but I think I know where the risks are."[50] Congress might have been too conflicted to actually legislate, but Volcker's warning suggests that Congress's ability to channel public anger against the Fed helped to set the boundaries of monetary policy in fighting stagflation and historically high interest rates.

Conclusion

The Accord of 1951 was the high-water mark of the Federal Reserve's relationship with Congress. Having sided with the Fed rather than the Treasury in the midcentury struggle over the separation of monetary policy and debt management, Congress enabled the Fed to reestablish its own authority vis-à-vis the Treasury and White House. Still, the Accord could not guarantee that the Fed would operate independently of political considerations, and it made the Fed much more likely to heed the concerns of its congressional overseers. Collaborating on debt management and fiscal policy issues might still make sense under certain conditions, but the Accord clearly signaled that the Fed was ultimately accountable to the legislature that created it, not to the Treasury that had subordinated its monetary policy tools.

Congress in the 1970s exploited its power as the Fed's boss, reshaping the legislature's relationship with the central bank. Upset with the persistence of stagflation and disappointed with the Fed's policy response, a Democratic Congress backed by a Democratic White House in 1977 blamed the Fed and imposed a new regime of accountability. Congress gave the Fed a clearer set of goals, placing into the Federal Reserve Act a durable dual mandate to pursue both employment and price stability. Congress required presidents to seek the consent of the Senate in deciding who should steer the Fed. And lawmakers required the Fed chair and FOMC to follow new rules for greater transparency and accountability.

The newly created communications regime between the Fed and Congress created incentives for the Fed to heed Congress's policy views (to the extent that lawmakers could agree). By requiring the Fed to set targets and defend them in public before Congress, the Fed could not ignore the expectations of lawmakers' and their constituencies. In short, the new transparency requirements gave an edge to lawmakers seeking to hold the Fed accountable for the efficacy of the Fed's own policy target.

We get a glimpse of the consequences of the newly mandated semiannual testimony in July 1977 just before Burns was scheduled to testify before Congress. As he explained to his fellow FOMC members,

> Gentlemen, we're faced with a very hard decision. Speaking personally for a moment, I wish I could join my colleagues who were inclined to move toward somewhat lower growth rates. I wish I could—temperamentally, yes; that's what I would prefer to do. But I do have an obligation to this Committee and to the System as well as to the country. I'll have to testify before the Committee, I will have to defend whatever this Committee decides.[51]

In confidence to his FOMC colleagues, Burns expressed an existential question about the proper role of the central bank in a democratic society. Can a central bank hold firm to pursue the policies that it considers to be optimal in economic terms if prevailing voices in the political system prefer a different policy outcome? By imposing new transparency requirements on the Fed, Congress forced the central bank to balance its own views against the policies it believed the Congress and broader public would support.

On balance, the reporting arrangements called for in 1975 that became law in 1977 institutionalized clearer channels of communication between Congress and the Fed. As Kettl (1986, 165) observed, H. Con. Res. 133 and subsequent measures created opportunities for the sending of signals "rich in explicit and implicit political messages, in both directions." Lawmakers could use their perch to broadcast to the Fed, the public, and markets their concerns about the contours of monetary policy. Most important, legislators gained a regular means of signaling their concerns to the Fed, making it harder for the Fed to make policy choices without at least a nod to the views of its legislative bosses and justifying why it might deviate from them. Overall, congressional reforms put the Fed on notice that lawmakers would periodically demand more aggressive action from the Fed to address macroeconomic conditions.

Ultimately, the political pressure proved too much for the feckless Burns. Unable to balance the president's electoral ambitions with appropriate policy, Burns failed to pursue a policy agenda that might have resolved the economy's dire situation. Volcker, on the other hand, favored tough corrective action and had the steely temperament to carry it through. Moreover, he was aided by the downturn's persistence, a sufficiently supportive Congress, and ultimately a Republican White House eager to blame its predecessor. That alignment gave the ascendant Volcker political cover to deliver massive monetary tightening and finally defeat stagflation. Volcker contextualized the Fed's political challenge some years later:

The Federal Reserve is meant to be independent of parochial political interests. But it's got to operate . . . within the range of understanding of the public and the political system. You just can't go do something that is just outside the bounds of what people can understand, because you won't be independent for very long if you do that (quoted in Samuelson 2008, 112).

Congress would again raise the prospects for serious reform of the Federal Reserve Act, this time with Bernanke at the head of the Fed facing economic and political challenges in the wake of the global financial crisis as well as the Great Recession that ensued between 2007 and 2009. As we explore in the next chapter, financial and economic crises renewed the cycle of crisis, policy failure, blame, and reform; a Democratic Congress and White House would respond to crises by giving the Fed more power, and imposing more transparency on the institution. Such moves, as we will discuss next, once again reshaped the relationship between Congress and the Fed, making both institutions ever more dependent on the other.

7

The Only Game in Town

Congress's response to the global financial crisis and Great Recession offers a recent test of our political-economic theory of reform. In this chapter, we probe the cycle of blame and reform that led lawmakers to reopen the Federal Reserve Act in the wake of another financial crisis. Starting in late 2008, the Fed's unconventional, untested, and exigent central bank tools blurred the lines between monetary and fiscal policy, exacerbating the Fed's already-tense relationship with Congress at a time of severe economic stress. Controlling Congress and the White House, new Democratic majorities in 2010 responded to economic and policy failures by revamping the powers and governance of the Fed. In a recurring pattern, lawmakers gave the Fed more responsibility and imposed more transparency, demanding more accountability in return.

We use contemporary press coverage, interviews with top Fed officials, and congressional votes to pinpoint the economic, political, and institutional forces that drove Congress and the president to rewrite the Federal Reserve Act. In enacting the Dodd-Frank Wall Street Reform and Consumer Protection Act in 2010, lawmakers overcame ideological and partisan barriers to legislative action. And after a blast of fiscal stimulus early in 2009, Republican capture of the

House in November 2010 undermined additional spending—despite pleas from the Fed for a healthier mix of fiscal and monetary policy. Instead, the Fed became "the only game in town" (Menza 2012), for years providing unprecedented and almost-unlimited monetary accommodation.

The Fed currently remains locked in congressional cross hairs. Liberals call for additional limits on emergency lending, greater public control of the reserve system, and sustaining monetary accommodation, while conservatives advocate additional, even formulaic, constraints on monetary policy and greater power for the regional reserve banks. Even as the economy recovers and headwinds associated with the financial crisis fade, the Fed's political standing remains precarious. In 2017, a new president and legislature continue to pursue reforms that would reshape the Fed's congressional mandate as well as the tools to meet it.

Political-Economic Roots of the Financial Crisis

The collapse of New Century Financial Corporation—a large subprime mortgage lender—in early 2007 was a wake-up call to Congress and federal regulators and marked the onset of the worst financial crisis since the Great Depression. The "poster child for bad practices in the mortgage industry" (Keoun and Church 2007), New Century helped to drive both a remarkable boom and catastrophic bust of the US housing market. The late 1990s' expectation of ever-rising housing prices encouraged many lenders to lower credit standards—generating a new class of borrowers with subprime mortgages. Lax underwriting further fueled the housing bubble, pushing prices even higher and encouraging more people to enter the housing market. Between 1994 and 2005, subprime lending increased from a $35 billion to $665 billion market, constituting nearly a quarter of all mortgages by 2006 (Aaron 2009).

As housing became less affordable, mortgage payments grew more onerous, thereby lessening demand, lowering house prices between 2005 and 2006, and eventually popping the housing bubble in 2008. As demand was dropping, companies like New Century lowered their mortgage-underwriting standards even further as they sought to generate more business (Keoun and Church 2007). As lending standards dropped credit worthiness of new borrowers deteriorated. The burst of the housing bubble (largely unexpected, even with the decline in house prices) left millions of homeowners underwater: they had put so little money down and borrowed against their homes only to discover that millions of mortgages were now greater than the value of the underlying properties. Defaults and then foreclosures surged, peaking at more than four million foreclosed homes between 2007 and 2012 (Keil 2012).

Had mortgage lenders followed a traditional model of retaining mortgages made in their communities, which would have given them some "skin in the game," the damage caused by the collapse of the subprime mortgage market might have been contained. By sharing the risks of the mortgages they underwrote, local lenders might have been more circumspect in making loans in the first place—in effect, self-regulating local mortgage markets. Instead, local banks bundled and sold mortgages to financial firms, which then repackaged them for investors, who in turn were lulled into buying securities that rating agencies (fraudulently) stamped with triple-A ratings (Lattman 2013). Investors then borrowed against the securities, while collecting interest payments from the holders of the original mortgage. With local loans off their books, mortgage lenders had (seemingly) little reason to worry about the credit worthiness of their borrowers. Moreover, companies such as AIG sold insurance (in the form of "credit default swaps") to investors in mortgage-backed securities and other, more complicated financial products. So long as house prices kept rising, AIG made money-collecting premiums with seemingly little risk of having to cover losses. In reviewing the causes of the financial crisis, the government-sponsored Financial Crisis Inquiry Commission (2011, xxiv) said that "it appeared to financial institutions, investors, and regulators alike that risk had been conquered: the investors held highly rated securities they thought were sure to perform, the banks thought they had taken the riskiest loans off their books; and regulators saw firms making profits and borrowing costs reduced."

The risks were hardly contained. When the housing bubble popped and homeowners defaulted, losses flushed throughout the global financial system—affecting individuals and institutions exposed in any way to the underlying mortgages or related securities and financial instruments. Losses stemming from the burst of the housing bubble were especially concentrated in a set of systemically important financial institutions—typically deemed to be "too big to fail" (ibid.). Indeed, the US financial crisis came to a head in September 2008 as financial instability spread throughout US credit markets. The precipitating event was a decision by the Treasury and Federal Reserve that the Fed lacked the legal authority to prevent the financial giant Lehman Brothers from going bankrupt.[1] Lehman's collapse nearly brought down the global financial system, provoking the Treasury and Fed just days later to seemingly reverse course and engineer a multibillion-dollar rescue of AIG. The ensuing economic disaster fueled the world's worst recession since the Great Depression; one government study pegged the total cost of the crisis (including the value of lost economic output, jobs, and household wealth) at over $20 trillion (Melendez 2013).

Notably, the media paid little attention to the rise in subprime lending until 2007. Figure 7.1 displays media attention to the subprime lending, as measured by counts of *New York Times* articles that mention "subprime" over the postwar period. Ripples of attention first appear when house prices start falling in 2006. But a sustained focus on the effects of subprime lending occurs only as the bubble bursts and firms like New Century go bankrupt in 2007. Like the media, the public (as measured by a count of Google searches) seems to dismiss the brewing crisis until 2007 (figure 7.2).

The lack of public and media attention to the explosive growth in subprime lending no doubt reflected Congress's and government regulators' failure to recognize the signs as well as identify the causes of (let alone stop) the brewing financial crisis. Few believed that the housing market would completely unravel. Some prescient regulators, such as Federal Reserve Board governor Edward Gramlich, warned Fed chair Greenspan as early as 2000 about the dangers of ignoring the rapidly growing subprime lending business; as the

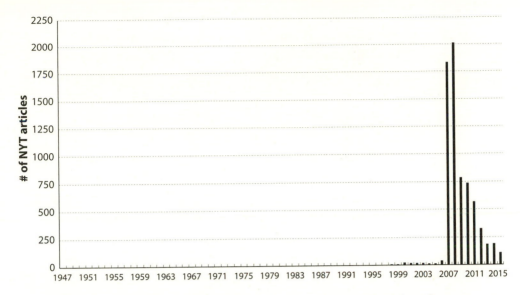

FIGURE 7.1. Number of *New York Times* "subprime" mentions. *New York Times* Chronicle, accessed February 4, 2017, http://chronicle.nytlabs.com/; search for "subprime."

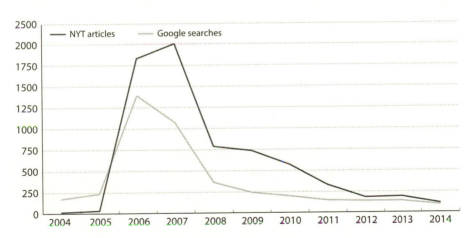

FIGURE 7.2. Public versus media attention to the subprime crisis, 2004–14. *New York Times* Chronicle, accessed February 4, 2017, http://chronicle.nytlabs.com/; Google Trends (US only).

Federal Reserve Bank of San Francisco observed in 2001, subprime originations rose from $35 billion in 1994 to $140 billion in 2000, for an average annual growth rate of 26 percent (Laderman 2001). Concerns by Gramlich and others fell on deaf ears within the Fed. Greenspan would later claim that the Fed lacked the tools to investigate predatory lending (Andrews 2007). Bernanke (2015, 101), however, observes that the Fed in the years before the crisis "failed to stop some questionable practices," arguing that the Fed could have used its authority more aggressively under the Home Ownership and Equity Protection Act to limit predatory lending (even though the Fed lacked the authority to enforce any rules it wrote to implement the act).

Even fewer recognized that securitizing subprime mortgages and the interconnectedness of those loans within the economy could fuel global financial contagion. Fed chair Bernanke underestimated the potential consequences of declining house prices when he testified in early 2007 before Congress's Joint Economic Committee. Emblematic of the struggles that both fiscal and monetary policy makers would have in grasping the enormity of the financial crisis and appropriate responses, Bernanke (2007) contended that

> although the turmoil in the subprime mortgage market has created severe financial problems for many individuals and families, the implications of these developments for the housing market as a whole are less clear. . . . At this juncture . . . the impact on the broader economy and financial markets of the problems in the subprime market seems likely to be contained.

Before 2007, Congress raised few red flags about developments in the housing market underlying the rise of subprime lending. Recalling Congress's electorally driven, countercyclical attention, figure 7.3 illustrates the low salience of precrisis, mortgage-related issues in both the House and Senate. Summing up the total number of committee hearings each year that addressed mortgage-related issues in both chambers, the figure shows that it took a record financial crisis to spark congressional attention. Putting those hearings into perspective (figure 7.4), mortgage-related hearings as a proportion of all hearings focused on consumer finance, bankruptcy, and mortgage markets begin to rise in the early 2000s. Congress does not pay a disproportionate level of attention to mortgage issues until 2007. Lawmakers' lack of interest likely reflected both parties' support for both the 1999 Financial Services Modernization Act that deregulated the finance industry and broadening national homeownership across

FIGURE 7.3. Number of mortgage-related congressional committee hearings, 1947–2014. Policy Agendas Project, http://www.policyagendas.org/. The data are drawn from the Policy Agendas Project compilation of congressional committee hearings, and include all committee hearings in the policy areas of consumer finance, bankruptcy, and secondary mortgage markets whose titles mention mortgage-related issues. The data used here were originally collected by Frank R. Baumgartner and Bryan D. Jones, with the support of National Science Foundation grant numbers SBR 9320922 and 0111611, and were distributed through the Department of Government at the University of Texas at Austin. Neither the National Science Foundation nor the original collectors of the data bear any responsibility for the analysis reported here.

the period. Furthermore, the few warning flags raised by Democratic legislators over the 2000s failed to gain traction with Republicans in control of Congress and the White House (McCarty, Poole, and Rosenthal 2013; Aaron 2009).

After the crisis and recession ebbed, Bernanke (2012a) delivered a clear-eyed appraisal of the Fed's mistakes. We quote at length his discussion with students at George Washington University in spring 2012, delivered as part of Bernanke's efforts to demystify the Fed (Goldfarb 2014). Bernanke (2012, 11) first assessed the role of the Fed as supervisor:

> The Fed made mistakes in supervision and regulation. I think two I would point out. One would be in our supervision of banks and bank holding companies. We didn't press hard enough on this

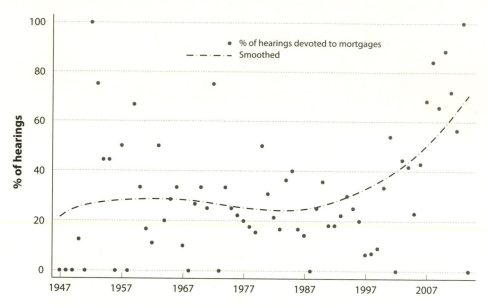

FIGURE 7.4. Mortgage-focused issues as percentage of related congressional hearings, 1947–2014. Policy Agendas Project, http://www.policyagendas.org/. The data are drawn from the Policy Agendas Project compilation of congressional committee hearings, and report the percentage of all committee hearings in the policy areas of consumer finance, bankruptcy, and secondary mortgage markets whose titles mention mortgage-related issues. The data used here were originally collected by Frank R. Baumgartner and Bryan D. Jones, with the support of National Science Foundation grant numbers SBR 9320922 and 0111611, and were distributed through the Department of Government at the University of Texas at Austin. Neither the National Science Foundation nor the original collectors of the data bear any responsibility for the analysis reported here.

issue of measuring your risks. . . . A lot of banks simply didn't have the capacity to thoroughly understand the risks that they were taking. The supervisor should have pressed them harder to develop that capacity and if they didn't develop that capacity, should have restricted their ability to take these risky positions. I think the Fed and other bank supervisors didn't press hard enough on this and that turned out to be obviously a serious problem.

Bernanke (ibid.) also pinpointed the Fed's failures to pursue its statutory responsibility to protect consumers:

Another area where the Fed I think performed poorly was in consumer protection. The Fed had some authorities to provide some protections to mortgage borrowers that would have, if used effectively, . . . reduced at least some of the bad lending that occurred during the latter part of the housing bubble. But for [a] variety of reasons that wasn't done, not nearly to the extent it should have been. The really hard thing, at least in my view, to anticipate fully, was that the effects of the decline in house prices would be so much more severe than the . . . sort of similar decline in dot-com stocks. And again, the reason is . . . the ways in which decline at [sic] house prices affected mortgages, affected the soundness of the financial system and created a panic which in turn led to the instability of the financial system.

The Financial Crisis Inquiry Commission (2011, xvii) concurred with Bernanke's analysis, blaming the Fed for its failure to "stem the flow of toxic mortgages . . . by setting prudent mortgage-lending standards."

In contrast, experts continue to disagree about whether monetary policy helped to fuel the run-up in house prices and financial instability that generated the global financial crisis. As chair of the Fed for nearly two decades (1987–2006), Greenspan led the central bank for a period subsequently dubbed the Great Moderation: the almost quarter-century period of economic growth and financial stability ending in 2007 during which the Fed enjoyed low and stable inflation. Many argue that the Fed's move to lower interest rates after the popping of the 2000 Internet bubble fueled a rise in house prices by lowering mortgage rates and thus directly boosting housing demand. As the Financial Crisis Inquiry Commission report notes, Greenspan testified before Congress in November 2002 that the Fed's accommodative monetary policy stirred the economy with "mortgage interest rates that are at lows not seen in decades."[2] The commission concluded that while the Fed's low rates generated conditions that fostered the housing bubble, stronger regulatory action could have constrained its calamitous burst. Conservative critics of the Fed, such as Stanford economist John Taylor, are more likely to blame monetary policy directly for the crisis. "Monetary excesses were the main cause of the boom," Taylor opined in the *Wall Street*

Journal. "The Fed held its target interest rate, especially in 2003–5, well below known monetary guidelines that say what good policy should be based on historical experience" (Taylor 2009).[3]

Bernanke (2012a) questioned the impact of the Fed's reluctance to raise rates between 2002 and 2004 on the run-up in house prices. First, other countries (such as the United Kingdom) experienced booms and busts in their housing sector in the same period, although subject to tighter monetary policy. Nor did housing markets in the euro area perform similarly, despite being subject to a single monetary policy set by the European Central Bank. Second, Bernanke argued that the magnitude of the increase in house prices was too big to be explained by relatively small changes in interest rates at the time. Finally, the timing of the rise in house prices preceded the Fed's loosening of policy after the burst of the dot-com bubble in 2000. Still, as Bernanke acknowledged in 2012, the jury was out on whether and how monetary policy might have contributed to the boom and bust in house prices during the Great Moderation.

In contrast, lawmakers already had their scapegoats, replaying the pattern of blame and reform in the wake of crisis. Republicans singled out the affordable housing mission that was added to the charters of Fannie Mae and Freddie Mac for encouraging more as well as cheaper lending to low-income individuals entering the housing market. Critics on th Left and Right targeted the Fed's overly accommodative monetary policy along with its supervisory and regulatory lapses as direct causes of the housing bubble and onset of crisis. In addition, the Fed's policy choices in the wake of the crisis failed to mollify congressional critics—leaving the Fed especially vulnerable to legislative efforts to increase accountability and congressional oversight. Below, we look at the Fed's policy responses in the wake of the crisis and its political reverberations in Congress.

Unconventional Monetary Policy at the Zero Bound

"Extraordinary times call for extraordinary measures," Bernanke (2009) said, justifying the Fed's initial response to the financial crisis. Because the FOMC had lowered interest rates to zero in

December 2008, the Fed could no longer use traditional monetary policy tools to inject further stimulus into the economy. Unwilling to push rates below zero, the FOMC needed more unconventional monetary policy solutions to generate economic growth. Even keeping rates near zero—for years after the end of the recession—generated intense (often-irrational) criticism of the Fed from Republicans on the Hill and presidential campaign trail in 2008, many of whom asserted that the Bernanke Fed was "debasing the currency" and would ultimately generate uncontrollable inflation (Ip 2011). Even into early 2017, the Fed's preferred inflation metric remained below the 2 percent target—undermining critics' charges against prolonged, near-zero rates.

To supplement the effects of keeping rates low indefinitely, the Bernanke Fed turned to even more innovative monetary tools. The Fed prioritized three key policy innovations: the adoption of forward guidance (a commitment to keep rates low into the future), quantitative easing (more formally known as LSAPs), and novel lender of last resort programs. First, forward guidance offered the Fed a tool for setting market and public expectations about the future path of interest rates. Rather than push rates below zero, the Fed told markets that it would leave rates low into the future—hoping to spur investments to generate economic activity and demand. The Fed experimented with varying forms of forward guidance, committing to keep rates low for "an extended period" (2009), until a calendar date certain (2011), and until unemployment and expected inflation hit specified benchmarks (2012).

Second, the Fed's quantitative easing program drew on the Fed's statutory authority to conduct open market operations (buying and selling government securities). The Fed's three rounds of LSAPs pumped trillions of dollars into the economy during and after the crisis. The FOMC first bought Treasuries to push down long-term interest rates and compel investors to seek riskier, higher-returning assets. Then, the FOMC purchased mortgage-backed securities (assets underwritten by the housing finance giants Fannie Mae and Freddie Mac) to further depress mortgage rates and revive the housing market. Overall, LSAPs expanded the Fed's balance sheet by nearly $3 trillion between December 2007 and November 2014, ballooning the Fed's holdings to roughly four times the average size of the prerecession balance sheet (Ricketts and Waller 2014).

Quantitative easing supporters asserted that because housing finance was at the heart of the financial crisis, bolstering housing markets by reducing long-term rates was essential. Critics, including the president of the Federal Reserve Bank of Richmond, Jeffrey Lacker, countered that "when the central bank buys private assets, it can tilt the playing field toward some borrowers at the expense of others, affecting the allocation of credit" (Lacker and Weinberg 2014). Unconventional monetary policies, in other words, blurred the line between monetary and fiscal policy, putting the Fed in the politically fraught position of choosing economic winners and losers. Capitol Hill skeptics of LSAPs maintained that distributional issues were better left to politicians. Many conservative critics viewed quantitative easing as outright debt monetization, leading Republicans to object that the Fed was simply financing the federal deficit by printing money (Appelbaum 2015).

Third, the Fed devised a series of programs to inject short-term liquidity into frozen credit markets. Programs targeting the Fed's traditional borrowers—banks and other depository institutions—were conducted via the regional reserve banks' discount windows. Such programs included the opening of "currency swap lines" with foreign central banks, intended to inject US dollars into foreign banks to discourage them from dumping their holdings of US mortgages (which in turn would have increased the cost of credit for US borrowers).[4] These plans allowed the Fed and its regional reserve banks to provide loans to a broader range of counterparties than under noncrisis conditions, and on the basis of a broader range of collateral than the Fed would typically allow.

The Board of Governors created additional lending facilities to address liquidity problems beyond the conventional banking system. These programs relied on the Fed's 13(3) statutory authority under the Federal Reserve Act (named for the section of the act in which the authority is granted), empowering the Fed to be the lender of last resort in "unusual and exigent circumstances." Put simply, these programs supplied loans to borrowers and investors in credit markets. The Commercial Paper Funding Facility was typical of such lending plans: the New York Fed financed the purchase of commercial paper (e.g., short-term corporate promissory notes), thereby pushing liquidity into corporate credit markets that depended on commercial paper. These programs reached well beyond the banking sector, providing liquidity for the "shadow" banking system—mutual funds, hedge funds, investment banks, and other nonbank financial institutions.[5]

The Fed's response to the crisis followed the advice of Walter Bagehot, who in 1873 wrote *Lombard Street: A Description of the Money Market*, a treatise on how the Bank of England responded to a credit crisis in the late 1860s. Bagehot's "dictum," as it is known, is typically summarized as follows: "To avert panic, central banks should lend early and freely (i.e., without limit), to solvent firms, against good collateral, and at 'high rates'" (Tucker 2009). Assuming that recipients of the Fed's lending were solvent, the Fed responded predictably to the crisis by finding innovative ways to inject liquidity into frozen credit markets within both traditional and shadow banking systems. The solvency requirement was essential, and later contested (Wallach 2015). If major institutions lacked capital and acceptable collateral, then additional fiscal—not monetary—intervention would have been required and was assumed by 2009 to be beyond Congress's political reach.[6]

In lending to a broad range of bank and nonbank institutions—including traditional depository institutions, investment firms, insurance companies, industrial companies, and foreign central banks—the Fed sparked public and elite outrage. First, critics demanded public disclosure of the recipients of the Fed's loans. Given the Fed's resistance to disclosure, it took legal and ultimately congressional action to force the Fed to reveal the recipients of its emergency loans—those from both its discount windows and the special facilities established through the Board's 13(3) powers (Bloomberg Business 2011a). Lawmakers from both parties rejected the Fed's position that disclosure would undermine the effectiveness of their emergency lending programs.

Corporate America and global finance dominated the list of emergency loan recipients (Bloomberg Business 2011b). Bloomberg News totaled the lending at $1.2 trillion, including loans to Ford Motor Company, Toyota, Morgan Stanley, and Citigroup as well as major banks in Europe and the Gulf States. Lawmakers in 2011 objected to the imbalance of loans between Wall Street and Main Street. Asked Walter Jones (R–North Carolina) at a June 2011 congressional hearing, "Why in hell does the Federal Reserve seem to be able to find the way to help these entities that are gigantic? They get help when the average businessperson down in eastern North Carolina, and probably across America, they can't even go to a bank they've been banking with for 15 or 20 years and get a loan" (ibid.). Critics charged that the Fed—operating under a cloak of secrecy with no expectation that its lending would be made public—cared only about saving Wall Street and global financial giants, with little concern for resolving the credit crisis more broadly in the US economy.

Bernanke responded by reaching out to Main Street. He explained and defended monetary policy choices in college lectures, town hall meetings, national televised interviews, and even after-hours sessions in the Fed's boardroom with local DC-area high school teachers (Federal Reserve 2012; Goldfarb 2014). As Bernanke acknowledged in an interview, "I learned in the crisis that transparency served broader purposes, including maintaining the right relationship with Congress and explaining the Fed's policy choices to the public."[7] His efforts in the immediate wake of the crisis and during the Great Recession, however, failed to dissuade Congress from curtailing the Fed's lending powers and imposing greater transparency when it revamped the financial regulatory system in 2010. Ultimately, bipartisan agreement that the Fed had failed to prevent the financial crisis undermined lawmakers' trust that the Fed's unconventional policies would be effective—let alone fair—tools for restoring the nation's economic health.

A Renewed Cycle of Blame and Reform

As established in previous chapters, Congress and the Fed are interdependent institutions. The Fed's policy-making power depends directly on the strength of its congressional support. Lawmakers' backing in turn is shaped by the Fed's performance in managing the economy consistent with its statutory mandates. True to form, after nearly two decades of benign neglect of the Fed during the Great Moderation, many lawmakers blamed the Fed for the global financial crisis and criticized its policy choices in the aftermath. Indeed, the Fed's unconventional monetary policies—especially its broad application of its 13(3) emergency lending authority— provoked congressional anger across party and ideological lines.[8] While demanding greater transparency for past and future lending decisions, Democrats gave the Fed more power to supervise systematically important financial institutions; Republicans sought to curtail monetary policy discretion, decentralize more power to the reserve bank presidents on the FOMC, and impose greater transparency on FOMC deliberations.

Still, bipartisan anger generated partisan responses. Controlling both chambers and the White House, and over the loud objection of Republican legislators, Democrats backed an overhaul of the financial regulatory system—including changes to the Federal Reserve Act. In this section, we take a closer look at the political alignments that shaped congressional efforts to empower the Fed and impose greater transparency in the wake of the crisis. We examine in detail three challenges to the Fed's authority: a successful effort to impose reforms via Dodd-Frank in 2010, a failed attempt to deny Bernanke a second term as chair, and an unsuccessful GOP effort to impose new audits on the Fed (reviving the Democrats' campaign from the 1970s). The intersection of financial crisis and intense political polarization allows us to evaluate congressional reactions to the Fed's failures when both parties can conveniently blame the Fed for the crisis, but hold conflicting views about appropriate fiscal and monetary policy.

LEGISLATING IN THE WAKE OF CRISIS

Dodd-Frank partially rewired how the government supervises and regulates the nation's financial system. Among other Dodd-Frank provisions, lawmakers sought to improve supervision of too big to fail financial institutions, provide new avenues for winding down—rather than bailing out—such institutions, protect consumers from predatory lending, and impose new limits and transparency on banks' proprietary trading practices (Kaiser 2014). By failing to force the breakup of too big to fail financial institutions or concentrate supervisory authority into fewer agencies (to prevent financial institutions from shopping for more lenient regulators), the law did not go as far as many critics wanted. Several years after Dodd-Frank's enactment, the rules to implement it were still incomplete. But proponents argued that the new law would reduce the level of risk in the financial system and give regulators greater legal authority to resolve the inevitable, future financial crises.

In reopening the Federal Reserve Act, lawmakers gave the Fed more responsibility while imposing more transparency and clipping some of its powers. First, Congress designated the Fed as the regulator of systemically important financial institutions (but granted the authority to determine which institutions are systematically important to a new council of existing regulators). Second, Dodd-Frank stripped the Fed of its consumer protection authority, created the Consumer Financial Protection Bureau, and mandated that the Fed fund it from its own revenue stream. Third, over the Fed's objections, the new law required disclosure of borrowers from the Fed's financial crisis credit facilities as well as (with two-year lags) any future borrowers from the Fed's regular discount window and emergency lending programs. Fourth, the law curtailed the Fed's 13(3) emergency lending by prohibiting Fed loans to individual firms, except as part of lending programs with broad eligibility, and crucially, conditional on permission from the Treasury secretary.[9] Bernanke (2015, 464) reflected in his memoirs that "it was one authority I was happy to lose"—perhaps because the change would shield the Fed from blame during future, inevitable bailouts.

The House and Senate did not vote directly on each of the provisions that limited the Fed's monetary policy autonomy. Recorded votes, however, took place in both chambers on the adoption of Dodd-Frank as well as measures to impose greater transparency on the Fed's emergency lending and monetary policy decision making.[10]

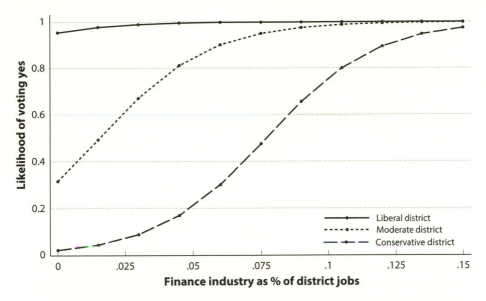

FIGURE 7.5. Likelihood of voting in favor of financial regulatory reform, Democrats only, 2009. House roll call vote no. 968, December 11, 2009, on the final passage of the Dodd-Frank Wall Street Reform and Consumer Protection Act of 2009. Predicted support generated with *prgren* command in Stata 11.2.

The December 2009 House vote to adopt a comprehensive financial regulatory reform bill was the House's precursor to the final Dodd-Frank conference agreement. Near party-line splits occurred on the question of adopting the House measure. Consistent with GOP votes on most of the major Democratic initiatives during President Obama's first two years in office, no Republican crossed the line to vote for the bill; Democrats divided 227–27 in favor.[11]

Democratic defections look similar to previous intraparty divisions over reforming the powers and responsibilities of the Fed.[12] More conservative members and those from more conservative districts were more likely to join Republican colleagues to vote against new government limitations on the financial sector (figure 7.5). Support for reform among House Democrats was concentrated within liberal districts and districts more dependent on jobs within the financial industry. To the extent that the bill was intended to stabilize the financial sector, lawmakers with a greater share of constituents whose jobs depended on returning the sector to health were more likely to vote in favor of the bill. Even in the more conservative Democratic districts, the economic relevance of the financial sector diminished those members' likelihood of opposing the bill.

When the Senate considered its version of financial regulatory reform, back-to-back votes were taken on amendments offered by Senators Sanders and Vitter to impose greater transparency on the Fed. The Vitter amendment would have added a tough audit the Fed program, removing the 1976 provision in the Federal Reserve Act that exempted monetary policy from GAO audits. The Sanders amendment, though, was voted on first, and it proposed a compromise between supporters and opponents of a full Federal Reserve audit. Instead of allowing the GAO to audit the FOMC's monetary policy decisions, the Sanders amendment required a onetime disclosure of the Fed's emergency lending programs beginning in December 2007, including loans made to stabilize Bear Stearns in March 2008. The amendment was adopted ninety-six to zero (McGrane and Crittenden 2010).

The unanimous adoption of Sanders's amendment took the wind out of Vitter's sails. Vitter's amendment failed, thirty-seven to sixty-one. Partisan and electoral motivations drove support for Vitter's amendment. Republicans generally favored the challenge to the Democratic bill, supporting the amendment by a margin of thirty to ten. Of the ten Republican senators opposing the audit bill, roughly half hailed from the moderate end of the GOP conference. None of them—save Robert Bennett of Utah—faced voters in 2010. Three days prior, Bennett had lost the nomination of Utah Republicans to run for reelection in November—eliminating the electoral cost of siding with the Fed and against supporters of a full audit. Democrats broke fifty-one to seven against Vitter's amendment. The seven Democrats breaking party lines were generally moderates, with two (Russ Feingold and Blanche Lincoln) anticipating a close election that fall. Despite voting for a right-wing, populist challenge to the Fed's autonomy, both lost their races in November to conservative challengers. The two votes suggest bipartisan support for increasing Fed transparency, but only more conservative senators and those risking reelection favored a more intrusive audit of the Fed's decision making on monetary policy.

REAPPOINTING BERNANKE

Amid debates over new limits on the Fed's monetary policy discretion, President Obama nominated Bernanke for a second four-year term as Fed chair. In January 2010, thirteen Democrats and seventeen Republicans voted not to confirm Bernanke.[13] The seventy to thirty tally was the closest margin for any Fed chair since nominees were first subject to separate votes on confirmation in 1977 (Irwin 2010). Partisanship, ideology, and electoral risk again shaped lawmakers votes on giving Bernanke a second term. Senators voting to reconfirm Bernanke were less likely to be running for reelection (76 versus 53 percent), more likely to be chamber centrists than on the ideological wings (78 versus 62 percent), and more likely to represent states highly dependent on the financial services industry (91 versus 56 percent).[14] Although Bernanke amassed a supermajority of the Senate for confirmation, the historically small margin demonstrated that electorally vulnerable lawmakers were still eager to blame the Fed, and by proxy, Bernanke, for the crisis, the country's weak recovery, and the unconventional policy remedies the Fed championed.

REPUBLICANS AND THE FED

Democrats lost their House majority in the 2010 elections, creating two new challenges for the Fed. First, as the price for raising the federal government's debt ceiling, Republicans pushed Congress and the president to significantly curtail fiscal spending over the course of 2011—most significantly with enactment of the Budget Control Act in August that year. The new law imposed caps on discretionary spending that would be enforced by mandatory cuts in entitlement spending for a decade unless Congress and the president could cut over $1 trillion from the federal deficit over that ten-year period. While Congress and the president ultimately raised the debt limit, partisan pyrotechnics in summer 2011 provoked Standard & Poor's to downgrade US Treasuries, compounded fiscal headwinds, and compromised the nascent recovery.

Second, Republican control of the House unleashed attacks on the Fed by a new Republican majority highly critical of the Fed's performance. As Bernanke (2015, 492) reminds us in his memoir, the November elections coincided with the FOMC meeting at which the Fed commenced its second round of LSAPs, committing to buy $600 billion in Treasury bonds through June 2011. By mid-November, GOP leaders in both chambers had penned a letter to Bernanke decrying asset purchases, and warning that the move could debase the currency and fuel inflation. Moreover, now in control of the House agenda, GOP critics continued to campaign to audit the Fed, bringing audit bills to the House floor in both July 2012 and September 2014. With Democrats in control of the Senate and White House, few anticipated enactment. Still, such legislative efforts offered lawmakers another chance to blame the Fed and amend the act.

In 2012, the House bill passed, 327–98; all but a single Republican and 89 Democrats voted in favor. Familiar voting alignments within the Democratic Caucus emerged. Electoral and ideological forces shaped Democratic votes on the audit bill (figure 7.6).[15] First, lawmakers who barely won their elections in 2010 (securing less than 55 percent of the two-party vote) were on average thirty points more likely to support new audits. Representing more conservative districts (in the wake of large Democratic losses in conservative-leaning states and districts), Blue Dog (conservative) Democrats broke 20–3 in favor of the bill—generating almost a forty-point gap in the likelihood that Blue Dogs (compared to other Democrats) would support new audits. Finally, we detect a small loyalty to the reserve system from Democrats who represent regional reserve bank cities. Controlling for other factors that shaped Democrats' votes, Democrats representing reserve bank cities were slightly more likely to rally to the Fed's defense and oppose new audits. A century later, the original decision to locate reserve banks far from Wall Street still paid dividends to the Fed, generating pockets of support for the Fed around the country—albeit not from the GOP bench.

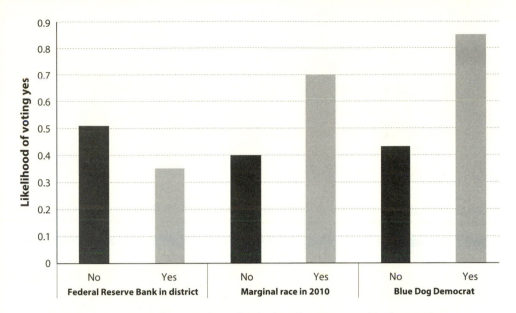

FIGURE 7.6. Likelihood of voting in favor of Audit the Fed, Democrats only, July 2012. House roll call vote no. 513, July 25, 2012. The estimates are computed from the logit model of the Democrats' votes. We estimate the likelihood of a yes vote as a function of whether or not the member was in their first term, retiring, won a marginal race (55 percent of the vote or less in 2010), belonged to the Blue Dog coalition, represented a Federal Reserve Bank state or city, and the percentage of the state employed in the finance industry. Predicted support calculated with *margins* command in Stata 14.2

Confirmed by the Senate in early 2014, Yellen became the first woman to head the Fed. By fall, the third round of LSAPs had been completed, interest rates remained near zero, and inflation stayed below the Fed's formal target rate of 2 percent. Still, Republicans continued to warn that the Fed's unconventional policies would soon unleash runaway inflation and thus urged the Fed to hike rates. Signaling the GOP's continued dissatisfaction with the Fed's performance, GOP leaders called up the audit bill for a new floor vote in September. It was perhaps a farewell gesture to retiring Representative Paul, who had spent his legislative career advocating for a return to the gold standard and repeal of the Federal Reserve Act.

Compared to the 2012 bill, advocates of expanded Fed audits picked up a few more supporters, generating a final tally of 332–92. This time, 106 Democrats joined all but a solitary Republican

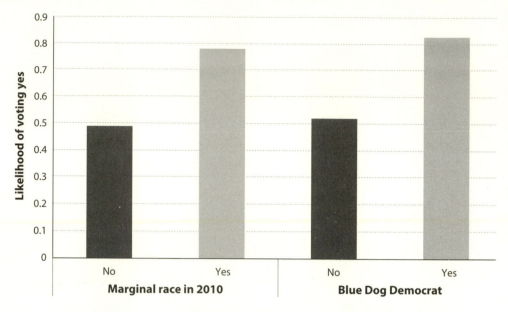

FIGURE 7.7. Likelihood of voting in favor of Audit the Fed, Democrats only, September 2014. House roll call vote no. 504, September 17, 2014. The estimates are computed from the logit model of the Democrats' votes on Audit the Fed bill. We estimate the likelihood of a yes vote as a function of whether or not the member was in their first term, retiring, won a marginal race (55 percent of the vote or less in 2012), belonged to the Blue Dog coalition, represented a Federal Reserve Bank state or city, and the percentage of the state employed in the finance industry. Predicted support calculated with *margins* command in Stata 14.2.

to vote in favor of the bill. Democrats favoring the audit bill again hailed from the right tail of the House Democratic Caucus.[16] Of the Blue Dog Democrats, 13 (of the remaining 15) voted for the bill— yielding about a thirty-point gap in the likelihood that Blue Dogs would support the bill compared to their non–Blue Dog Democratic colleagues (see figure 7.7). Lawmakers in tight November elections also disproportionately favored Paul's bill, generating nearly a thirty-point difference in their likelihood of supporting the bill compared to electorally safe Democrats. Unlike the vote in 2012, however, we find little evidence that lawmakers from districts with a reserve bank city diminished Democratic support for the bill. Despite the expanded Democratic support for the measure, it stood little chance of enactment so long as the parties split control of the branches. That might explain why Democratic support for the measure increased: better to take a stand on a popular position with conservative constituencies—particularly if lawmakers knew it would fail—rather than risk being caught on the wrong side of a vote.

Democrats lost their Senate majority in the 2014 elections, handing Republicans control of Congress for Obama's last two years in office. Few expected Republicans (lacking a filibuster-proof majority in the Senate) to impose more restraints on the Fed with a Democrat in the White House still eager to defend the Fed's performance in the wake of the crisis and recession. Nevertheless, lawmakers from both parties continued to advocate for Fed reform. House Republicans offered a bill that would require the FOMC to embrace a policy formula (or rule) for setting interest rates, mandating that the Fed defend any policy rule that deviated from a prescribed rule and authorizing new GAO audits to ensure Fed compliance with its rule. The House Financial Services Committee also provoked a legal fight with the Fed when the panel's chair (without the support of any committee Democrats) subpoenaed Fed records pertaining to an FOMC leak in September 2012 (Harrison 2015a). Facing both a Department of Justice criminal investigation and congressional probe, Yellen struggled in summer 2015 to balance demands from the Fed's congressional overseers against advice from the Fed's inspector general, who warned that complying with the Hill subpoena might compromise the Justice Department's criminal investigation (Davidson 2015).

Across the Capitol, the Senate banking panel approved a financial regulatory relief bill on a party-line vote that included proposals to increase the Fed's accountability to Congress for its policy choices. In addition to reversing parts of Dodd-Frank, the bill would make the president of the Federal Reserve Bank of New York a presidential appointee (subject to Senate confirmation), require the Fed to report any monetary policy rule to Congress used to set interest rates, mandate more testimony to Congress by Fed officials, and force release of FOMC transcripts within three years. Lacking any support from Democrats, the bill died at the close of the Congress.

Finally, in spring 2015, ideological foes Senators Elizabeth Warren (D-Massachusetts) and Vitter proposed further limits on the

Fed's emergency lending powers (Harrison 2015b). The senators charged that the Fed's draft rule to implement new limitations on 13(3) lending fell short of congressional intent when lawmakers clipped the Fed's 13(3) wings in Dodd-Frank. Instead, the Warren-Vitter bill would mandate a more specific definition of "broad-based" lending programs for the Fed to follow, require the Fed to certify the solvency of potential borrowers, and impose a penalty rate on any future emergency loans. The Fed could waive those restrictions only with congressional approval. The Senate failed to act on the Warren-Vitter measure, but the bipolar pair from the parties' left and right flanks surely signaled to the Fed that even years after the crisis, monetary politics was alive and well on Capitol Hill.

The Power of Legislative Threats

Politicians targeting the Fed with new legislative limits lost leverage with the enactment of Dodd-Frank and onset of a divided government. Judging from Bernanke's reflections after leaving the Fed and FOMC transcripts of the period, Fed officials remained sensitive to criticism from the Hill. Some Fed officials may have worried about the legislative consequences of Republicans regaining control of Congress and the White House in the future. In a June 2014 interview, Bernanke reflected on the threat posed to the Fed by aggressive measures to limit Fed independence. He acknowledged the limited chance that GOP critics could secure their legislative goals while government remained divided. But he raised the prospect of future legislative efforts that could limit the capacity of the Fed: "The last three presidents—Clinton, Bush, and Obama—have all been proponents of Fed independence. Absent the support of some future White House, although it might be difficult to get passed and signed legislation that poses a serious challenge to the basic powers of the Fed, it unfortunately would not be impossible."[17] As Bernanke's observation suggests, Congress retains the power to remake the nation's monetary regime. Given this, central bankers have to remain alert to the possibility—however remote—of existential threats to the institution.

Bernanke's decade-long effort to build consensus within the Fed for the adoption of a formal, numerical inflation target provides additional evidence that Fed officials at times seek political support from Congress even when considering internal changes. Bernanke (2015, 526) notes that a key goal when he first joined the Board in 2002 was to encourage his colleagues to consider a numerical inflation target—a benchmark that would anchor both monetary policy and inflation expectations in the medium term. Under inflation targeting, a central bank compares its forecast for the future path of inflation against its inflation goal and adjusts monetary policy accordingly. In Bernanke's (2003) words, inflation targeting allowed for "constrained discretion" by the central bank. The Fed in January 2012 finally adopted a 2 percent inflation target—a *full decade* after Bernanke first broached the subject with Board colleagues.

Why did it take so long for the Fed to adopt a target? Economists after all often distinguish between central bank goals and instrument independence (Debelle and Fischer 1994). Because Congress writes the Fed's mandate into law, the Fed lacks goal independence. But central bankers typically argue that the Fed has instrument independence: the Fed should be "free to choose the means by which it seeks to achieve its goals" (ibid., 197). To the extent that an inflation target is an instrument to achieve price stability, then an independent Fed should have been able to adopt a target with little concern about the congressional reaction. And yet during several years of debating the adoption of a target, FOMC officials showed acute sensitivity to the degree of political support from Congress for such a move.

FOMC transcripts over the course of Bernanke's two terms reveal the political dynamics that underscored the process of adopting a formal target. Consider, for example, the concerns voiced in October 2006 by Michael Moskow, then president of the Federal Reserve Bank of Chicago, when the FOMC discussed whether to adopt a numerical inflation target:

For me the biggest issue is the dual mandate responsibility and our relationship to the Congress. Clearly, a persuasive case must be made that we will continue to fulfill our dual mandate responsibilities. The challenge is how to make an explicit numerical specification of price stability operationally compliant with the dual mandate, and to do so, we need to clarify the flexibility of the time period for bringing inflation back to its target, as [Federal Reserve Bank of Richmond president] Jeff [Lacker] just talked about. The amount of time to do this would depend on the size of the current inflation deviation and the deviations from maximum sustainable growth and employment. So I think the intermediate step of explaining longer-term forecasts would help us learn how to communicate these difficult dual mandate issues more effectively.[18]

Governor Frederic Mishkin echoed Moskow's concerns, warning FOMC colleagues not "to get too far ahead of the Congress on this." As then Boston Fed president Cathy Minehan, put it, "We do need to consider the likely interaction with the Congress as we set a target for one of our goals but not another. . . . What else might that interaction with the Congress provoke? The possibility for unintended consequences is clear."[19] Two years later, then Fed vice chair Don Kohn voiced a similar concern about adopting an inflation target without consulting first with Congress: "Having an inflation target won't have any effect if it is repudiated by the Congress. As soon as we make it, it could have a negative effect."[20]

Bernanke explains in his memoir why it took the Fed a decade to adopt an inflation target. In January 2009, Bernanke recalls, he consulted with Representative Frank—then chair of the House Financial Services Committee—about adopting a target. Frank declared that he would oppose the change. According to Bernanke (2015, 526–27), Frank understood the policy logic favoring an inflation target, but he also recognized the poor political optics of adopting a target for only half the Fed's statutory mandate in the midst of recession: "He [Frank] thought that the middle of a recession was the wrong time to risk giving the impression, by setting a target for inflation but not employment, that the Fed didn't care about jobs." Frank's opposition helped to convince Bernanke to defer the formal adoption of an inflation target until unemployment had dropped significantly.

Remarkably, even in 2010 when Bernanke felt that the FOMC had sufficiently managed the potential political risks of adopting a formal inflation target, the committee balked. As Bernanke summed up that December during the last FOMC meeting:

> One of the main issues has been whether we could succeed politically in creating an inflation target or whether there would be pushback from the Congress, etc. I think we're at a moment that if we wanted to do something like that, it would actually be welcomed by the political world. I see absolutely no problem whatsoever from a political perspective if we want to go ahead and put some more structure, whether it's an inflation target or some other kind of structure, on our policymaking. Yet . . . we just kind of talked ourselves out of it somehow. (Federal Open Market Committee 2010a, 109)

Concern about the political risks of adopting an explicit target for just half the Fed's congressional mandate derailed the target for yet another year.

We also have at least anecdotal evidence that the threat of transparency can make central bankers more cautious policy makers. Consider the perspective offered by the president of the St. Louis Federal Reserve Bank, William Poole, in September 2007 during a FOMC meeting—after the onset of the financial crisis. In discussing potential moves by the Fed to increase liquidity in the financial system, Poole encouraged his FOMC colleagues to think carefully about how lawmakers might perceive the beneficiaries of emergency lending:

> I just say that I think there's a transparency issue here that might have to be explained. . . . There is certainly a risk that this facility will not be . . . available to small banks, and the large banks would be getting access to discount window funds at a rate potentially well below that available to small banks. If this were to become a political controversy with some of those who are less friendly to us in the Congress than others, it would complicate the value of this.[21]

Such debate during the crafting of monetary policy, especially in the midst of a financial crisis, raises the possibility that imposing more accountability offers Congress an avenue for indirectly influencing the Fed's policy choices. Concern about how a program will be viewed seems to generate a pause within the FOMC. Three years later, we hear the same worries within the FOMC about the potential political pitfalls of paying interest on reserves held at the Fed—a power Congress granted the Fed before the crisis. Such payments, Philadelphia reserve bank president Charles Plosser notes to his FOMC colleagues, could generate

> accusations that the Fed is continuing taxpayer bailouts of our largest banks. . . . Of course, this does not mean that we should back away from using these tools, and I believe we should use them when the time comes, but I think we must be cognizant of the potential cost, namely, the risk to the institution and our independence of managing such an overly large balance sheet going forward. (Federal Open Market Committee 2010a, 84)

Concerns about the political optics of unconventional policy came mostly from the Fed's hawks, who by definition preferred less accommodative policy. But even Bernanke warned his colleagues in spring 2010 during an FOMC discussion of opening dollar swap lines with foreign central banks: "We can't ignore the politics of this by any means" (Federal Reserve Open Market Committee 2010b, 6). In that meeting, Fed spokesperson Michelle Smith offered a strategy for lowering the political costs of potentially controversial swap lines: "If we could somehow say that we're doing this in some newer, more transparent, quicker way, I think that would help us to mitigate some of the political risk. I don't know if we can do that, but if we could, I think that would be helpful" (ibid., 22). Arguing that political concerns should not dissuade the Fed from acting, Governor Betsy Duke made it plain why the committee was so concerned about political risk: "Frankly, the fact that we have to discuss the political risk underscores the seriousness of the GAO audit provision" (Federal Open Market Committee 2010b, 40). With a cycle of blame and reform in full swing, Fed officials treaded carefully with their congressional overseers. The furor against the Fed in the wake of the financial crisis suggests that the Fed pays a cost for failing to anticipate Congress's views.

Conclusion

Congress's reaction to the global financial crisis mirrors its response to previous episodes of dire financial and economic crises. Electoral imperatives lead legislators to blame the Fed for the sour economy, reevaluate the central bank's powers and governance, and try to make the Fed more accountable to Congress. At the same time, Congress often bestows the Fed with new responsibilities, albeit frequently coupling such grants with new limits on the Fed. In the wake of the most recent financial crisis, the public's angry reaction to Wall Street bailouts moved Congress to constrain the Fed's lender of last resort power and demand greater accountability from the Fed in its supervisory role (by creating a vice chair for supervision and mandating that they testify before Congress twice a year).[22] Heightened criticism from both political parties compelled the Fed to become more transparent about its unconventional monetary policies, pushing the Fed to make new efforts to explain its policies to the public. A truly autonomous central bank should have felt little compulsion to do so. But partisan polarization in the wake of the crisis made it clear to the Fed that its own precarious political standing required greater responsiveness to the (often-conflicting) demands of its congressional bosses. Seen in this light, the Fed's extended deliberations about adopting an inflation target reflect in part the Fed's reluctance to exacerbate congressional anger as a result of the crisis.

The Fed's rocky relationship with Congress (what one reporter dubbed "a cold war") continues (Torres 2016). Persistent low inflation, growth, and interest rates confound Fed policy makers and their congressional overseers, raising doubts about the efficacy of the Fed's unconventional (and unprecedented) monetary policy innovations. At the same time, many lawmakers remain skeptical of the Fed's policy objectives. Some liberals argue the Fed is moving too fast to raise rates; some conservatives believe it is going too slowly. And unhappy lawmakers threaten to enact additional limits on the Fed and even take away a key monetary tool that Congress gave the Fed before the crisis.

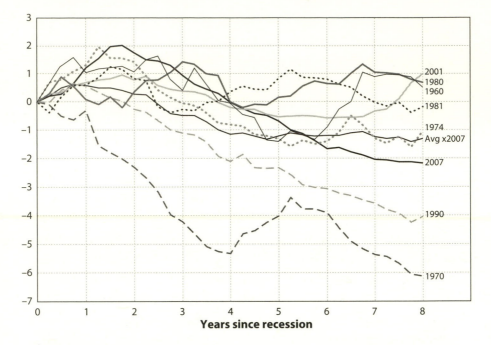

FIGURE 7.8. Cumulative change in government spending as a percent of total GDP, years since recession began. Authors' calculations from US Bureau of Economic Analysis. N.d.

The Federal Reserve shoulders the burden to restore its political capital and reputation in the long shadow of the global financial crisis. Unfortunately, when the Democrats lost control of the House in 2010, the Fed became the lone economic policy activist in Washington. In figure 7.8, we show the cumulative change in federal, state, and local spending (as a share of the total economy) in the wake of each postwar recession. Following the Democrats' 2008 electoral bonanza and an initial burst of stimulus, fiscal policy had been stymied—particularly in comparison to robust government spending as a result of most postwar recessions. And while Bernanke and his successor, Yellen, contended throughout this period that monetary policy was "not a panacea," a divided government failed to heed the call for significantly more stimulus.[23] Absent additional tax cuts or spending measures, it is hard to see how the Fed can engineer a more normal economic recovery given the macroeconomic challenges of low inflation, demand, and productivity. Monetary policy nihilists worry that the Fed may be "out of ammunition."[24] The prospect of another recession presents an economic challenge that would be particularly hard for the Fed to fight without more political support.

As Sir Paul Tucker (2015, 24), a former deputy governor of the Bank of England, observed more generally about the mix of monetary and fiscal policies:

> Given their mandates, central banks have little or no choice— under democratic principles and under the rule of law—to do what they can to restore economic recovery consistent with keeping medium-term inflation expectations anchored. Elected policymakers know that and, further, are under no obligations to act themselves.

Tucker's observation captures the Fed's dilemma in the wake of electoral change in Congress. Republican lawmakers elected on a promise to shrink the size and role of government had little incentive to pursue policies that might have reduced the Fed's burden in trying to restore the economy. Democrats retained some leverage to push back against fiscal restraint before they lost control of the Senate in 2014. But a divided and polarized Congress ultimately made monetary policy the only game in town to restore the economy. Blaming the Fed for the crisis, clipping its wings to fight future recessions, and still imposing new supervisory responsibilities on the Fed, Congress made it plain to the Fed in light of the global financial crisis and Great Recession who was the boss.

8

The Myth of Independence

> If I had learned one thing in Washington, it was that no
> economic program can succeed, no matter how impeccable
> the arguments supporting it, if it is not politically feasible.
> —BEN S. BERNANKE, THE COURAGE TO ACT

Bernanke's reflection after a dozen years at the Fed buries the notion
of Fed independence. As we have shown throughout the book, Congress and the Federal Reserve are interdependent institutions—the
inevitable consequence of reelection-seeking, blame-avoiding politicians who hold the power to make and remake political institutions.
Legislators' interest in monetary policy is reactive and countercyclical. But episodic interest does not create an independent Federal
Reserve. Because Fed credibility is vulnerable to congressional-led
cycles of blame and reform, Fed success in managing an inherently
cyclical economy depends directly on maintaining political support.

In this final chapter, we consider the broader arc of the Fed's
historical and contemporary political relationships. We review the
blame game politics that drove the creation of the Fed and continues to shape its evolution as a quasi-public political institution. We
then look forward to the Fed's coming policy challenges in an era

of intense partisan polarization. A decade after the financial crisis, the Fed confronts the human costs of an uneven, historically slow recovery and institutional costs incurred with its Capitol Hill bosses. Hope for a more robust economy agenda and under fire from both ends of Pennsylvania Avenue requires the Fed to master monetary politics.

How the Fed Evolves

In 1913, President Wilson acknowledged the difficulty of creating a US central bank. His first inaugural address spurred lawmakers to establish a national reserve system, but warned that it would be impossible to wipe the slate clean in designing a central bank: "We shall deal with our economic system as it is and as it may be modified, not as it might be if we had a clean sheet of paper to write upon; and step by step we shall make it what it should be" (Wilson 1913). Wilson's admonition foreshadowed the new Democratic majority's challenges in crafting the Federal Reserve Act. Unable to successfully start from scratch, lawmakers layered their new, decentralized reserve system on top of existing monetary architecture: the gold standard, state and national banking laws, and a popular aversion to centralized monetary control.

These inherited political and institutional constraints shaped the newly formed Federal Reserve's early performance. As we showed in chapters 3 and 4, the compromises that generated a decentralized, regional reserve system in 1913 contributed to the onset and severity of the Great Depression. Politicians—as well as Fed officials—who urged more monetary accommodation and policy coordination across the reserve banks were often unable to corral or coerce regional colleagues to cooperate (Friedman and Schwartz 1963). Although it had been created to prevent the recurring panics of the nineteenth and early twentieth centuries, the Fed failed to stem or reverse the severity of the Great Depression.

During each cycle of Fed blame and reform, lawmakers rediscovered Wilson's warning about the difficulty of revamping the Fed. Even in the aftermath of the Great Depression, Roosevelt's handpicked Fed chair could not convince Congress to centralize the original, regional reserve system. Partially to blame, the Fed's suboptimal structure remained politically invaluable. Spreading control of credit far beyond Washington and Wall Street, the reserve system hardwired political and financial support for the Fed on Main Street. Even today, when there are few federal-style reserve systems around the world, reformers have never fully centralized the Fed. Long after the demise of the political coalitions that created a decentralized central bank, regionalism and quasi-public/private control remain unique features of the Federal Reserve System.

Still, despite limited beginnings and periodic proposals to alter its mandate, change its governance, and completely consolidate control, the Fed has become a global economic juggernaut. In chapter 2, we categorized eighteen major legislative reforms of the Fed over its first century. Amendments that increased Fed power were nearly balanced with amendments that reduced it. And in some years, Congress and the president simultaneously empowered and constrained the Fed. Even as Congress periodically clipped the Fed's wings or required more accountability, lawmakers rarely withdrew any of the Fed's inherited powers. In other words, the Fed continued to accrue power. Over time, the political-economic dynamic that generated more power for the Fed even after its policy failures enlarged its enormous economic impact.

To be sure, immense growth and the comparative strength of the US economy helped to expand the Fed's policy-making influence. International developments over the course of the past century have also contributed to the Fed's rise in global reputation and consequence. The Fed's cooperative monetary policy helped underwrite and sustain the United States' involvement in both world wars—conflicts that ultimately contributed to US economic prominence by midcentury. Late twentieth-century global growth and associated increases in global trade also helped to fuel Fed power. And because such exchange, especially oil, is often denominated in dollars, the Fed accrued more power by virtue of its position as the central bank of the world's largest economy with the world's reserve currency. Indeed, the world became reliant on dominant US monetary policy.

Until recently, with the rise of China and Europe, the United States' relative international status made the Fed the unambiguous leader in shaping monetary policy around the world.

Our analysis of the Fed's evolution has focused primarily on its monetary policy responsibilities. But congressional decisions to empower the Fed with regulatory and supervisory authority over banks—as well as the power to set interest rates and serve as the lender of last resort—vastly expanded the scope of the Fed's economic impact. Granted, the original Federal Reserve Act gave only limited regulatory powers to the Fed, authorizing the Fed to oversee the activities of national banks that were obligated to become members of the regional reserve system (Conti-Brown 2016). It was not until the 1951 Accord broke the Treasury's grip on monetary policy that Congress moved to cement and then expand the foundations of the Fed's regulatory authority. Enacting the Bank Holding Company Act in 1956, Congress gave the Fed power to regulate and supervise banking companies that had eluded state control.

Not all central banks hold both monetary and regulatory powers. In many ways, coupling the two makes for sounder policy: the monetary policy maker arguably has the optimal perspective to know how best to regulate financial institutions, which serve as the primary conduit through which monetary policy operates. As Bernanke defended the Fed's conjoint powers, "information and experiences helps [the Fed] to understand the economy and the financial system better." The political rationale for combining regulatory and monetary control is just as strong. Bernanke stressed that just as a regional reserve system potentially strengthens the Fed's standing across the country, the Fed is also well served having a widespread regulatory presence: "The Fed needs to have roots across the whole country, and not just in New York and Washington, or else it will get divorced politically from the country."[1]

That was precisely the argument used by Bernanke and the reserve bank presidents when they lobbied senators in 2010 against changes to the Federal Reserve Act that would limit the Fed's supervisory reach. Senator Chris Dodd (D-Connecticut) proposed to break up the Fed's monetary and regulatory authority by limiting the scope of the Fed's supervisory authority to the banks. Galvanized by the Fed, banking associations deployed hundreds of bankers to lobby on Capitol Hill against Dodd's proposal. Soon after, the Senate defeated Dodd's proposal ninety to ten, with senators from Texas and Missouri leading the charge.[2] The century-old public/private compromise continued to pay political dividends when the central bank sought to protect its accrued power.

Implications of Blame Game Politics

Interdependence—rather than independence—best characterizes the Fed's position within the broader political system, anchored by its post-1951 Accord relationship with Congress. Critical to that relationship is Congress's central role in driving the emergence of a remarkably more powerful and transparent Federal Reserve. In the wake of economic downturns that are often but not always a by-product of legislative or monetary failures, lawmakers' reactive attention to the Fed perpetuates a cycle of blame and reform. That behavior drove Congress to create the Fed in 1913, and regularly reconsider and even enhance the Fed's authority and public accountability.

Blame game politics predates the contemporary relationship between Congress and the Fed. Testifying before the House Banking and Currency Committee in 1964 when Congress reviewed the Fed's first half century, Fed chair Martin (1964) pinpointed the political value of the Fed to Congress:

> Now, we do bear the slings and arrows of the public. You are in the position of being able to blame us if it goes wrong. We are certainly not asking for your applause if it goes right, but to say that if things collapsed we would not bear the brunt of the public opprobrium I do not think is quite a fair approach to it. I think we will bear the opprobrium of the people if things go wrong, and we have to, this is part of our responsibility.

Viewed through our political-economic prism, Congress depends on the Fed to manage national monetary policy and provide political cover when the economy falters. Indeed, one study of the effect of economic conditions on legislators' electoral fortunes pinpoints 1913 as a key juncture (Lynch 2002). Before Congress created the Fed, macroeconomic conditions played a stronger and more consistent role in shaping midterm electoral outcomes. Once institutional responsibility for managing the national economy shifted to the Fed, lawmakers could more credibly escape blame for inevitable economic downturns. Legislators were also more willing to enhance the powers of the Fed when blame game politics led them to reform the Fed in light of policy failures.

Fed dependence on Congress is more intuitive, even if underappreciated. By repeatedly revising the Federal Reserve Act, Congress signals to Fed officials the costs of failing to meet congressional expectations. Fed chairs understand that the Fed's capacity to make politically unpopular—but economically necessary—policy requires building and maintaining congressional and presidential support. Failure to sufficiently engage lawmakers raises the risk that Congress and the president could retaliate by circumscribing future Fed autonomy or undermining monetary policy with counterproductive fiscal policy.

The reactive nature of congressional attention to monetary policy may seem obvious to legislative scholars accustomed to the pervasive impact of electoral motives on legislative behavior and outcomes. If there is little direct credit to be claimed when the Fed engineers a robust economy, then there is little payoff for electorally minded lawmakers to spend time or resources examining the Fed's performance. But the countercyclical nature of congressional attention has an important, nonobvious implication for the nature of the Fed's position within the political system: Fed autonomy grows when congressional interest in monetary policy subsides. So long as the Fed delivers mandate-consistent economic growth and stable prices, few lawmakers will focus on the Fed's conduct of monetary policy. Congressional indifference sustains Fed autonomy.

Conversely, Fed autonomy suffers as the economy falters and congressional interest climbs; Congress scapegoats the Fed for economic outcomes. As we have shown throughout the book, the

Fed is insufficiently insulated within the political system to make tough policy choices without gauging potential reactions from Congress and the public. As we explored in chapter 7, Bernanke delayed adopting an inflation target for years until he could secure the tacit support of influential lawmakers. As we recounted in chapter 6, even Volcker, who slayed inflation with unprecedented rate hikes and a steep recession, knew to keep a finger on the public's pulse.

To be sure, the Fed is partially insulated within the political system, regardless of the state of the economy. Staggered terms for the Fed chair, budgetary autonomy from Congress, and private sector involvement in the reserve system—these and other statutory features buffer the Fed. But the Fed is not immune to public, presidential, or congressional criticism. Such attacks are consequential because they directly harm the Fed's credibility, the most important asset for an organization seeking to sustain as well as maintain its power and autonomy (Carpenter 2010). The more its reputation suffers, the harder it is for the institution to fend off attempts to saddle it with more responsibility, clip its wings, or impose more transparency. The enactment of a multiyear transportation bill late in 2015 illustrates the Fed's dilemma. After several years of congressional stalemate over raising the gas tax to fuel federal highway spending, the parties swiftly agreed to a proposal that would raid the Federal Reserve's capital surplus (Hughes and Page 2015). If the Fed's public standing had been stronger at the time, we doubt the Fed would have been such easy prey for congressional, fiscal slight of hand.

Ultimately, there is some irony in the Fed's conditional independence. In 1913, the framers of the Fed created a central bank to focus on the nation's long-run financial and economic health. In writing the Federal Reserve Act, lawmakers devised a compromise intended to build durable political support for what had failed twice before and remained a controversial idea: a central bank. Despite building an institution to secure financial stability in the longer term, legislators soon revealed to central bankers that they remained equally concerned about the short run. The Fed found itself beholden to congressional majorities that cared—and continue to care—at least as much about avoiding blame for a poor economy. Always a creature of

Congress, the Fed has no choice but to ensure that it chooses policies broadly palatable to public and congressional majorities, lest its legislative bosses threaten to reconsider its powers and policy-making capacity. By the end of its first century, the Fed has developed into a political institution fully cognizant of the limits and conditionality of its autonomy: strongest when policy efficacy delivers robust growth, and blamed by politicians when the economy underperforms.

Forward Guidance

The Fed enters its second century bedeviled by what one reporter called the "Mystery of Missing Inflation" (Zumbrum 2015). With unemployment hovering just under 5 percent and the Fed beginning to normalize its unconventional policies, inflation remains below the Fed's formal, 2 percent target. The persistence of slow growth, low rates, and little inflation—nearly a decade after the financial crisis—raises real questions about the effectiveness of monetary policy (Torres and Kennedy 2015). Compounding the Fed's current monetary challenges, it faces continuing, often-conflicting congressional criticism from both political parties. Today, the Fed's weakened reputation leaves the institution vulnerable to legislative attacks—especially in the wake of the 2016 elections that gave Republicans full control of Congress and the White House after years of blame-the-Fed criticism by the GOP. Such attacks further weaken the Fed in public and political eyes, amplifying doubts about its capacity to fight the next, inevitable recession.

As the Fed mulled its policy choices in late 2016, Fed officials—as well as economists, Fed watchers, and politicians—offered competing proposals in light of slow growth and low inflation (Blinder 2016; Hilsenrath and Timiraos 2015). Some stressed conventional monetary policy tools such as normalizing interest rates—thinking, among other reasons, that low rates were more the problem than the solution. Others advocated new, less well-understood tools such as lower or even negative interest rates. Still others encouraged unprecedented cooperation between Congress, the president, and the Fed: Congress and the president would enact expansionary fiscal policy (some mix of broad-based tax cuts and increased public spending) that would be financed by the Fed with new money (rather than by the Treasury issuing more debt or Congress hiking taxes in the future).[3] Most important, Fed chair Yellen (2016) argued that the Fed could reuse the successful, though controversial, tools developed during and after the financial crisis.

All these strategies require significant cooperation between fiscal and monetary authorities. More generally, the weaker the Fed's ammunition for generating growth or fighting future recessions, the more Fed officials depend on tenuous political support for unorthodox policy tools and complementary fiscal stimulus. In today's ideologically polarized and electorally competitive environment, however, stalemate on constructive tax and spending policies along with Republican proposals to limit Fed discretion undermine cooperation. Effective economic policy requires a functional polity, especially so when traditional policy tools lose their firepower. Absent a robust, sustainable economic recovery, the Fed will need a stronger collaborative relationship with Congress, not greater autonomy or new limits on its discretion.

The 2016 elections revealed the deep political reverberations of economic shortfalls and policy failures. Through legislation, Congress directs the Fed to pursue long-term economic outcomes consistent with the public's evolving priorities, and repeatedly blames and reforms the Fed when it fails to deliver. So long as lawmakers remain risk-averse reelection seekers, blame game dynamics will shape the Federal Reserve. Ultimately, Congress's countercyclical focus endows the Fed with some autonomy when the economy is strong, but hems it in when the economy falters. At best, the Federal Reserve earns partial and contingent independence from Congress, and thus, we conclude, barely any independence at all.

NOTES

Chapter 1: Monetary Politics

1. On the relationship between Congress and the Fed more generally, see Kettl 1986; Morris 2000; Woolley 2004.

2. The Fed's purchase of government debt during and after the financial crisis was alternately called *quantitative easing, large-scale asset purchases* (LSAPs), or *credit easing.* Between 2008 and 2014, the Fed purchased over three trillion dollars in mortgage-backed securities, other agency debt, and US Treasury securities. See Irwin 2014.

3. Here, we compare the results of a Harris poll in January 1998 that asked "How would you rate the job Alan Greenspan and the Federal Reserve are doing?" to the results of a Gallup Poll in July 2009 that asked "How would you rate the overall job each of the following are doing: The Federal Reserve?" Priming respondents' evaluations with a reference to Greenspan may have inflated confidence in the central bank. Louis Harris and Associates, Harris Poll, September 1988 (survey question). USHARRIS.111388.R3, Louis Harris and Associates (producer). Storrs, CT: Roper Center for Public Opinion Research, iPOLL (distributor), accessed December 30, 2015, https://ropercenter.cornell.edu/CFIDE/cf/action/home/index.cfm.

4. The Fed engages in open market operations when it buys and sells government bonds either directly (pursuant to statutory authorization from Congress) or indirectly through bond dealers. Regional reserve banks still operate discount windows that provide loans for member banks within their districts. Each reserve bank's discount lending rate, however, must be approved by the Board of Governors, which often rejects requests for changing the loan rate.

5. Macroprudential regulation refers to policy tools that are aimed at reducing risk that originates within and across the financial system. (In contrast, microprudential regulation targets individual consumers or firms.)

6. The Federal Reserve's 13(3) powers are detailed in Board of Governors of the Federal Reserve System 2013b. We explore the powers more extensively in chapters 4 and 7, including changes in Dodd-Frank that limited their reach.

7. For the most recent treatment of the origins of the Federal Reserve, see Lowenstein 2015.

8. See, among others, Alesina and Summers 1993; Alt 1991; Bernhard, Broz, and Clark 2002; Broz 1997; Fernandez-Albertos 2015.

9. For the platforms, see http://www.presidency.ucsb.edu/platforms.php.

10. Bernanke (2013a) explores the persistence of deflation after 1913. The threat of deflation in this period stemmed partially from the inadequacies of the international gold standard that tied the availability of credit to the nation's stock of gold (Eichengreen and Sachs 1985; Bernanke and James 1991). With an international gold standard, trade deficits and the accompanying outflow of gold would automatically reduce the issuance of currency, thereby constricting the money supply while deflating prices and demand.

11. As political scientist Terry Moe (1995, 143) once put it, "Bureaucratic structure emerges as a jerry-built fusion of congressional and presidential forms, their relative role and particular features determined by the powers, priorities, and strategies of the various designers."

12. For a review of the Fed's thinking in this period about its public critics, see Goldfarb 2014.

13. On nineteenth-century partisan disagreements over economic policy, see, among others, Ritter 1997.

14. Adoption of the Treasury-Fed Accord in 1951 did not actually involve legislation. As we discuss in detail in chapter 5, though, legislative threats and lawmakers' actions clearly drove the adoption of the Accord.

Chapter 2: The Blame Game

1. We estimate an ordinary least squares model to regress the approval rating (typically combining "strong" and "somewhat strong" approval) on the average annual unemployment and inflation rates, controlling for lagged approval and a "rookie effect" (whether or not the chair is in their first year in office). The results are available from the authors. Note that some years have multiple observations while others have none (due to the absence of polling about the Fed in those years).

2. We estimate approval as a function of unemployment, inflation, and a "rookie effect" of a Fed chair's first year in office, and then generate predicted approval from the model. The results are available from the authors. Bernanke's average annual approval fell five and six points shy of his predicted approval in 2010 and 2011, respectively, before rebounding in 2012.

3. Gallup Organization, Gallup Poll, November 2014 (survey question). USGALLUP.112014A.R01C, Gallup Organization (producer). Ithaca, NY: Cornell University, Roper Center for Public Opinion Research, iPOLL (distributor), accessed July, 10, 2016.

4. We estimate approval (combining good and excellent ratings) as a function of respondent partisan identification, monthly household income, highest educational level obtained, and whether or not the respondent reported that they were retired. We code respondents who lean toward one party or the other as identifying with that party, dropping pure independents. The results are available from the authors.

5. See, for example, Schiller 1995; Sulkin 2005, 2011; Volden, Wiseman, and Wittmer 2013.

6. For the period 1947–2008 (80th–110th Congresses), we rely on the congressional bills data set maintained by E. Scott Adler and John Wilkerson (1947–2008) to identify bills that would amend the Federal Reserve Act. For the period 2009–14, we locate relevant bills via Thomas.loc.gov. The content of each bill after 1972 can be determined from Thomas.loc.gov. For the period before 1973, we consult bill texts available in CIS congressional bills, resolutions, and laws on microfiche (1933–2008).

7. Except where noted, bill counts include bills focused on both the monetary and regulatory dimensions of the Federal Reserve Act.

8. The misery index sums the unemployment and inflation rates. We obtain annual inflation rates (change in the Consumer Price Index for All Urban Consumers maintained by the Bureau of Labor Statistics) from McMahon 2014. For the annual unemployment rates, see Bureau of Labor Statistics 2014.

9. After 2011, a majority of Republican-sponsored bills focused primarily on the Fed's regulatory rather than monetary policy authority.

10. If a bill includes provisions to both constrain and empower the Fed, we code the provisions separately, and determine whether on net, the bill constrains or empowers the Fed. The drawback of the method is that we treat each provision equally, regardless of substantive significance. The benefit of the method is that we avoid subjective determinations of the relative importance of provisions in a single bill.

11. When the bars rise above zero on the y-axis, lawmakers on balance favor constraining the Fed; when the bars fall below zero, lawmakers prefer to empower the Fed.

12. We estimate a negative binomial regression given the count nature of the data, including lagged versions of both economic indicators. We reject the alternative Poisson model, given that the overdispersion parameter (alpha) is significantly greater than zero. We also control for the creation of the dual mandate, since requiring the Fed to pursue both maximum employment and stable prices should reduce at least Democrats' attention to the Fed's conduct of monetary policy. The data include bills that address either the monetary or regulatory policy dimensions of the Fed.

13. The dependent variable in table 2.2 is the overall number of House and Senate bills targeting the Fed introduced each quarter. We estimate a negative binomial regression, including as regressors the number of bills introduced in the previous quarter, the quarterly change in the unemployment rate, a dummy variable to demark the adoption of the dual mandate (Q178), a dummy variable coded 1 to mark FOMC rate hikes during the current or previous quarter (0 if rates are left unchanged or lowered), and a dummy variable coded 1 if the incumbent president appointed the sitting Fed chair (0 otherwise). We also include a control variable to demark the quarter (coded 1 through 8) since lawmakers introduce declining numbers of bills over the eight quarters of each Congress. The target rate decisions are from the Federal Reserve, accessed from Bloomberg LP, May 16, 2016. When we re-run the analysis using increases in the quarterly average effective Federal Funds rate (rather than increases in the target rate), the results are

similar: Lawmakers tend to introduce more bills in quarters when the effective funds rate goes up. Finally, we find little evidence of reciprocal Fed behavior: an uptick in bills targeting the Fed does not typically compel the Fed to alter rates.

14. Table 2.3 shows the results from three logit models that estimate which lawmakers are more likely to introduce bills that target the Fed. We model House Democrats and Republicans in separate models, and all senators in a single one. We control for political forces (electoral margin, ideology, and first-term status) and institutional position (member of relevant banking committee, and whether or not the Fed has a reserve bank within the member or senator's state). Ideology is measured via DW-NOMINATE scores made available by Keith T. Poole; see https://voteview.polisci.ucla.edu/. Higher scores represent more conservative legislators.

15. These partisan effects generally hold up when we rerun the analysis including only bills that address the Fed's monetary policy responsibilities. The results are available from the authors.

16. In 2015, the GAO conducted twelve nonmonetary policy audits of the Federal Reserve System. For details, see http://www.federalreserve.gov/newsevents/reform_audit_gao.htm (accessed February 24, 2016).

17. We measure ideology with Keith T. Poole and Howard Rosenthal's first-dimension Common Space scores). Common Space scores position House and Senate lawmakers along the same Left-Right spectrum. For the scores, see http://voteview.com/basic.htm (accessed February 29, 2016).

18. We consider 1913 a "reform" year due to the adoption of the original Federal Reserve Act.

19. We do not include the 1951 Treasury-Fed Accord, because no law was enacted, or the 1956 Bank Holding Company Act, since the changes were directed toward the Fed's bank supervisory powers.

20. We treat each incidence of reform equivalently, even though some amendments to the act have more direct and long-lasting effects than others.

21. We use the FRED series for the civilian unemployment rate, percent, annual, seasonally adjusted (1948–2014), and inflation, consumer prices for the United States, percent, annual, not seasonally adjusted (1961–2014). We draw unemployment rate data for 1913–47 from Stanley Lebergott (1957) and calculate the annual inflation rate for 1913–60 from the Bureau of Labor Statistics, consumer price index history, table 24 (http://www.bls.gov/cpi/#tables). For FRED data, see https://research.stlouisfed.org/fred2/. Unemployment and months in recession run in tandem, but not excessively so (Pearson's r = 0.4).

22. Presidents and Fed chairs have staggered four-year terms, so there is no guarantee in any given year that the same party both holds the White House and, initially appointed, the sitting Fed chair. That said, over the Fed's first century, partisan mismatch occurred just 16 percent of the time. For coding, see the following note. For evidence that the partisanship of the Fed chair matters in setting interest rates, see Clark and Arel-Bundock 2013.

23. We code mismatched president–Fed chair pairs as 1, and 0 otherwise. For example, Bernanke is coded as a match for President Bush in 2006, 2007,

and 2008, and a mismatch with President Obama in 2009. Because Obama re-appointed Bernanke as chair in 2010, we resume coding the pair as a match in 2010–13. This coding strategy allows us to test whether Congress targets the Fed for reform when the head of the Fed is out of step with the president's party. Alternatively, one could assume that the Fed chair's party matches the party of the president who first appointed them. Any other party pairing would count as a mismatch. Thus, every Bernanke-Bush pair would be a match, and every Bernanke-Obama pair a mismatch, even though Obama reappointed Bernanke for a second term.

24. Ben S. Bernanke, interview with the authors, Brookings Institution, Washington, DC, June 13, 2014.

Chapter 3: Creating the Federal Reserve

1. For the party platforms, see Woolley and Peters, n.d.

2. As we explore in chapter 4, reforms of the Fed in the wake of the Great Depression stripped the president's lieutenants of their seats on the Board and gave the Board more power.

3. For a detailed review of the conflicts, see Jeong, Miller, and Sobel 2009; Lowenstein 2015.

4. On the procedural steps that brought two versions of the bill to the floor, see "Senate to Tackle Three Money Bills," *New York Times*, November 21, 1913, 13.

5. Despite the binding vote in the Democratic Caucus, two Democrats defected to support Hitchcock's alternative. See "Senators Waver on Currency Bill," *New York Times*, November 28, 1913, 16.

6. For the House vote, see Sixty-Third Congress, House roll call vote no. 73, accessed February 22, 2017, ftp://k7moa.com/dtl/63.dtl. For the Senate vote, see Sixty-Third Congress, Senate roll call vote no. 185, accessed February 22, 2017, ftp://k7moa.com/dtl/63s.dtl.

7. "Wilson Is Blamed for Currency Halt," *New York Times*, November 11, 1913, 3.

8. We consider the eighteen legislators (including eight Republicans) who voted for Victor Murdock (P-Kansas) for speaker in 1913 as Progressives (of whom fifteen cast a vote on the final conference report establishing the Fed).

9. The Federal Reserve Act allowed for subsequent changes by the Federal Reserve Board to the boundaries of the reserve districts, but did not permit the creation of new districts once twelve districts had been designated.

10. Michael R. McAvoy (2006) offers an account of the organization of the system that highlights the economic rationale followed by the RBOC.

11. For the cities' submission materials, see RBOC 1914b.

12. "Affixes His Signature at 6:02 pm, Using Four Gold Pens," *New York Times*, December 24, 1913, 1.

13. Board of Governors of the Federal Reserve System 2013a.

14. A series of reserve banks had been designated in a nineteenth-century national banking system, with a pyramid of small national banks, larger banks

in several dozen reserve cities, and the largest banks in the initial three central reserve cities. With fluctuating demand, but a relatively fixed currency supply, the national banking system proved unable to stem periodic financial panics. For details, see Bordo, Rappoport, and Schwartz 1992.

15. On the financial underdevelopment of the South and challenges it posed for the placement of the reserve banks, see Odell and Weiman 1998.

16. On insurgent Progressives' antipathy toward the Federal Reserve Act, see Link 1954, chapter 2. Alan Ware (2006, 131–32) argues that Wilson reached out to conservative Democrats rather than to Progressive Republicans.

17. We estimate a logit model using Stata 11.2's logit routine. The dependent variable is thus whether or not the applicant city was selected by the RBOC (1 = yes; 0 = otherwise).

18. For instance, the Maryland–New York dyad would be coded 1, since the RBOC placed a reserve bank in New York; the Maryland-Baltimore dyad would be coded 0, since the RBOC did not place a reserve bank in Baltimore.

19. Conditional logit models estimate choices among alternatives in groups, conditional on the decision maker selecting at least one from each group of observations. Figure 3.2, for example, shows the votes of state banker delegations that were ultimately assigned to the Richmond Federal Reserve district: Maryland; Washington, DC; Virginia; the Carolinas; and portions of West Virginia. By modeling banker choices within each of the twelve reserve districts, we make the (reasonable) assumption, based on Willis's (1923) study, that the RBOC planned to select the maximum number of cities (twelve).

20. We obtained the volume of check clearings in each city in 1913 from *Dun's Review*.

21. According to the 1910 census, Dallas ranked fifty-seventh out of the one hundred most populous cities.

22. The overall fit of the model is good, and we safely reject the hypothesis that the coefficients are jointly equal to 0.

23. "Huge Bank Advocated," *New York Times*, January 6, 1914, 9.

24. Again, the overall fit of the model is good, and we safely reject the hypothesis that the coefficients are jointly equal to 0.

25. Willis (1923, 585) would have concurred: "In none of the preliminary survey . . . was the establishment of a bank at Richmond, Virginia, ever seriously considered."

Chapter 4: Opening the Act in the Wake of the Depression

1. For commercial bank suspension data, see Friedman and Schwartz 1963, 438. Not all of these banks were members of the Federal Reserve System. For estimates of the unemployment data, see Bernstein, n.d.

2. Other economists highlight alternative causes of the Depression, including the impact of the Republicans' Smoot-Hawley tariff increases, President Herbert Hoover's call for higher taxes in 1931, and the malfunctioning of the international gold standard as European economies went into decline in the late 1920s.

3. For a further review of this period of change in Fed history, see Meltzer 2000; 2003, 127.

4. For details on changes to the Federal Reserve Act before the 1930s, see Dykes and Whitehouse 1989.

5. But Chang-Tai Hsieh and Christina D. Romer (2006) find little evidence that the public at home or abroad harbored such fears.

6. Changes to the Federal Reserve Act over time have been chronicled in issues of the annual reports of the Federal Reserve Board (until 1935) and afterward in the annual reports of the Board of Governors of the Federal Reserve System; accessed August 3, 2016, https://fraser.stlouisfed.org/title/117#!2472.

7. As Nolan McCarty, Keith T. Poole, and Howard Rosenthal (2013, 153) have similarly argued, legislative responses to financial and economic crises have often been limited, and stronger responses have typically required a transition in political power—the Great Depression being the "quintessential illustration of our claim."

8. Supporters of the Thomas Amendment thought that its mere adoption would make it unnecessary to deploy it. See "House Will Speed Inflation-Farm Aid," *New York Times*, April 30, 1933, 8. This view proved wrong: Roosevelt would make full use of his new powers to reduce the gold content of the dollar and take the United States off the gold standard.

9. See "Inflation Schemes Held in Abeyance," *New York Times*, March 24, 1933, C29.

10. To measure the importance of farming to state economies, we use agricultural census data available in table 11 of the 1935 Census of Agriculture, published by the US Department of Agriculture. We use the per capita value of manufacturing to measure the relative importance of manufacturing in each state. Manufacturing value data are available in table 3 of the Biennial Census of Manufacturers (1933 and 1935), published by the US Department of Commerce. Population data for 1930 are available in the Fifteenth Census of the United States, table 32, published in 1931 by the Department of Commerce.

11. Note that the parameter estimate for the southern representative variable does not reach statistical significance. We use Ira Katznelson and Quinn Mulroy's (2012) definition of the South, which includes all seventeen states that mandated racial segregation via Jim Crow laws. Because almost all southerners were Democrats (save for two Republicans elected from Tennessee), we do not detect distinctive southern support for the bill when we include party as a predictor. Once party is removed from the equation, southern lawmakers disproportionately support passage of the bill.

12. See "New Tack Planned by Inflationists," *New York Times*, March 23, 1933, 3.

13. See "Political Battle Resumed in Senate," *New York Times*, April 11, 1933, 2.

14. Ibid.

15. Calculated with Stata 11.2 *margins* command, which generates predicted probabilities at particular values of each independent variable, holding the other variables constant at their mean values.

16. "Inflation Fight Is Warm," *New York Times*, April 28, 1933, 2–3.

17. "House Will Speed Inflation-Farm Aid," *New York Times*, April 30, 1933, 8.

18. "Excerpts from the Press Conference, April 19, 1933," American Presidency Project, accessed February 20, 2017, http://www.presidency.ucsb.edu/ws/index.php?pid=14620.

19. See "Move for Closure on Banking Bill," *New York Times*, January 18, 1933, 1.

20. See "Roosevelt Favors Pushing Bank Bill," *New York Times*, May 6, 1933, 19.

21. Standing votes were recorded in the House, but such vote tallies do not record members' votes. The Senate voted at each stage by unrecorded voice votes.

22. Senator Carter Glass, *Congressional Record*, May 19, 1933, S3725.

23. Ibid.

24. "Bank Bill Held Up for Woodin Views," *New York Times*, April 18, 1933, 23.

25. "Roosevelt Backs Bank Compromise," *New York Times*, June 8, 1933, 35.

26. *Business Week*, April 12, 1933, 3.

27. Roosevelt had been setting a daily gold price for the previous three months as well. Despite efforts to discern the rhyme or reason of FDR's gold prices, most accounts (Blum 1959; Ahamed 2009) suggest that prices were utterly random. Ahamed (2009, 473) calls that three-month period "one of the most bizarre episodes of the history of currency policy."

28. "Bill Is Sent to Congress," *New York Times*, January 16, 1934, 1.

29. "Morgenthau Sees Managed Currency," *New York Times*, January 16, 1934, 1.

30. "Meeting at White House: President and Advisers Map Policy on Reserve Bank Gold Holdings," *New York Times*, January 12, 1934, 1.

31. "Bill Is Sent to Congress," *New York Times*, January 16, 1934, 1.

32. "House in Noisy Session," *New York Times*, January 21, 1934, 1.

33. The results are available from the authors. We model Republican votes on the gold reserve bill as a function of whether or not the member hailed from a reserve bank state, controlling for the value of manufacturing and importance of farming in their home states.

34. "House in Noisy Session," *New York Times*, January 21, 1934, 30.

35. "Critics Open Fire on Banking Phases of the Money Bill," *New York Times*, January 20, 1934, 1.

36. "Testimony of Owen D. Young before Senate Committee on Money Bill," *New York Times*, January 23, 1934, 10.

37. US Treasury, n.d.

38. Eccles's original proposal for the FOMC would have given voting rights to three members of the Board and two reserve bank presidents. But when Eccles testified before the House banking panel in support of his bill, he suggested that an FOMC comprised only of Board members would be preferable: sharing authority between the Board and reserve system would potentially undermine Board control of monetary policy. See "Eccles Favors Banking Bill Changes," *Wall Street Journal*, March 5, 1935, 2.

39. For a discussion of the impact of a mandatory retirement rule, see "New Deals May Yet Get Reserve Board," *Wall Street Journal*, February 6, 1935, 3.

40. For a discussion of the relationship of House Republicans and bankers opposed to the original Eccles bill, see "Ready to Redraft Banking Bill," *New York Times*, March 29, 1935, 33.

41. See "House Banking Vote May Be Delayed Until Next Week," *Wall Street Journal*, May 2, 1935, 2.

42. "Bank Bill Fight Expected to End in Glass Victory," *New York Times*, July 3, 1935.

43. Quoted in *Congressional Record*, July 26, 1935, S11917.

44. "Bankers Accused of Coercing House," *New York Times*, July 30, 1935, 27.

45. The Board alone retained authority to alter member bank reserve requirements on a vote of four Board members. For details on the conference committee's decisions, see "House Managers' Analyses of Banking Bill, Filed with Conferees' Report," *New York Times*, August 20, 1935, 14.

46. Diaries of Henry Morgenthau Jr., vol. 8:15, July 3, 1935, accessed August 3, 2016, http://www.fdrlibrary.marist.edu/archives/collections/franklin/?p=collections/findingaid&id=535&q=&rootcontentid=188897#id188897.

47. Diaries of Henry Morgenthau Jr., vol. 6:68, June 13, 1935, accessed August 3, 2016, http://www.fdrlibrary.marist.edu/archives/collections/franklin/?p=collections/findingaid&id=535&q=&rootcontentid=188897#id188897.

48. FOMC Executive Committee Meeting Notes, March 13, 1937, accessed August 3, 2016, http://www.federalreserve.gov/monetarypolicy/files/FOMChminecl19370313.pdf.

Chapter 5: Midcentury Modern Central Banking

1. "Federal Reserve Dispute," *CQ Almanac*, 7th ed. (Washington, DC: Congressional Quarterly, 1952), accessed January 30, 2017, http://library.cqpress.com/cqalmanac/cqal51-8889-29657-1405148.

2. Diaries of Henry Morgenthau Jr., vol. 8:15, July 3, 1935, accessed August 3, 2016, http://www.fdrlibrary.marist.edu/archives/collections/franklin/?p=collections/findingaid&id=535&q=&rootcontentid=188897#id188897.

3. FOMC Executive Committee Meeting Notes, March 13, 1937, accessed August 3, 2016, http://www.federalreserve.gov/monetarypolicy/files/FOMChminecl19370313.pdf.

4. Diaries of Henry Morgenthau Jr., vol. 62:267, April 3, 1937, accessed August 3, 2016, http://www.fdrlibrary.marist.edu/archives/collections/franklin/?p=collections/findingaid&id=535&q=&rootcontentid=188897#id188897.

5. "Morgenthau Hits Drop in U.S. Bonds," *New York Times*, January 10, 1941, 29.

6. For the public debt as a percentage of (nominal) GDP (1939–present), see Federal Reserve Bank of St. Louis 2016c.

7. Federal Open Market Committee 1933–2016, "Meeting, June 10, 1941."

8. Federal Open Market Committee 1933–2016, "Meeting, September 27, 1941."

9. See, for example, the discussion in which Governor John K. McKee references the war period; Federal Open Market Committee 1933–2016, "Meeting, December 12, 1941."

10. Robert Higgs, quoted in Katznelson 2013, 343.

11. "Direct Bond Deals Urged for Senate," *New York Times*, February 5, 1942, 10.

12. "Economists Score Eccles Bond Plan," *New York Times*, February 9, 1942, 25.

13. Partisanship and ideology correlated at 0.6.

14. We measure the importance of the financial sector by the volume of banking assets in the state, drawing data on the number of national banks, and total dollars of assets or liabilities in those banks, by state, from US Department of Commerce 1942.

15. The figures show the likelihood that senators voted to curtail direct purchases. Based on the estimates in table 5.1, we simulate the likelihood of senators voting to curtail direct purchases, controlling for party, ideology, state economic interests, and region.

16. Interestingly, Patman complained on the floor when the House took up the conference report that he had been led to believe that the conferees would strip the Smith amendment in conference. Yet the Senate conferees instead acceded to the House, and simply clarified the language of the Smith amendment to make it clear that the $5 billion limit applied only to bond purchases from the Treasury, not in the open market. Patman threatened to derail the conference report to address the amendment in question. But reminded by the speaker of the House that the chamber would have to reject the entire conference report and vote anew to go back to conference, Patman quickly folded and simply voted against the conference report. The final vote was 315–22. See *Congressional Record*, 77th Cong., 2nd sess., House, March 16, 1942, 2502–13.

17. The direct purchase authority turned out to be an exceedingly small tool in the Fed's arsenal during the war. Between 1942 and the end of the war in 1945, the Fed bought just over $2 billion in securities directly from the Treasury (Garbade 2014, table 4)—a mere 2 percent of the nation's GDP in 1945. Had Senator Taft's amendment to limit direct purchases to $2 billion been adopted, it would actually have had some bite.

18. For unemployment rates (1930–40), see Santoni 1986. For unemployment rates after 1944, see US Bureau of Labor Statistics 2016.

19. "Rejects Changes in Full-Job Bill," *New York Times*, September 20, 1945, 19.

20. Senate roll call votes no. 82 and no. 83, Seventy-Ninth Senate, September 28, 1945.

21. Senate roll call vote no. 84, Seventy-Ninth Senate, September 28, 1945. We regress the final vote on senators' party affiliation and DW-NOMINATE ideological score. Only the ideology parameter estimate is statistically significant. (Party and ideology are correlated at just 0.56 in the Seventy-Ninth Congress.)

22. Associated Press, "Plot in Congress to Kill Truman's Job Bills Reported," *Washington Post*, November 20, 1945, 7.

23. House roll call vote no. 100, Seventy-Ninth House, December 14, 1945. We model the final vote as a function of party and racial ideology (as measured by lawmakers' second dimension DW-NOMINATE scores; http://www.voteview .com). Both variables' parameter estimates are statistically significant at $p < 0.05$.

24. *Congressional Record*, September 27, 1945, 9204.

25. The *New York Times* remarked that this was the first time since the creation of the Fed in 1913 that a president had tried to influence monetary policy by calling the whole Board to the White House (Belair 1951d, 1).

26. As part of the agreement, McCabe agreed to step down and was replaced as chair by Martin. Reflective of historians' focus on personalities, Hetzel and Leach (2001, 37n9) observe that in Leach's view, McCabe made the Accord possible "through the professional, honest way that he presented the case for monetary independence to the executive branch and Congress." In 1951, Leach was serving as a staff economist at the Fed's Board of Governors.

27. "Monetary, Credit, and Fiscal Policies," Report of the Subcommittee on Monetary, Credit, and Fiscal Policies of the Joint Committee on the Economic Report of the Congress of the United States, 81st Cong., 2nd sess., January 24, 1950.

28. Ibid., 432.

29. Ibid., 232.

30. US Congress 1951, 175. But note, the Douglas report included one of Patman's pet issues with the Fed: he wanted Congress to reinstate the 90 percent franchise tax on the reserve banks' earnings that had been eliminated by statute in 1933. So there was certainly a basis for Patman's support for some of the report, although he clearly had established himself already as a foe of the Fed.

31. "Monetary, Credit, and Fiscal Policies," 31.

32. "Talks Fail to End Monetary Policy Dispute," *New York Times*, December 9, 1949, 46.

33. The *New York Times* reported at the time: "It is known, for instance, that Senator Robert A. Taft . . . has interested himself in the dispute and has asked the Federal Reserve for particulars"; "Senator Shelves Treasury Dispute," *New York Times*, February 7, 1951, 20.

34. "Monetary Policy and Management of the Public Debt," hearings before the Subcommittee on General Credit Control and Debt Management, Joint Committee on the Economic Report of the Congress of the United States, 82nd Cong., 2nd sess., 1952, 97.

35. See "Fiscal Confusion: Reserve Board Hikes Discount Rate to Curb Credit; Treasury Still Backs Cheap Money on Refunding Bonds," *Wall Street Journal*, August 19, 1950, 2.

36. Ibid.

37. "The Money Market: Firm Money Apparently Wins First Round in Clash of Fiscal Policies," *Wall Street Journal*, August 28, 1950, 7.

38. "Fiscal Confusion," 2.

39. Ibid.

40. Allan Sproul, letter to James E. Shelton, February 28, 1951, reprinted in Ritter 1980, 83.

41. Allan Sproul, "The 'Accord': A Landmark in the First Fifty Years of the Federal Reserve System," reprinted in Ritter 1980, 64.

42. Oral history interview by Richard A. Baker, Senate Historical Office, with Grover W. Ensley, executive director, Joint Economic Committee, US Congress, Washington, DC, October 29–November 1, 1985.

43. Allan Sproul, letter to James E. Shelton, February 28, 1951, reprinted in Ritter 1980, 83.

Chapter 6: The Great Inflation and the Limits of Independence

1. William McChesney Martin testimony in US Senate, Committee on Banking and Currency, *Nomination of William McChesney Martin Jr.*, hearings, 84th Cong., 2nd sess., 1956, 5.

2. Gallup's "Most Important Problem" responses are compiled by the Policy Agendas Project, http://www.policyagendas.org/page/datasets-codebooks #gallups_most_important_problem.

3. Cambridge Reports / Research International, "Cambridge Reports National Omnibus Survey," Roper Center for Public Opinion Research, Storrs, Connecticut, July 1978.

4. "2 Democrats Seek Arthur Burns' Hide," *Chicago Tribune*, November 5, 1977, G7.

5. The Phillips curve proposed a negative relationship between inflation and unemployment. James Forder (2014) explores the Phillips curve and its historical treatment by macroeconomists.

6. See, in particular, Meltzer 2005; Abrams 2006; Weise 2012.

7. "Federal Reserve Holds the Helm," *New York Times*, January 16, 1966, 131.

8. Whip Inflation Now largely called for fiscal restraint—proposals Congress rejected out of hand in the midst of a recession.

9. Federal Reserve Act, Section 2a, accessed August 10, 2016, http://www .federalreserve.gov/aboutthefed/section2a.htm.

10. For explorations of the original mandate of the Federal Reserve, see Bernanke 2013a; Reinhart and Rogoff 2013.

11. Public Law 63–43, accessed July 30, 2015, http://www.llsdc.org/FRA-LH.

12. Marriner Eccles, "Banking Act of 1935," hearings before the Committee on Banking and Currency, House of Representatives, 74th Cong., 1st sess., February 21, 22, 26, 27, and 28, and March 1, 4, 5, 6, 11, 12, 13, and 14 (Washington, DC: Government Printing Office, 1935), 238.

13. Ibid., 238.

14. Federal Reserve Act, Section 2a, accessed July 29, 2015, http://www .federalreserve.gov/aboutthefed/section2a.htm.

15. Measuring ideology with Keith T. Poole and Howard Rosenthal's DW-NOMINATE scores for the Ninety-Fifth House (ranging from most liberal −1 to most conservative +1), Ohio Republican Charles W. Whalen scored −0.269 and Maryland's Newton Steers scored −0.151. In comparison, the median Republican

in that Congress scored 0.197; the median Democrat, −0.290. Accessed August 8, 2016, http://voteview.com.

16. Ninety-Fifth Congress, House of Representatives, vote 806, March 9, 1978, accessed August 8, 2016, http://voteview.com/HOUSE95.html. Number of unemployed, number of district residents working in the finance, real estate, and insurance industries, and percent of district residents unionized drawn from Adler, n.d. The results of the logit model are available from the authors.

17. The difference in unemployed for Democratic supporters and opponents of the Jeffords amendment is statistically significant (p < 0.001).

18. "Senate Seeking Compromise on Employment Bill," *Washington Post*, October 11, 1978, A9.

19. Ninety-Fifth Congress, US Senate, votes 1129 and 806, October 13, 1978, accessed August 8, 2016, http://voteview.com/SENATE95.html.

20. We model the vote as a function of party, number of unemployed in the state, number of district residents working in the finance, real estate, and insurance industries, and percent of district residents unionized. Data are drawn from Adler, n.d. Only senators' party affiliation and strength of unions in their state are statistically significant at conventional levels. The results of the logit model are available from the authors.

21. According to the Bank of International Settlements (2009, chapter 2, table 1), a study of forty-five Bank of International Settlements–member central banks found thirty-three central banks with a price stability mandate or priority given to price stability. The Bank of International Settlements serves as the de facto bank for sixty member central banks.

22. Reuss began his campaign with a more audacious bill that would have commanded the Fed to expand the money supply at a rate of 6 percent per year, set an interest rate target for the Fed, and require the central bank to hit the target within a particular time limit. Strongly opposed by Burns, the proposal divided Reuss's banking panel colleagues, including several senior Democrats. The committee defeated Reuss's bill by a vote of nineteen to twenty, with seven Democrats bucking Reuss's leadership and all Republicans opposed. "Reuss Withdraws Bill Hit by Burns," *New York Times*, February 21, 1975, 39.

23. Supporters of the resolution doubted that President Ford would sign the bill. "Federal Reserve Policies," in *CQ Almanac, 1975*, 31st ed. (Washington, DC: Congressional Quarterly, 1976), 166–69, accessed July 24, 2015, http://library.cqpress.com/cqalmanac/document.php?id=cqal75-1213467.

24. "Federal Reserve Policies," in *CQ Almanac, 1975*, 31st ed. (Washington, DC: Congressional Quarterly, 1976), 166–69, accessed July 24, 2015, http://library.cqpress.com/cqalmanac/document.php?id=cqal75-1213467.

25. Ninety-Fourth Congress, House of Representatives, House vote 60, March 24, 1975. We model the vote as a function of lawmakers' partisanship and the impact of the recession back home (as measured by the unemployment rate by House district). The number of unemployed is only measured roughly, given the use of the census to determine district-level unemployment. Thus, the measure

actually taps the level of unemployment in the 1970 census. For data and sources, see Adler, n.d. The results are available from the authors.

26. "Transcript," Federal Open Market Committee meeting, July 19, 1977, 35, accessed February 3, 2017, http://www.federalreserve.gov/monetarypolicy /fomchistorical1977.htm.

27. *Federal Reserve Act of 1977*, hearings before the Committee on Banking, Finance, and Urban Affairs, House of Representatives, 95th Cong., 1st sess., on H.R. 8094, a bill to promote the accountability of the Federal Reserve system, July 18 and 26, 1977, 59, accessed December 31, 2015, https://fraser.stlouisfed .org/scribd/?title_id=377&filepath=/docs/historical/fr_act/hearing_hr8094 _hr_19770718.pdf#scribd-open. Burns makes reference to quarterly reports, but the proposed legislation referenced semiannual testimony about quarterly projections.

28. "Bank Unit Bill Proposes Fed Appointment Changes," *New York Times*, July 29, 1977, 72.

29. "Interest Rate Ceilings," in *CQ Almanac, 1977*, 33rd ed. (Washington, DC: Congressional Quarterly, 1978, accessed February 2, 2017, http://library.cqpress .com/cqalmanac/document.php?id=cqal75-1213467.

30. Senator John Tower, 123 *Congressional Record* 36203 (1977), Senate, November 1.

31. Senator William Proxmire, 123 *Congressional Record* 36203 (1977), Senate, November 1.

32. The 1977 amendments that compelled semiannual testimony were absorbed the next year into the Humphrey-Hawkins statute. Humphrey-Hawkins itself expired a decade later. Congress subsequently amended the Federal Reserve Act in 2000 to revise the requirement for semiannual testimony. Congress stripped the specific forecasts originally required under Humphrey-Hawkins. Instead, the law was revised to require appearances and reports to Congress at semiannual hearings regarding "the efforts, activities, objectives, and plans of the Board and the Federal Open Market Committee with respect to the conduct of monetary policy; and economic developments and prospects for the future." Public Law 106–569, Title X, accessed December 31, 2015, http://www.gpo.gov /fdsys/pkg/PLAW-106publ569. The semiannual testimony today is still delivered at what is informally known as the "Humphrey-Hawkins hearings," despite the law's demise.

33. In 2004, Congress changed the legal name of the GAO from the General Accounting Office to the Government Accountability Office.

34. Such a lobbying campaign would become a staple of future Federal Reserve efforts to dilute legislative proposals deemed threatening to the Fed's autonomy. We review one such attempt in the wake of the global financial crisis of 2007–8 when lawmakers sought again to audit the Fed.

35. Ninety-Fifth Congress, House of Representatives, vote 606, October 14, 1977. We use Keith T. Poole and Howard Rosenthal's first dimension DW-Nominate score to measure legislators' ideologies; accessed August 7, 2015, http://voteview.com/house95.htm.

36. Monthly unemployment rates obtained from Federal Reserve Board of St. Louis. 2016a. Monthly inflation rate (year-to-year percentage change) from Federal Reserve Bank of St. Louis. 2016b.

37. Ronald Reagan TV Ad: "Prouder, Stronger, Better," accessed August 12, 2016, https://www.youtube.com/watch?v=EU-IBF8nwSY.

38. For a detailed account of Volcker's performance at the Fed—and his ability to resist political pressures to end the anti-inflation campaign—see Silber 2012. Conti-Brown (2016, 41) attributes much of the Fed's credibility in combating inflation in this period to the "exercise of slow, cautious, painstaking leadership within the Federal Reserve System."

39. For the longer (and consistent) story of the Fed chair Greenspan's obfuscation to Congress about the tape recordings, see Auerbach 2008, chapter 6. For an account of the final agreement to release verbatim transcripts, see Wessel 1993.

40. For further evidence of participants' expectation that meeting deliberations would not be made public in this period, through an analysis of verbal FOMC dissents before and after the 1993 decision to make transcripts available with a five-year lag, see Meade and Stasavage 2008.

41. "Transcript," Federal Open Market Committee meeting, October 6, 1979, 10, accessed August 8, 2016, http://www.federalreserve.gov/monetarypolicy /fomchistorical1979.htm.

42. "Transcript," Federal Open Market Committee meeting, March 18, 1980, 36, accessed August 8, 2016, http://www.federalreserve.gov/monetarypolicy /fomchistorical1980.htm.

43. "Transcript," Federal Open Market Committee meeting, July 7, 1981, 55, accessed August 8, 2016, http://www.federalreserve.gov/monetarypolicy /fomchistorical1981.htm.

44. "Transcript," Federal Open Market Committee meeting, October 6, 1981, 19, accessed August 8, 2016, http://www.federalreserve.gov/monetarypolicy /fomchistorical1981.htm.

45. "Transcript," Federal Open Market Committee meeting, October 6, 1981, 25, accessed August 8, 2016, http://www.federalreserve.gov/monetarypolicy /fomchistorical1981.htm.

46. "Broad Banking Deregulation Bill Approved," *CQ Almanac, 1980*, 36th ed. (Washington, DC: Congressional Quarterly, 1981), 275–77.

47. Richard Timberlake (1993, 364–65) notes that because the Fed maintains a monopoly on the creation of the money supply, its leverage over the monetary base is independent of the number of member banks or volume of reserves held in Fed coffers.

48. "Monetary Policy," in *CQ Almanac, 1982*, 38th ed. (Washington, DC: Congressional Quarterly, 1983), 64–65.

49. Senator William Proxmire, 125 *Congressional Record* 29356 (1979), Senate, October 24.

50. "Transcript," Federal Open Market Committee meeting, October 5, 1982, 50–51, accessed August 8, 2016, http://www.federalreserve.gov/monetarypolicy /fomchistorical1982.htm.

51. "Transcript," Federal Open Market Committee meeting, July 19, 1977, 42, accessed August 8, 2016, http://www.federalreserve.gov/monetarypolicy /fomchistorical1977.htm.

Chapter 7: The Only Game in Town

1. Laurence Ball (2016) challenges the Fed's claims, arguing that political pressures against bailing out Lehman Brothers led the Fed and Treasury to stand pat.

2. Alan Greenspan, "The Economic Outlook," prepared testimony before the Joint Economic Committee, 107th Cong., 2nd sess., November 13, 2002, quoted in Financial Crisis Inquiry Commission 2011, 88.

3. For additional views about the impact of monetary policy on the housing boom and bust, see Baily and Taylor 2014.

4. These credit lines allowed the Fed to lend dollars to other central banks, which then offered dollar-denominated loans to their own countries' banks. On currency swap lines, see Hilsenrath and Sparshott 2011.

5. For a summary of the full range of the Fed's crisis response policies, see "The Federal Reserve's Response to the Financial Crisis and Actions to Foster Maximum Employment and Price Stability," Board of Governors of the Federal Reserve System, accessed August 15, 2016, http://www.federalreserve.gov /monetarypolicy/bst_crisisresponse.htm.

6. Congress and President George W. Bush in October 2008 had already struggled to enact the $700 billion Troubled Assets Relief Program, designed to purchase toxic assets from bank balance sheets, but ultimately used to inject capital into the banks. Few believed that Congress would renew such funding in the near future.

7. Ben S. Bernanke, interview with the authors, Brookings Institution, Washington, DC, June 13, 2014.

8. For the charge that the Fed favored the financial industry in designing 13(3) programs, see Jacobs and King 2016.

9. It took more than five years after the adoption of Dodd-Frank for the Fed to finalize a rule in November 2015 to implement the new limitations on 13(3) lending (Board of Governors of the Federal Reserve System 2015). Senators' dissatisfaction with the Fed's draft rule provoked liberals and conservatives to charge that the draft rule failed to address Congress's intended changes to the Fed's authority (Schroeder 2015).

10. We recognize that in voting for omnibus reform measures, lawmakers' votes could have been shaped by more than the provisions affecting the Fed.

11. 111th Congress, House roll call vote no. 968, December 11, 2009, on final passage of the Dodd-Frank Wall Street Reform and Consumer Protection Act of 2009.

12. We measure House members' votes as a function of their district's conservatism (John McCain's share of the two-party vote in their district in 2008), their own ideology (whether or not they belong to the moderate Blue Dog coalition within the Democratic Caucus), and the economic salience of the financial industry in their district (the percent of the district employed in finance, based on the US census of 2000).

13. 111th Congress, Senate roll call vote no. 16, January 28, 2010.

14. The percentages represent the marginal probabilities of each type of senator voting to confirm, controlling for each senator's party.

15. 112th Congress, House roll call vote no. 513, July 25, 2012. Figure 7.6 shows the simulated probabilities that Democrats will support the bill. We first estimate a logit model of the forces shaping Democrats' votes, focusing on the effects of elections (whether or not the member is retiring, barely won their 2010 election, or in their first term), ideology (a Blue Dog member or not), salience of the financial industry to their state (the percent of the state employed in financial services), and commitment to the Federal Reserve (whether or not a regional reserve bank is located in each lawmaker's district and/or state). For the Blue Dog membership from the 112th Congress, see http://self.gutenberg.org/articles/blue_dog_coalition #Membership (accessed August 15, 2015). Financial services employment data are drawn from the US census of 2010. The results are available from the authors.

16. 113th Congress, House vote no. 504, September 17, 2014. We again model the audit the Fed vote as a function of ideology and electoral forces, controlling for a lawmaker's representation of a regional reserve bank. Specifically, we control for whether or not the member is retiring, barely won their 2012 election, is in their first term, is a Blue Dog member or not, the percent of the state employed in financial services, and whether or not a regional reserve bank is located in each lawmaker's district and/or state. For the Blue Dog membership for the 113th Congress, see http://ballotpedia.org/Blue_Dog_Coalition#113th _Congress_2 (accessed August 15, 2016).

17. Bernanke, interview with the authors.

18. Federal Open Market Committee 1933–2016, "Meeting, October 24–25, 2006," 131.

19. Ibid., 138, 153.

20. Federal Open Market Committee 1933–2016, "Meeting, December 14, 2008, 68.

21. Federal Open Market Committee 1933–2016, "Meeting, September 18, 2007."

22. The Obama administration never nominated anyone for the position. Instead, Board governor Daniel Tarullo informally served in the role.

23. See, for example, Bernanke 2012b.

24. For an exploration of the constraints on monetary and fiscal policy responses, see Hilsenrath 2015.

Chapter 8: The Myth of Independence

1. Ben S. Bernanke, interview with the authors, Brookings Institution, Washington, DC, June 13, 2014.

2. Scott Lanman and Craig Torres (2010) recount the full-court press mounted by Fed officials to defend their supervisory authority.

3. Bernanke (2016) explains the concept and potential implementation of "helicopter money."

REFERENCES

Aaron, Kat. 2009. "Predatory Lending: A Decade of Warnings." Center for Public Integrity. Accessed September 29, 2015, http://www.publicintegrity.org/2009/05/06/5452/predatory-lending-decade-warnings.

Abrams, Burton A. 2006. "How Richard Nixon Pressured Arthur Burns: Evidence from the Nixon Tapes." *Journal of Economic Perspectives* 20 (4): 177–88.

Adler, E. Scott. N.d. "Congressional District Data File, [Ninety-Fourth and Ninety-Fifth Congresses]." University of Colorado at Boulder.

Adler, E. Scott, and John D. Wilkerson. N.d. Congressional Bills Project (1947–2008), NSF 00880066 and 00880061.

Ahamed, Liaquat. 2009. *Lords of Finance: The Bankers Who Broke the World.* New York: Penguin Books.

Alesina, Alberto, and Lawrence H. Summers. 1993. "Central Bank Independence and Macroeconomic Performance: Some Comparative Evidence." *Journal of Money, Credit and Banking* 25 (2): 151–62.

Alt, James. 1991. "Leaning into the Wind or Ducking out of the Storm: U.S. Monetary Policy in the 1980s." In *Politics and Economics in the Eighties,* edited by Alberto Alesina and Geoffrey Carliner, 41–82. Chicago: University of Chicago Press.

Andrews, Edmund L. 2007. "Fed Shrugged as Subprime Crisis Spread." *New York Times,* December 18. Accessed September 29, 2015, http://www.nytimes.com/2007/12/18/business/18subprime.html?hp&_r=1&.

Appelbaum, Binyamin. 2015. "In Republican Attacks on the Fed, Experts See a Shift." *New York Times,* April 7, B1. Accessed September 29, 2015, http://www.nytimes.com/2015/04/08/business/economy/in-republican-attacks-on-the-fed-experts-see-a-shift.html.

Auerbach, Robert D. 2008. *Deception and Abuse at the Fed.* Austin: University of Texas Press.

Bailey, Stephen. 1950. *Congress Makes a Law: The Story behind the Employment Act of 1946.* New York: Columbia University Press.

Baily, Martin Neil, and John B. Taylor, eds. 2014. *Across the Great Divide: New Perspectives on the Financial Crisis.* Hoover Institution Press. Accessed September 21, 2015, http://www.hoover.org/research/across-great-divide-new-perspectives-financial-crisis-0.

Ball, Laurence. 2016. "The Fed and Lehman Brothers." Paper presented at a meeting of the NBER Monetary Economics Program, July 14. Accessed February 4, 2017, http://www.econ2.jhu.edu/People/Ball/Lehman.pdf.

Bank of International Settlements. 2009. *Issues in the Governance of Central Banks.* Basel, Switzerland: Bank of International Settlements. Accessed August 1, 2015, http://www.bis.org/publ/othp04.htm.

Barkley, Frederick R. 1941. "For a Firm Dollar." *New York Times,* January 2, 1.

———. 1945. "'Full' Employment Out of House Bill." *New York Times,* December 5, 21.

Belair, Felix, Jr. 1945. "Truman Battles for Full-Job Bill." *New York Times,* December 21, 4.

———. 1950a. "Congress Is Urged to Curb Treasury on Credit Control." *New York Times,* January 13, 1.

———. 1950b. "Reserve Board Set to Cut Bank Credit as Inflation Brake." *New York Times,* October 8, 1, 93.

———. 1951a. "Bond Agreement Viewed as 'Truce.'" *New York Times,* March 5, 16.

———. 1951b. "Six Senators Urge New Credit Policy." *New York Times,* March 7, 26.

———. 1951c. "Truman Puts Rein on Reserve Board." *New York Times,* February 2, 1.

———. 1951d. "Truman 'Thanks' Reserve Board for 'Assurance' on Fiscal Policy." *New York Times,* February 3, 25.

Bensel, Richard Franklin. 1984. *Sectionalism and American Political Development, 1880–1980.* Madison: University of Wisconsin Press.

Bernanke, Ben S. 2002. "Remarks by Governor Ben S. Bernanke." Presented at the conference to Honor Milton Friedman, University of Chicago, November 8. Accessed December 29, 2015, http://www.federalreserve.gov/boarddocs/Speeches/2002/20021108/default.htm.

———. 2003. "A Perspective on Inflation Targeting." Remarks at the annual Economic Policy Conference of the National Association for Business Economics, Washington, DC, March 25. Accessed November 2, 2015, http://www.federalreserve.gov/Boarddocs/Speeches/2003/20030325/default.htm.

———. 2007. "The Economic Outlook." Testimony before the Joint Economic Committee, US Congress, March 28. Accessed September 20, 2015, http://www.federalreserve.gov/newsevents/testimony/bernanke20070328a.htm.

———. 2009. "Federal Reserve Policies to Ease Credit and Their Implications for the Fed's Balance Sheet." Speech delivered at the National Press Club Luncheon, National Press Club, Washington, DC, February 18. Accessed September 8, 2015, http://www.federalreserve.gov/newsevents/speech/bernanke20090218a.htm.

———. 2012a. "The Federal Reserve after World War II." Chairman Bernanke's College Lecture Series: The Federal Reserve and the Financial Crisis, lecture 2, George Washington University School of Business, March 22. Accessed September 20, 2015, http://www.federalreserve.gov/newsevents/lectures/the-Federal-Reserve-after-World-War-II.htm.

———. 2012b. "U.S. Monetary Policy and International Implications." Address delivered at the Challenges of the Global Financial System: Risks and Governance under Evolving Globalization seminar sponsored by the Bank of Japan–International Monetary Fund, Tokyo, October 14. Accessed February 29, 2016, http://www.federalreserve.gov/newsevents/speech/bernanke20121014a.htm.

———. 2013a. "A Century of U.S. Central Banking: Goals, Frameworks, Accountability." Paper presented at the First 100 Years of the Federal Reserve: The Policy

Record, Lessons Learned, and Prospects for the Future conference, sponsored by the National Bureau of Economic Research, Cambridge, MA.

———. 2013b. "Concluding Remarks." Speech at the ceremony commemorating the centennial of the Federal Reserve Act, Federal Reserve. Accessed November 13, 2105, http://www.federalreserve.gov/newsevents/speech/bernanke20131216b.htm.

———. 2015. *The Courage to Act: A Memoir of a Crisis and Its Aftermath*. New York: W. W. Norton and Company.

———. 2016. "What Tools Does the Fed Have Left? Part 3: Helicopter Money." Brookings, April 11. Accessed February 4, 2017, https://www.brookings.edu/blog/ben-bernanke/2016/04/11/what-tools-does-the-fed-have-left-part-3-helicopter-money/.

Bernanke, Ben S., and Harold James. 1991. "The Gold Standard, Deflation, and Financial Crisis in the Great Depression: An International Comparison." In *Financial Markets and Financial Crises*, edited by R. Glenn Hubbard, 33–68. Chicago: University of Chicago Press.

Bernhard, William, J. Lawrence Broz, and William R. Clark. 2002. "The Political Economy of Monetary Institutions." *International Organization* 56:693–723.

Bernstein, Irving. N.d. "Chapter 5: Americans in Depression and War." US Department of Labor. Accessed July 27, 2016, https://www.dol.gov/general/aboutdol/history/chapter5.

Binder, Sarah A. 2003. *Stalemate: Causes and Consequences of Legislative Gridlock*. Washington, DC: Brookings Institution Press.

Blinder, Alan. 2016. "What to Do about the Federal Reserve." Equitablog. Washington Center for Equitable Growth, October 31. Accessed February 21, 2017, http://equitablegrowth.org/monetary-policy/what-to-do-about-the-federal-reserve/.

Bloomberg Business. 2011a. "Secret Fed Loans Gave Banks $13 Billion Undisclosed to Congress." Bloomberg Business, November 21. Accessed September 26, 2015, http://www.bloomberg.com/news/articles/2011-11-28/secret-fed-loans-undisclosed-to-congress-gave-banks-13-billion-in-income.

———. 2011b. "Wall Street Aristocracy Got $1.2 Trillion in Secret Loans." Bloomberg Business, August 21. Accessed September 26, 2015, http://www.bloomberg.com/news/articles/2011-08-21/wall-street-aristocracy-got-1-2-trillion-in-fed-s-secret-loans.

Blum, John Morton. 1959. *From the Morgenthau Diaries: Years of Crisis, 1928–1938*. Boston: Houghton Mifflin.

Board of Governors of the Federal Reserve System. N.d. Industrial Production Index. Accessed August 3, 2016, https://www.federalreserve.gov/releases/g17/About.htm.

———. 2013a. Federal Reserve Act, Section 2. Federal Reserve Districts. Accessed December 28, 2015, http://www.federalreserve.gov/aboutthefed/section2.htm.

———. 2013b. Federal Reserve Act, Section 13. Powers of the Federal Reserve Banks. Accessed December 19, 2015, http://www.federalreserve.gov/aboutthefed/section13.htm.

———. 2015. "Press Release." November 30. Accessed January 1, 2016, http://www.federalreserve.gov/newsevents/press/bcreg/20151130a.htm.

Bordo, D. Michael, Owen F. Humpage, and Anna J. Schwartz. 2015. *Strained Relations: US Foreign–Exchange Operations and Monetary Policy in the Twentieth Century*. Chicago: University of Chicago Press.

Bordo, D. Michael, Peter Rappoport, and Anna J. Schwartz. 1992. "Money versus Credit Rationing: Evidence for the National Banking Era, 1880–1914." In *Strategic Factors in Nineteenth Century American Economic History*, edited by Claudia Goldin and Hugh Rockoff, 189–224. Chicago: University of Chicago Press.

Bremner, Robert. 2004. *Chairman of the Fed: William McChesney Martin Jr. and the Creation of the Modern American Financial System*. New Haven, CT: Yale University Press.

Broz, J. Lawrence. 1997. *The International Origins of the Federal Reserve System*. Ithaca, NY: Cornell University Press.

Burns, Arthur F. 1979. "The Anguish of Central Banking." Per Jacobsson Lecture, Belgrade, Yugoslavia, September 30. Accessed August 7, 2015, http://www.perjacobsson.org/lectures/1979.pdf.

Calomiris, Charles W., and Gary Gorton. 1991. "The Origins of Banking Panics: Models, Facts, and Bank Regulation." In *Financial Markets and Financial Crises*, edited by R. Glenn Hubbard, 109–74. Chicago: University of Chicago Press.

Calomiris, Charles W., and Stephen H. Haber. 2014. *Fragile by Design: The Political Origins of Banking Crises and Scarce Credit*. Princeton, NJ: Princeton University Press.

Carlson, Mark A., and David C. Wheelock. 2014. "Navigating Constraints: The Evolution of Federal Reserve Monetary Policy, 1935–59." Finance and Economics Discussion Series, Divisions of Research and Statistics and Monetary Affairs, Federal Reserve Board, Washington, DC, June 9.

Carpenter, Daniel. 2010. *Reputation and Power: Organizational Image and Pharmaceutical Regulation at the FDA*. Princeton, NJ: Princeton University Press.

Chandler, Lester. 1958. *Benjamin Strong: Central Banker*. Washington, DC: Brookings Institution Press.

Clark, William, and Vincent Arel-Bundock. 2013. "Independent but not Indifferent: Partisan Bias in Monetary Policy at the Fed." *Economics and Politics* 25 (1): 1–25.

Clifford, A. Jerome. 1965. *The Independence of the Federal Reserve System*. Philadelphia: University of Pennsylvania Press.

Congressional Budget Office. 2010. *Historical Data on Federal Debt Held by the Public*. July. Accessed January 30, 2017, http://www.cbo.gov/publication/21728.

Conti-Brown, Peter. 2014. "The Institutions of Federal Reserve Independence." Rock Center for Corporate Governance, Working Paper Series No. 139, January 2.

———. 2016. *The Power and Independence of the Federal Reserve*. Princeton, NJ: Princeton University Press.

Cowan, Edward. 1977. "The Humphrey-Hawkins Bill." *New York Times*, November 19, 14.

Davidson, Kate. 2015. "Rep. Hensarling to Yellen: Ignoring Subpoena Is 'Inexcusable.'" *Wall Street Journal*, July 15. Accessed November 2, 2015, http://blogs.wsj.com/economics/2015/07/15/rep-hensarling-to-yellen-ignoring-subpoena-is-inexcusable/.

———. 2016. "Donald Trump's Comments on the Fed, Interest Rate Policy, and Janet Yellen." *Wall Street Journal*, November 9. Accessed November 21, 2016, http://www.wsj.com/articles/donald-trumps-comments-on-the-fed-interest-rate-policy-and-janet-yellen-1478724767.

Debelle, Guy, and Stanley Fischer. 1994. "How Independent Should a Central Bank Be?" Center for Economic Policy Research, Stanford University. Accessed November 2, 2015, www.bostonfed.org/economic/conf/conf38/conf38f.pdf.

De Long, J. Bradford. 1996. "Keynesianism, Pennsylvania Avenue Style: Some Economic Consequences of the Employment Act of 1946." *Journal of Economic Perspectives* 10 (3): 41–53.

———. 1997. "America's Peacetime Inflation: The 1970s." In *Reducing Inflation: Motivation and Strategy*, edited by Christina D. Romer and David H. Romer, 247–80. Chicago: University of Chicago Press.

Dubner, Stephen. 2015. "Ben Bernanke Gives Himself a Grade: A New Freakonomics Radio Podcast." *Freakonomics: The Hidden Side of Everything*, December 3. Accessed December 13, 2015, http://freakonomics.com/2015/12/03/ben-bernanke-gives-himself-a-grade-a-new-freakonomics-radio-podcast/.

Dugan, Andrew. 2014. "Fed Chairman Bernanke Leaves with Mixed Verdict." Gallup, January 29. Accessed November 16, 2015, http://www.gallup.com/poll/167099/fed-chairman-bernanke-leaves-mixed-verdict.aspx.

Dun's Review. 1913. Various issues. New York: R. G. Dun and Co. Accessed December 29, 2015, http://www.loc.gov/rr/business/duns/duns15.html#db15a.

Dykes, Sayre Ellen, and Michael A. Whitehouse. 1989. "The Establishment and Evolution of the Federal Reserve Board: 1913–23." *Federal Reserve Board Bulletin*, April. Accessed 29, 2015, https://fraser.stlouisfed.org/docs/meltzer/dykest89.pdf.

Eccles, Marriner. 1951. *Beckoning Frontiers: Public and Personal Recollections*. New York: Alfred A. Knopf.

Eichengreen, Barry. 1992. *Golden Fetters: The Gold Standard and the Great Depression, 1919–1939*. New York: Oxford University Press.

Eichengreen, Barry, and Jeffrey Sachs. 1985. "Exchange Rates and Economic Recovery in the 1930s." *Journal of Economic History* 45 (4): 925–46.

Farhang, Sean, and Ira Katznelson. 2005. "The Southern Imposition: Congress and Labor in the New Deal and Fair Deal." *Studies in American Political Development* 19:1–30.

Farnsworth, Clyde H. 1977. "Washington and Business: Legislation for G.A.O. Auditing of Fed." *New York Times*, October 27, D1, D5.

———. 1980. "More Clout for the Fed." *New York Times*, March 17, D2.

Federal Open Market Committee. 1933–2016. *Federal Open Market Committee Meeting Minutes, Transcripts, and Other Documents*. Accessed August 3, 2016, https://fraser.stlouisfed.org/title/?id=677#!22661.

Federal Open Market Committee. 2010a. "Meeting of the Federal Open Market Committee on December 14." In *Transcripts and Other Historical Materials*. Accessed February 21, 2017, https://www.federalreserve.gov/monetarypolicy/files/FOMC20101214meeting.pdf.

―――. 2010b. "Conference Call of the Federal Open Market Committee on May 9." In *Transcripts and Other Historical Materials*. Accessed February 21, 2017, https://www.federalreserve.gov/monetarypolicy/files/FOMC20100509confcall.pdf.

Federal Reserve Board. 1914–2014. *Annual Report of the Board of Governors of the Federal Reserve System*. Accessed December 29, 2015, https://fraser.stlouisfed.org/title/117.

―――. 2012. "Conversation with the Chairman: A Teacher Town Hall Meeting." Accessed September 29, 2015, http://www.federalreserve.gov/newsevents/conferences/chairman-bernanke-teacher-town-hall.htm.

―――. 2013. Transcript of chairman Ben Bernanke's press conference, December 18. Accessed November 15, 2015, http://www.federalreserve.gov/monetarypolicy/fomcpresconf20131218.htm.

Federal Reserve Bank of Richmond. N.d. *Treasury–Federal Reserve Accord*. Historical Documents. Accessed December 30, 2015, https://www.richmondfed.org/publications/research/special_reports/treasury_fed_accord/historical_documents/index.cfm.

Federal Reserve Board of St. Louis. 2015a. "Bank Prime Loan Rate." Accessed August 10, 2015, https://fred.stlouisfed.org/series/WPRIME/.

―――. 2015b. "Effective Federal Funds Rate." Accessed August 10, 2015, https://research.stlouisfed.org/fred2/series/DFF/.

―――. 2016a. "Civilian Unemployment Rate." Accessed July 19, 2015, https://research.stlouisfed.org/fred2/series/UNRATE/.

―――. 2016b. "Consumer Price Index for All Urban Consumers: All Items." Accessed August 4, 2016, https://research.stlouisfed.org/fred2/series/CPIAUCNS/.

―――. 2016c. "Gross Federal Debt as Percent of Gross Domestic Product." Accessed August 4, 2016, https://research.stlouisfed.org/fred2/series/GFDGDPA188S/.

―――. N.d. "Industrial Production Index." Accessed August 3, 2016, https://research.stlouisfed.org/fred2/series/INDPRO/.

Fernandez-Albertos, Jose. 2015. "The Politics of Central Bank Independence." *Annual Review of Political Science* 18:217–37.

Financial Crisis Inquiry Commission. 2011. *The Financial Crisis Inquiry Report: Final Report of the National Commission on the Causes of the Financial and Economic Crisis in the United States*. Washington, DC: Government Printing Office. Accessed September 20, 2015, http://fcic.law.stanford.edu/.

Fitch, Asa. 2014. "In First Post-Fed Public Appearance, Bernanke Defends Crisis Record." *Wall Street Journal*, March 15. Accessed July 19, 2015, http://blogs.wsj.com/middleeast/2014/03/05/in-first-post-fed-public-appearance-bernanke-defends-crisis-record/.

Forder, James. 2014. *Macroeconomics and the Phillips Curve Myth*. Oxford: Oxford University Press.

FRASER. 2015. "Annual Report of the Board of Governors of the Federal Reserve System, 1914–2015." Accessed August 3, 2016, https://fraser.stlouisfed.org/title/117.

―――. N.d. Marriner S. Eccles Papers, University of Utah. Accessed August 3, 2016, http://fraser.stlouisfed.org/archival/1343.

Friedman, Milton. 1968. "The Role of Monetary Policy." *American Economic Review* 58, no. 1 (1968): 1–17.

Friedman, Milton, and Anna Jacobson Schwartz. 1963. *A Monetary History of the United States, 1876-1960*. Princeton, NJ: Princeton University Press.

———. 1971. *A Monetary History of the United States, 1867–1960*. Princeton, NJ: Princeton University Press.

Friendly, Alfred. 1950. "Congress Unit Favors Broad Budget Change." *Washington Post*, January 13, 1.

Garbade, Kenneth D. 2012. *Birth of a Market: The U.S. Treasury Securities Market from the Great War to the Great Depression*. Cambridge, MA: MIT Press.

———. 2014. "Direct Purchases by U.S. Treasury Securities by Federal Reserve Banks." Federal Reserve Bank of New York Staff Report No. 684, August.

Goldfarb, Zachary. 2014. "Michelle Smith, Working behind the Scenes to Shape the Fed's Public Image." *Washington Post*, January 25. Accessed December 30, 2015, http://www.washingtonpost.com/business/michelle-smith-working-behind-the -scenes-to-shape-the-feds-public-image/2014/01/24/293cedf2-82d4-11e3-9dd4 -e7278db80d86_story.html.

Hackley, Howard H. 1973. *Lending Functions of the Federal Reserve Banks: A History*. Accessed December 29, 2015, https://fraser.stlouisfed.org/scribd/?title _id=128&id=0&filepath=%2Fdocs%2Fpublications%2Fbooks%2Flendfunct _hackley1973o.pdf.

Harrison, David. 2015a. "Key House Lawmaker Sends Subpoena to Fed over 2012 Leak." *Wall Street Journal*, May 21. Accessed November 2, 2015, http://www.wsj.com /articles/key-house-lawmaker-sends-subpoena-to-fed-over-2012-leak-1432248908.

———. 2015b. "Senate Duo Takes Aim at Fed's Lending Powers." *Wall Street Journal*, May 13. Accessed November 2, 2015, http://blogs.wsj.com/economics/2015/05 /13/senate-duo-takes-aim-at-feds-lending-powers/.

Hess, Jerry N. 1969. "Oral History Interview with John W. Snyder." Harry S. Truman Library and Museum. Accessed January 31, 2017, http://www.trumanlibrary.org /oralhist/snyder25.htm.

Hetzel, Robert L., and Ralph F. Leach. 2001. "The Treasury-Fed Accord: A New Narrative Account." *Economic Quarterly* 87 (Winter): 33–55.

Hilsenrath, Jon, and Nicholas Timiraos. 2015. "U.S. Lacks Ammo for Next Economic Crisis." *Wall Street Journal*, August 17. Accessed February 2, 2017, https://www .wsj.com/articles/u-s-lacks-ammo-for-next-economic-crisis-1439865442.

Hilsenrath, Jon, and Jeffrey Sparshott. 2011. "Central Banks Move to Calm Fears." *Wall Street Journal*, December 1. Accessed September 25, 2015, http://www.wsj.com /news/articles/SB10001424052970204012004577069960192509068.

Hoover, Herbert. 1952. *The Memoirs of Herbert Hoover, Volume 3: The Great Depression 1929–1941*. New York: Macmillan.

Houston, David F. 1926. *Eight Years with Wilson's Cabinet, 1913 to 1920*. Vol. 1. New York: Double Day Page.

Hsieh, Chang-Tai, and Christina D. Romer. 2006. "Was the Federal Reserve Constrained by the Gold Standard during the Great Depression? Evidence from the 1932 Open Market Purchase Program." *Journal of Economic History* 66 (1): 140–76.

Huff, W. R. "Senate Adopts Banking Measure without Change." *Wall Street Journal,* July 27, 1935, 1.

Hughes, Siobhan, and Paul Page. 2015. "Lawmakers Reach Compromise on Five-Year Highway Bill." *Wall Street Journal,* December 1. Accessed December 19, 2015, http://www.wsj.com/articles/congress-strikes-compromise-on-5-year-highway -bill-1449001406.

Humphrey, Hubert H. 1977. "The Jobs Bill: An 'Indispensable First Step.'" *Washington Post,* December 4, 85.

Ip, Greg. 2011. "The Republicans' New Voodoo Economics." *Washington Post,* August 19. Accessed September 29, 2015, https://www.washingtonpost.com/opinions /the-republicans-new-voodoo-economics/2011/08/18/gIQAxhyRQJ_story.html.

Irwin, Neil. 2010. "Bernanke Confirmed by Senate for 2nd Term as Fed Chairman." *Washington Post,* January 29. Accessed November 1, 2015, http://www.washingtonpost .com/wp-dyn/content/article/2010/01/28/AR2010012800103.html.

Jackson, Andrew. 1832. "Bank Veto (July 10)." Presidential Speech Archive, Miller Center. Accessed February 7, 2017, http://millercenter.org/president/speeches /speech-3636.

Jacobs, Lawrence R., and Desmond King. 2016. *Fed Power: How Finance Wins.* New York: Oxford University Press.

James, Scott. 2000. *Parties, Presidents, and the State: A Party System Perspective on Democratic Regulatory Choice, 1884–1936.* Cambridge: Cambridge University Press.

Jarrett, Vernon. 1978. "Push Is on to Pass Employment Bill." *Chicago Tribune,* B3.

Jeong, Gyung-Ho, Gary J. Miller, and Andrew C. Sobel. 2009. "Political Compromise and Bureaucratic Structure: The Political Origins of the Federal Reserve System." *Journal of Law, Economics, and Organization* 25 (2): 472–98.

Kaiser, Robert. 1978. "Senate Passes a 'Sunset Bill.'" *Washington Post,* October 12, A1.

———. 2014. *Act of Congress.* New York: Vintage Publishers.

Katznelson, Ira. 2013. *Fear Itself: The New Deal and the Origins of Our Time.* New York: Liverright.

Katznelson, Ira, and Quinn Mulroy. 2012. "Was the South Pivotal? Situated Partisan- ship and Policy Coalitions during the New Deal and Fair Deal." *Journal of Politics* 74 (2): 604–20.

Keil, Paul. 2012. "The Great American Foreclosure Story: The Struggle for Justice and a Place to Call Home." *ProPublica,* April 10. Accessed September 28, 2015, http:// www.propublica.org/article/the-great-american-foreclosure-story-the-struggle -for-justice-and-a-place-t/single.

Keoun, Bradley, and Stephen Church. 2007. "New Century, Biggest Subprime Ca- sualty, Goes Bankrupt." Bloomberg News, April 2. Accessed February 22, 2017, https://www.nachi.org/forum/f13/new-century-biggest-subprime-casualty-goes -bankrupt-15340/.

Kettl, Donald. 1986. *Leadership at the Fed.* New Haven, CT: Yale University Press.

Keyes, Scott. 2011. "Perry on Bernanke: 'I Dunno What Y'all Would Do to Him in Iowa but We Would Treat Him Pretty Ugly Down in Texas.'" ThinkProgress,

August 15. Accessed February 8, 2014, http://thinkprogress.org/politics/2011/08/15/296552/perry-on-bernanke-pretty-ugly-down-in-texas/.

Kirshner, Jonathan. 2007. *Appeasing Bankers: Financial Caution on the Road to War.* Princeton, NJ: Princeton University Press.

Lacker, Jeffrey M., and John A. Weinberg. 2014. "The Fed's Mortgage Favoritism. " *Wall Street Journal,* October 7. Accessed September 26, 2015, http://www.wsj.com/articles/jeffrey-lacker-and-john-weinberg-the-feds-mortgage-favoritism-1412721776.

Laderman, Liz. 2001. "Subprime Mortgage Lending and the Capital Markets." *FRBSF Economic Letter* 2001-38 (December 28). Accessed February 4, 2017, http://www.frbsf.org/economic-research/publications/economic-letter/2001/december/subprime-mortgage-lending-and-the-capital-markets/.

Lanman, Scott, and Craig Torres. 2010. "Here It Comes: Consider Yourself Warned." *Bloomberg News,* January 7.

Lattman, Peter. 2013. "Suit Charges 3 Credit Ratings Agencies with Fraud in Bear Stearns Case." *New York Times,* November 11. Accessed September 28, 2015, http://dealbook.nytimes.com/2013/11/11/suit-charges-3-credit-rating-agencies-with-fraud-in-bear-stearns-case/.

Lebergott, Stanley. 1957. "Annual Estimates of Unemployment in the United States, 1900–1954." In *The Measurement and Behavior of Unemployment,* edited by the National Bureau of Economic Research. Accessed November 28, 2015, http://www.nber.org/chapters/c2644.

Link, Arthur. 1954. *Woodrow Wilson and the Progressive Era, 1910–1917.* New York: Harper and Brothers.

Lippmann, Walter. 1951. "Federal Reserve Issue Subjected to Pressure." *Los Angeles Times,* March 4, B5.

Lowenstein, Roger. 2015. *America's Bank: The Epic Struggle to Create the Federal Reserve.* New York: Penguin Press.

Lynch, G. Patrick. 2002. "Midterm Elections and Economic Fluctuations: The Response of Voters over Time. *Legislative Studies Quarterly* 27:265–294.

Martin, William McChesney. 1964. *The Federal Reserve System after Fifty Years.* Hearings before the Subcommittee on Domestic Finance of the Committee on Banking and Currency, House of Representatives, 88th Cong., 2nd sess., January 22, 96.

Mayhew, David R. 1974. *Congress: The Electoral Connection.* New Haven, CT: Yale University Press.

McAvoy, Michael R. 2006. "How Were the Federal Reserve Bank Locations Selected?" *Explorations in Economic History* 43 (July): 505–26.

McCarty, Nolan, Keith T. Poole, and Howard Rosenthal. 2013. *Political Bubbles: Financial Crises and the Failure of American Democracy.* Princeton, NJ: Princeton University Press.

McCubbins, Mathew, and Thomas Schwartz. 1984. "Congressional Oversight Overlooked: Police Patrols versus Fire Alarms." *American Journal of Political Science* 28:16–79.

McGrane, Victoria, and Michael Crittenden. 2010. "Senate Passes Amendment for One-Time Audit of Fed." *Wall Street Journal,* May 11. Accessed October 31, 2015, http://

www.wsj.com/articles/SB10001424052748704250104575238130707230588
?alg=y.

McMahon, Tim. 2017. "Historical Inflation Rate." Accessed February 22. http://inflationdata.com/Inflation/Inflation_Rate/HistoricalInflation.aspx.

Meade, Ellen E., and David Stasavage. 2008. "Publicity of Debate and the Incentive to Dissent: Evidence from the US Federal Reserve." *Economic Journal* 118 (April): 695–717.

Melendez, Eleazar David. 2013. "Financial Crisis Cost Tops $22 Trillion, GAO Says." Huffington Post, February 14. Accessed February 4, 2017, http://www.huffingtonpost.com/2013/02/14/financial-crisis-cost-gao_n_2687553.html.

Meltzer, Allan H. 2000. "Lessons from the Early History of the Federal Reserve." Presidential address to the International Atlantic Economic Society, March 17, Munich. Accessed December 29, 2015, http://www2.tepper.cmu.edu/afs/andrew/gsia/meltzer/Munich.PDF.

———. 2003. *History of the Federal Reserve.* Vol. 1. Chicago: University of Chicago Press.

———. 2005. "Origins of the Great Inflation." *Federal Reserve Bank of St. Louis Review,* no. 2 (March–April): 145–75.

———. 2009. *History of the Federal Reserve.* Vol. 2. Chicago: University of Chicago Press.

Menza, Justin. 2012. "With Congress in Gridlock, 'Fed's the Only Game in Town.'" CNBC, July 12. Accessed February 8, 2014, http://www.cnbc.com/id/48210558.

Moe, Terry M. 1995. "The Politics of Structural Choice: Toward a Theory of Public Bureaucracy." In *Organization Theory: From Chester Barnard to the Present and Beyond,* edited by Oliver E. Williamson, 116–53. New York: Oxford University Press.

Moley, Raymond. 1939. *After Seven Years.* New York: Harper and Brothers Publishers.

Morgenthau, Henry Jr. 1938. *Diaries of Henry Morgenthau, Jr., April 27, 1933–July 27, 1945.* Vol. 111 (February 16–22). Accessed March 11, 2015, http://www.fdrlibrary.marist.edu/archives/collections/franklin/index.php?p=collections/findingaid&id=535.

Morris, J. Irwin. 2000. *Congress, the President, and the Federal Reserve: The Politics of American Monetary Policymaking.* Ann Arbor: University of Michigan Press.

Murphy, Henry C. 1950. *The National Debt in War and Transition.* New York: McGraw-Hill Book Company.

National Bureau of Economic Research. 2010. *Report of the Business Cycle Dating Committee.* September 20. Accessed November 17, 2015, http://www.nber.org/cycles/sept2010.html.

Nelson, Clarence W. 1973. "Defining the Districts: Where to Draw the Lines." Excerpt from *Reflections from History: The Minneapolis Federal Reserve Bank.* Federal Reserve Bank of Minneapolis. Accessed December 25, 2015, https://www.minneapolisfed.org/about/more-about-the-fed/history-of-the-fed/defining-the-districts.

Odell, Kerry A., and David F. Weiman. 1998. "Metropolitan Development, Regional Financial Centers, and the Founding of the Fed in the Lower South." *Journal of Economic History* 58 (March): 103–25.

Office of the Comptroller of the Currency. 1914. *Annual Report of the Comptroller of the Currency to the Second Session of the Sixty-Third Congress of the United States.* Washington, DC: Government Printing Office.

Orphanides, Athanasios, and John C. Williams. 2002. "Robust Monetary Policy Rules with Unknown Natural Rates." *Brookings Papers on Economic Activity* 2:63–118.

Pierson, Paul. 2004. *Politics in Time: History, Institutions, and Social Analysis.* Princeton, NJ: Princeton University Press.

Pine, Art. 1977. "Was Humphrey-Hawkins Bill Worth it?" *Washington Post*, November 24, D1.

Proquest. N.d. "CIS Congressional Bills, Resolutions, and Laws on Microfiche (1933–2008)." Accessed February 25, 2017, http://cisupa.proquest.com/ws_display.asp ?filter=cis_leaf&item_id=%7B1D481C6F-CA7A-4929-B4B0-BC90D20FAC71%7D.

Reinhart, Carmen M., and Kenneth S. Rogoff. 2013. "Shifting Mandates: The Federal Reserve's First Centennial." *American Economic Review: Papers and Proceedings* 103 (3): 48–54.

Reserve Bank Organization Committee (RBOC). 1914a. *First-Choice Vote for Reserve-Bank Cities.* July 29. Accessed January 4, 2017, https://fraser.stlouisfed.org/scribd /?title_id=604&filepath=/files/docs/historical/federal reserve history/hr1914 _firstchoicevote.pdf.

———. 1914b. "Location of Reserve Districts in the United States: Letter from the Reserve Bank Organization Committee Transmitting the Briefs and Arguments to the Organization Committee of the Federal Reserve Board Relative to the Location of the Federal Reserve Districts." Accessed December 28, 2015, http://fraser .stlouisfed.org/publication/?pid=606.

———. 1914c. "Stenographer's Minutes: Federal Reserve District Divisions and Location of Federal Reserve Banks and Head Offices." January 23, Kansas City, MO. Accessed December 28, 2015, https://fraser.stlouisfed.org/docs/historical /federal%20reserve%20history/rboc/rbochearings_19140123_kansascity.pdf.

———. 1914d. *Report to the Reserve Bank Organization Committee by the Preliminary Committee on Organization.* June 1. Accessed December 28, 2015, https:// fraser.stlouisfed.org/scribd/?title_id=609&filepath=/docs/historical/federal %20reserve%20history/Reserve%20Bank%20Organization.pdf.

———. 1914e. *Decision of the Reserve Bank Organization Committee Determining the Federal Reserve Districts and the Location of Federal Reserve Banks under Federal Reserve Act Approved December 23, 1913. With Statement of the Committee in Relation Thereto.* Washington, DC: Government Printing Office, April 10. Accessed December 29, 2015, http://www.federalreservehistory.org/Media /Material/Event/16-125.

Richardson, Gary, Alejandro Komai, and Michael Gou. 2013. "The Gold Reserve Act." Accessed December 29, 2015, http://www.federalreservehistory.org/Events /DetailView/13.

Ricketts, Lowell R., and Christopher J. Waller. 2014. "The Rise and the (Eventual) Fall in the Fed's Balance Sheet." *Regional Economist*, January. Accessed September 29, 2015, https://www.stlouisfed.org/publications/regional-economist/january -2014/the-rise-and-eventual-fall-in-the-feds-balance-sheet.

Ritchie, Donald A., ed. 1999. *Minutes of the Senate Democratic Caucus: 1903–1964.* Washington, DC: Government Printing Office.

Ritter, Gretchen. 1997. *Goldbugs and Greenbacks: The Antimonopoly Tradition and the Politics of Finance in America.* New York: Cambridge University Press.

Ritter, Lawrence S. 1980. *Selected Papers of Allan Sproul.* New York: Federal Reserve Bank of New York.

Romer, Christina D. 2005. "Commentary: Origins of the Great Inflation," *Federal Reserve of St. Louis Review* 87, no. 2 (March–April): 177–85.

Romer, Christina D., and David H. Romer. 2002. "The Evolution of Economic Understanding and Postwar Stabilization Policy." In *Rethinking Stabilization Policy.* A symposium sponsored by the Federal Reserve Bank of Kansas City, Jackson Hole, Wyoming, August 29–31. Accessed August 4, 2015, https://www.kansascityfed.org/publications/research/escp/symposiums/escp-2002.

———. 2004. "Choosing the Federal Reserve Chair: Lessons from History." *Journal of Economic Perspectives* 18, no. 1 (Winter): 129–62.

Rose, Sanford. 1974. "The Agony of the Federal Reserve," *Fortune,* 186–88.

Russell, Mary. 1978. "Weaker Version of Jobs Measure Passed by House." *Washington Post,* March 17, A1.

Samuelson, Robert J. 2008. *The Great Inflation and its Aftermath: The Past and Future of American Affluence.* New York: Random House.

Sanders, Elizabeth. 1999. *Roots of Reform: Farmers, Workers, and the American State, 1877–1917.* Chicago: University of Chicago Press.

Santoni, G. J. 1986. "The Employment Act of 1946: Some History Notes." Federal Reserve Bank of St. Louis, November.

Schantz, Harvey L., and Richard H. Schmidt. 1979. "The Evolution of Humphrey-Hawkins." *Policy Studies Journal* 8, no. 3 (Winter): 368–77.

Schiller, Wendy J. 1995. "Senators as Political Entrepreneurs: Using Bill Sponsorship to Shape Legislative Agendas." *American Journal of Political Science* 39 (1): 186–203.

Schroeder, Peter. 2015. "Warren, Vitter Team Up on Fed Bills. *Hill,* May 15. Accessed October 31, 2015, http://thehill.com/policy/finance/241894-warren-vitter-team-up-on-fed-bills.

Shabecoff, Philip. 1978. "Humphrey-Hawkins Bill Backers Win a Key Test in House Voting." *New York Times,* March 10, D13.

Shiller, Robert J. 1989. *Market Volatility.* Cambridge, MA: MIT Press.

Shultz, George. 2002. "The Reagan Administration's Fight against Inflation." Interview, PBS: Commanding Heights. Accessed February 21, 2017, http://www.pbs.org/wgbh/commandingheights/shared/minitext/int_georgeshultz.html#6.

Silber, William. 2012. *Volcker: The Triumph of Persistence.* London: Bloomsbury Press.

Sparrow, Bartholomew. 1996. *From the Outside In: World War II and the American State.* Princeton, NJ: Princeton University Press.

Sproul, Allan. 1951. "Meeting Notes." February 26. Accessed December 30, 2015, https://www.richmondfed.org/publications/research/special_reports/treasury_fed_accord/historical_documents/.

Staiger, Douglas, James H. Stock, and Mark W. Watson. 1997. "How Precise Are Estimates of the Natural Rate of Unemployment?" In *Reducing Inflation: Motivation and Strategy*, edited by Christina D. Romer and David H. Romer, 195–246. Chicago: University of Chicago Press.

Stein, Herbert. 1996. *Fiscal Revolution in America*. Rev. 2nd ed. Washington, DC: American Enterprise Institute Press.

Stiglitz, Joseph. 1998. "Central Banking in a Democratic Society," *Economist* 146 (2): 199–226.

Streek, Wolfgang, and Kathleen Thelen. 2005. "Introduction: Institutional Change in Advanced Political Economies." In *Beyond Continuity: Institutional Change in Advanced Political Economies*, edited by Wolfgang and Kathleen Thelen, 1–39. Oxford: Oxford University Press.

Sulkin, Tracy. 2005. *Issue Politics in Congress*. New York: Cambridge University Press.

———. 2011. *The Legislative Legacy of Congressional Campaigns*. New York: Cambridge University Press.

Taylor, John B. 2009. "Commentary: How Government Created the Financial Crisis." *Wall Street Journal*, February 9. Accessed September 22, 2015, http://www.wsj .com/articles/SB123414310280561945.

Timberlake, Richard. 1993. *Monetary Policy in the United States: An Intellectual and Institutional History*. Chicago: University of Chicago Press.

Torres, Craig. 2016. "How the Fed's Cold War with Congress Could Harm the U.S. Economy." Bloomberg Business, February 26. Accessed February 21, 2017, https://www.bloomberg.com/news/articles/2016-02-26/how-the-fed-s-cold -war-with-congress-could-harm-the-u-s-economy.

Torres, Craig, and Simon Kennedy. 2015. "Central Banks Fight to Ensure That Crisis Tools Become the Norm." Bloomberg Business, November 19. Accessed December 19, 2015, http://www.bloomberg.com/news/articles/2015-11-19/central -banks-fight-to-ensure-crisis-toolkits-become-the-norm.

Tower, Samuel. 1946. "Compromise Bill on Jobs Is Evolved." *New York Times*, February 3, 32.

Truman, Harry S. 1945. "Special Message to the Congress Presenting a 21-Point Program for the Reconversion Period." September 6. Accessed December 30, 2015, http://www.presidency.ucsb.edu/ws/?pid=12359.

———. 1951. "Memorandum Requesting a Study of the Problems of Debt Management and Credit Controls." Public Papers of the Presidents, Harry S. Truman, 1945–1933. Accessed December 30, 2015, http://trumanlibrary.org/publicpapers /index.php?pid=252&st=&st1=.

Trussell, C. P. 1946. "Senate Approves Employment Bill." *New York Times*, February 4, 4.

Tucker, Paul. 2009. "The Repertoire of Official Sector Interventions in the Financial System: Last Resort Lending, Market Making, and Capital." Remarks at the Bank of Japan 2009 International Conference on the Financial System and Monetary Policy Implementation, Bank of Japan, Tokyo, May 27–28, 3. Accessed February 4, 2017, http://www.bis.org/review/r090608c.pdf.

————. 2015. "How Can Central Banks Deliver Credible Commitment and Be 'Emergency Institutions'?" Paper presented at Central Bank Governance and Oversight Reform: A Policy Conference, Hoover Institution, Stanford University, May 21. Accessed November 7, 2015, http://www.hoover.org/sites/default/files/tucker _conference_paper_0.pdf.

US Bureau of Economic Analysis. N.d. "National Economic Accounts." Accessed February 28, 2016, https://www.bea.gov/national.

US Bureau of Labor Statistics. 2016. "Labor Force Statistics from the Current Population Survey." Accessed August 4, 2016, http://www.bls.gov/cps/cpsaat01.htm.

————. N.d. "Consumer Price Index." Accessed August 3, 2016, http://www.bls .gov/cpi/.

US Congress. 1942a. *Congressional Record*, 77th Cong., 2nd sess. Various editions.

————. 1942b. *Executive Session Hearings on the Second War Powers Act*. House of Representatives, Committee on the Judiciary. Washington, DC: Government Printing Office.

————. 1951. Joint Committee on the Economic Report. Hearings, 82nd Cong., 1st sess., pursuant to Sec. 5 (a) of Public Law 304 (79th Congress), January 22, 24, 25, 26, 29, and 31, and February 2.

US Department of Commerce. 1942. "Table No. 282—National Banks—Summary, by States, December 31, 1940." Accessed August 4, 2016, https://www.census.gov /library/publications/time-series/statistical_abstracts.html.

US House Committee on Banking and Currency. 1971. *Federal Reserve Structure and the Development of Monetary Policy, 1915–1935*. Staff report of the Subcommittee on Domestic Finance, 92nd Cong., 1st sess. Washington, DC: Government Printing Office.

US Treasury. N.d. "Legislative Basis." Accessed August 3, 2016, http://www.treasury .gov/resource-center/international/ESF/Pages/basis.aspx.

Volden, Craig, Alan Wiseman, and Dana E. Wittmer. 2013. "When Are Women More Effective Lawmakers Than Men?" *American Journal of Political Science* 57 (2): 326–41.

Wallach, Philip. 2015. *To The Edge: Legality, Legitimacy, and the Responses to the 2008 Financial Crisis*. Washington, DC: Brookings Institution Press.

Warburg, Paul M. 1930. *The Federal Reserve System: Its Origin and Growth*. Vol. 1. New York: Macmillan.

Ware, Alan. 2006. *The Democratic Party Heads North, 1877–1962*. New York: Cambridge University Press.

Weise, Charles L. 2012. "Political Pressures on Monetary Policy during the US Great Inflation." *American Economic Journal: Macroeconomics* 4, no. 2 (April): 33–64.

Wells, Wyatt C. 1994. *Economist in an Uncertain World*. New York: Columbia University Press.

Wessel, David. 1993. "Federal Reserve to Release Transcripts of Past Sessions After Five-Year Delay." *Wall Street Journal*, November 18.

Wheelock, David C. 1991. *The Strategy and Consistency of Federal Reserve Monetary Policy, 1924–1933*. New York: Cambridge University Press.

Wicker, Elmus. 1971. "Roosevelt's 1933 Monetary Experiment." *Journal of American History* 57 (4): 864–79.

———. 2000. *Banking Panics of the Gilded Age*. New York: Cambridge University Press.

Willis, Henry Parker. 1923. *The Federal Reserve System*. New York: Ronald Press Co.

Wilson, Woodrow. 1913. Inaugural Address, March 4. American Presidency Project. Accessed December 1, 2015, http://www.presidency.ucsb.edu/ws/index.php?pid =25831.

Woolley, John. 1984. *Monetary Politics: The Federal Reserve and the Politics of Monetary Policy*. New York: Cambridge University Press.

Woolley, John, and Gerhardt Peters. N.d. "Political Party Platforms of Parties Receiving Electoral Votes: 1840–2012." American Presidency Project. University of California at Santa Barbara. Accessed December 25, 2015, http://www.presidency .ucsb.edu/platforms.php.

Yellen, Janet. 2016. "The Federal Reserve's Monetary Policy Toolkit: Past, Present, and Future." Speech at the Designing Resilient Monetary Policy Frameworks for the Future symposium sponsored by the Federal Reserve Bank of Kansas City, Jackson Hole, Wyoming, August 26. Accessed February 4, 2017, https://www .federalreserve.gov/newsevents/speech/yellen20160826a.htm.

Zumbrum, Josh. 2015. "The Mystery of Missing Inflation Weighs on Fed Rate Move." *Wall Street Journal*, December 13. Accessed December 13, 2015, http://www .wsj.com/articles/the-mystery-of-missing-inflation-weighs-on-fed-rate-move -1450056838.

INDEX

Note: Figures and tables are denoted by "f" and "t," respectively, following page numbers.

A NOTE ON THE TYPE

This book has been composed in Adobe Text and Gotham. Adobe Text, designed by Robert Slimbach for Adobe, bridges the gap between fifteenth- and sixteenth-century calligraphic and eighteenth-century Modern styles. Gotham, inspired by New York street signs, was designed by Tobias Frere-Jones for Hoefler & Co.